John R. Skinner

History of the Fourth Illinois Volunteers in Their Relation to the Spanish-American War

for the liberation of Cuba and other island possessions of Spain

John R. Skinner

History of the Fourth Illinois Volunteers in Their Relation to the Spanish-American War
for the liberation of Cuba and other island possessions of Spain

ISBN/EAN: 9783337243951

Printed in Europe, USA, Canada, Australia, Japan

Cover: Foto ©ninafisch / pixelio.de

More available books at **www.hansebooks.com**

HISTORY

OF THE

Fourth Illinois Volunteers

IN THEIR RELATION TO THE

SPANISH-AMERICAN WAR

FOR THE LIBERATION OF

CUBA AND OTHER ISLAND POSSESSIONS
OF SPAIN.

FULLY ILLUSTRATED WITH FINE TONED ENGRAVINGS SHOWING
OFFICERS AND MEN COMPOSING THE REGIMENT NEAR THE
DATE OF MUSTERING OUT, BESIDE SCENES CONNECTED
WITH THE CAREER OF THE REGIMENT.

BY
CHAPLAIN JOHN R. SKINNER

MAJOR-GENERAL FITZHUGH LEE.

COLONEL CASIMIR ANDEL.

COLONEL EBEN SWIFT.

DEDICATION.

TO

MY DEVOTED WIFE,

AND

LADY NURSES

OF THE

SEVENTH ARMY CORPS,

WHO WERE SO LONG ASSOCIATED TOGETHER IN THE HOSPITALS, WHERE THE SICK AND UNFORTUNATE OF THIS CORPS WERE TENDERLY CARED FOR,

IS THIS HUMBLE VOLUME DEDICATED.

BRIGADIER-GENERAL HENRY T. DOUGLAS.

CAPT. H. S. PARKER.

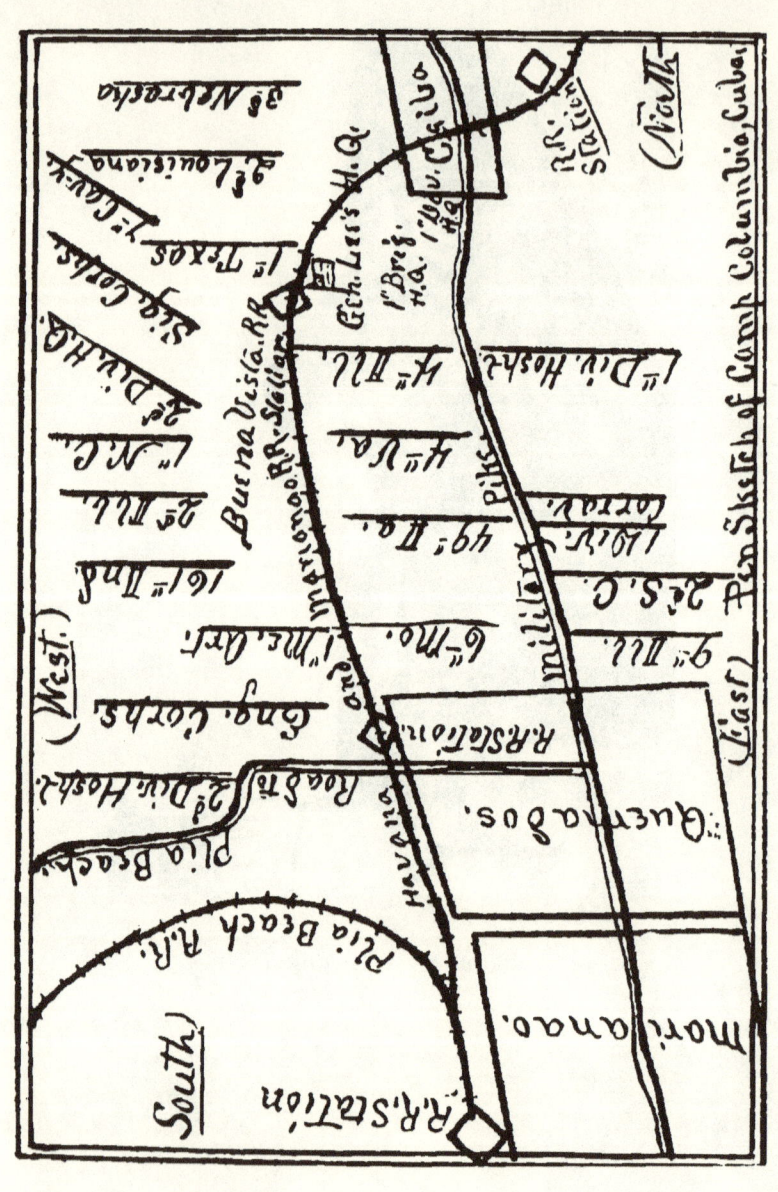

LIEUT-COLONEL S. A. D. MCWILLIAMS.

MAJOR L. E. BENNETT.   1ST LIEUT. CHARLES DOLE.

INTRODUCTION.

In undertaking to publish a history of the Fourth Illinois Volunteers I realize from the first the disadvantages under which I must labor from my comparative brief membership in the organization. In order, therefore, to prevent as far as possible any error of dates, facts or conditions, I at once sought relief from this embarrassment by soliciting help from those of the regiment who were more conversant with all the details connected with its history, and I now take this public way of tendering my most heartfelt gratitude to those who have either directly or indirectly rendered me assistance in this matter.

My effort and aim has been to secure and embody only facts and yet all facts of historic interest connected with the regiment in its career as United States Volunteers. That I have not been able to accomplish my desire in this respect, I fear will be discovered in the body of this book as I have been greatly disappointed in some, whose promises to aid in certain matters have failed to materialize in any helpful way, thus not only delaying the issue of the work, but as well reduced the number of cuts, biographies and facts of company history.

Still, with the hope that it may be worthy of your reception, not merely as a kind of souvenir of our campaign, but more, as a volume embodying history of faithful service, as well as real suffering, I submit it to the interested reader. While the reader will find facts repeated in this volume, yet the different settings given them by different writers will enable the reader to get a glimpse at them from several angles.

We have not striven to produce flowers of rhetoric, or beautiful symmetrical periods that please and charm the cultured literati. Nor have we attempted to give all the laughable incidents and jokes that passed, the misconstruction of which might cast reflections where they would give pain. So likewise we have withheld facts that could have no historic value to the reader, but on the other hand might be wrested to the embarrassment or serious hurt of individuals in their social, civil or political relations. Considering the great disadvantages under which we have labored in collecting the facts of the volume, which we hope are sufficiently reliable to be trusted and appreciated, we commit them to the public in this more permanent form, without an apology, yet asking that our imperfections as discovered will be pardoned as unintentional.

Arcola, Ill., June 30, 1899.   Respectfully,

J. R. SKINNER.

INDEX.

BIOGRAPHIES.

Abend, Lieut. E. J.	77
Andel, Col. Casimir	20
Andel, Lieut. W. C.	78
Blackwell, Sergt. S. B.	392
Clayton, Lieut. E. P.	113
Coen, Lieut. H. C.	37
Courtney, Capt. W. R.	196
Davis, Lieut. C. W.	237
Douglas, Brig.-Gen. H. T.	19
Evers, J. U.	410
Engelmann, Miss J.	405
Harris, Lieut. Lyman	170
Hersh, Capt. E. W.	168
Hilgard, Lieut. R. M.	78
Hilgard, Lieut. G. E.	399
Howell, Capt. W. A.	170
Lang, Maj. E. J	98
Lee, Brig.-Gen. Fitzhugh	17
McCord, Major T. C.	398
Moore, Lieut. R. J.	240
Parker, Capt. H. S	24
Pavey, Capt. N. P	50
Piper, Lieut. W. N	222
Rose, Lieut. P. J.	159
Satterfield, Lieut. W. E	52
Schrader, Capt. F. J.	75
Seaman, Lieut. A. O.	159
Swift, Col. Eben	23
Skinner, J. R.	409
Smith, Lieut. A. W.	196
Snyder, Capt. Al.	390
Todd, W. H.	408
Thompson, Lieut. F. E.	198
Voris, Lieut. A. C.	271
Washburn, Lieut. L. B.	195
Wilson, Lieut. I. N.	35

HISTORY.

Battalion, First	26
Battalion, Second	98
Band	393
Cheney, George, Address by	445
Chaplaincy	411
Hospital	401
Regiment	286
Company A	240
" B	171
" C	89
" C, Home Reception of	97
Company E	273
" F	53
Company H	222
" I	115
" K	161
" L	40
" M	199

COMPANY ROSTERS.

Company A	263
" B	186
" C	91
" D	81
" E	278
" F	70
" G	108
" H	228
" I	152
" K	163
" L	44
" M	214

PORTRAITS AND ILLUSTRATIONS.

Company A, Commissioned Officers	238
Company A	264
Company B, Commissioned Officers	169
Company B	187
Company C, Capt. E. E. Barton	89
Company C, Non-Com. Officers	92
Company D, Commissioned Officers	76
Company D	80
Company E, Commissioned Officers	272
Company E, Non-Com. Officers	279
Company F, Commissioned Officers	51
Company F, Non-Com. Officers	377
Company F	71
Company G, Commissioned Officers	109
Company G, Non-Com. Officers	376
Company G	462
Company H, Commissioned Officers	223
Company H	229
Company I, Commissioned Officers	142
Company I, Non-Com. Officers	116
Company I	151
Company K, Commissioned Officers	160

INDEX.

Company K.................. 162
Company L, Commissioned Officers................ 36
Company L, Non-Commissioned Officers............. 39
Company L...... 45
Company M, Commissioned Officers.................. 197
Company M, Non-Commissioned Officers............. 215
A Company Street in Camp Cuba Libre 300
A Company Street in Camp Columbia--Drill Hour..... 326
A Hungry Trio 349
A Mixed Race............... 426
Andel, Col. Casimir 7
Band......... 394
Barn, Ruins of a Cuban...... 341
Barbed Wire Defense 443
Before and After Fumigation. 106
Breaking Camp at Springfield, Jacksonville............... 301
Blanket Drill, or Kangaroo Court 305
Blackwell, Sam.............. 390
Bennett, Major L. E......... 10
Boneyard, Human 435
Boneventura Cemetery....... 439
Boarding a Transport 315
Block House. 425
Bugle Corps................. 285
Camp Barber Shop........... 357
Camp Columbia... 12
Camp McKenzie............. 372
Camp at Mountain Cut...... 335
Camp at Mountain Pass...... 343
Cathedral, Interior of........ 433
Corral, Fourth Illinois....... 356
Corduroy Bridge, Panama Park 298
Cuban Soldiers.............. 421
Cuban Soldiers' Camp.. 422
Donlan, Lieutenant.......... 397
Elliott, Major E. E.......... 194
Engelman, Miss J............ 406
Evers, J. U 410
Fast Mail................... 297
Foot-ball Team.............. 443
Fatigue Duty........ 302
Galbraith, Lieut. C. M....... 397
Guard Mount............... 324
Grayback, A................ 444
Giving an Order............. 351
Hangman's Tree............. 430
Hilgard, Lieut. G. E......... 397
Hospital, Fourth Ill., Cuba.... 402

Hungry Cubans....... 349
Lang, Major E. J............ 99
Lee, Brig. Gen. Fitzhugh.... 2
McWilliams, Lieut.-Col...... 9
McCord, Major M. D........ 397
Maine Graves................ 438
Margaret, Transport.... 371
Map of Camp Columbia..... 12
Military Road............... 332
Mobile Off for Cuba.......... 316
Mobile Entering Havana Harbor...................... 208
Moro Castle................. 388
Mountain Cut............ ... 334
North Gate, Camp Columbia.. 325
On Guard--Early Morning.. 354
Ox Cart, Georgia............. 428
Parker, Capt. H. S........ ..
Poems,..................... 378
Plowing in Cuba............ 427
Quartermaster's Store House, Quemados 432
Quarantine Camp............ 369
Ready for the March. (Referred to on page 302)...... 304
Ruins of a Cuban Barn...... 341
San Jose Espigon............ 321
Snakes and Other Trophies.. 347
Seasick..................... 104
Scene in Panama Park...... 299
Skinner, Capt. J. R......... 409
Skirmish Drill.............. 303
Swift, Col. Eben............ x
Swiping a Porker............ 339
Storm at Third Division Hospital...................... 294
Street Scene at Drill Hour, Cuba..................... 336
Sunset--From the Maine.... 30
Snyder, Capt. Al............ 390
Tandem Team............... 428
Transport Whitney.......... 365
Thatched Hut............... 429
Todd, Capt. H. W.......... 409
United States Military Cemetery...................... 389
Vento Springs............... 441
Wagon Train on the Way to Camp..................... 322
Wagon Train and North Mt.. 345
Washburn, Lieut............
Wreck of Water Tank...... 329
Wreck of the Maine........ 340
Whitney, The Transport.... 365
Yarmouth, The Transport.... 103
Y. M. C. A. Gospel Tent...... 414

SEVENTH ARMY CORPS.

FITZHUGH LEE.

Major-General Fitzhugh Lee, commanding the Seventh Army Corps, is one of the most conspicuous figures in the country to-day. For three years, as consul-general to Havana, he represented the United States in the unhappy island of Cuba during the desperate struggle that reduced it to a land of mourning and desolation.

He left the island with the withdrawal of diplomatic relations between this country and Spain on the eve of the outbreak of hostilities, and he now returns at the head of the army of occupation, and as military governor of Havana province will direct the fortunes of the people in that part of Spain's richest dependencies.

So eminent, courageous and diplomatic were his services that he possessed the confidence of not only two administrations, but of the whole country as well.

General Lee is a typical American, patriotic and magnanimous, as great in forbearance as he is valorous in the defense of the principles of justice and humanity, characteristics which made him invaluable to his country in the post which he held during the critical period preceding the Spanish-American war.

A soldier by birth and education, General Lee is a type of Virginia's best blood. He was born in Fairfax county November 19, 1835; was graduated from West Point in 1856, and commissioned second lieutenant of the Second Cavalry, serving in the west against the Indians, where he was severely wounded. Upon his return to duty he was ordered to West Point as instructor of cavalry, where he remained until the outbreak of the Civil war, when he exchanged the service of the Union for that of the Confederacy, and was commissioned first lieutenant of a cavalry corps. He served as adjutant-general of Ewell's brigade a short time, when he was made lieutenant-colonel of the First Virginia Cavalry, and after less than a year's service was advanced to a colonelcy. He was made a brigadier-general in July, 1862, and the following year a major-general. He was severely wounded at Winchester, after three horses had been shot under him, and was disabled for several months. During the closing days of the war he had command of the cavalry corps of Northern Virginia, which he surrendered to General Meade.

After some years of retirement following the declaration of peace, which he spent on his farm, he began to take an active part in the politics of his state, and was elected governor in 1885 for a term of four years. The year following the expiration of his term as governor, he led the troops of his state at the Washington centennial celebration in New York City, and received an ovation second to that accorded to no public man present. After that he retired from the public, and until his appointment as consul-general to Havana by President Cleveland in 1894 he led a quiet life.

It is one of the fortunes of war that General Lee should command the army of occupation in Havana province, where he was accorded such scant courtesy by the proud and haughty captain-generals of Spain, who afflicted with misrule and were a terror to its down-trodden and unhappy people, and should bring to them the protection of the United States, looking to a peaceful and stable government. During the months of December, 1898, and

January, 1899, General Lee and the regiments composing his command landed in the city of Havana, from which but a few months previous he had left under the frown of Spanish authority, but now receiving the welcome of a long-expectant and long-misruled people.

He took up his headquarters in a former Spanish-Cuban mansion at the Beuna Vista station, on the Marianao railroad, some four and a half miles northwest of Havana, where, in a beautiful and spacious camp, he was surrounded by the troops under his command, and where he remained until his corps was disbanded and returned to the United States in May, 1899.

[The above was copied in the main from a "History of the Seventh Army Corps," published in Savannah, Ga., in 1898.]

HENRY T. DOUGLAS.

Brig.-Gen. Henry T. Douglas was born and educated in Virginia. During the Civil war, having fitted himself for the work of a civil engineer, he was placed in the Corps of Engineers, C. S. A., serving on the staffs of Generals McGruder, A. P. Hill, G. W. Smith and E. Kirby Smith.

His military service began with the commission of second lieutenant of engineers, C. S. A., in which position his services were of such merit as led to his promotion to that of a colonelcy before peace was an assured fact between the contending states.

At the close of the civil strife, or in 1866, he resumed his chosen profession as civil engineer and continued in it until 1898, when he was commissioned brigadier-general of volunteers and assigned to duty as commander of the Second Brigade, First Division, Seventh Army Corps, and accompanied General Lee into the island of Cuba, remaining with his command until the army of occupation was broken up and returned to the states, from which a few months previously they had gone out.

General Douglas was filling the responsible position of chief engineer of the Baltimore and Ohio railroad and the Southern railway when he was called to the service of the United States.

CASIMIR ANDEL.

Col. Casimir Andel was born in Germany near Bingen on the Rhine in 1840. He came to this country in 1858, stayed in Evansville, Indiana, until 1859, when he came to Bellville, Illinois, where he entered upon mercantile pursuits. In response to President Lincoln's first call for seventy thousand volunteers, Colonel Andel enlisted as a private in Company A, of the Ninth Illinois Volunteers, April 17, 1861. A few days later he did his first guard duty at the main entrance to the fair grounds at Springfield, Illinois. He had orders not to let anybody pass after dark without the countersign. Shortly after dark a civilian, riding a military equipped horse tried to force his way, and not paying any attention to the sentinel's challenge, had his horse stabbed in the neck by the sentinel's bayonet. For this deed Andel was promoted corporal the next day by Col. August Mersy. When the Ninth Illinois Regiment was mustered out July 26, 1861, Andel joined the Twelfth Missouri Regiment, which was just organizing in St. Louis, as he was anxious to meet the enemy in the field and afraid that, if he would re-enlist in the Ninth Illinois Regiment, he would be doomed to remain in Cairo to the end of the war. August 8th he was mustered in as sergeant of Company B, Twelfth Missouri Infantry. After the battle of

Pea Ridge there were three lieutenancies vacant for which there were sixty applicants. Sergeant Andel, having passed the best examination, was commissioned second lieutenant of Company A.

At the bloody charge on the 22nd of May, 1863, Lieutenant Andel was shot through the upper right arm while charging a rebel battery near Vicksburg, Mississippi. He fell a few yards in front of the enemy's works while attempting to step over a large fallen tree. Seeing the impossibility of taking said battery, he lay flat on the ground with his command (his captain having been wounded and retired previously) from about one o'clock in the afternoon until dark, thereby keeping the rebels from firing upon our retreating columns, as the ground was very steep and the rebels were compelled to expose the whole upper part of their bodies in order to use their guns effectively. In this way the wounded and dead and even the scattered arms could be removed from the field without any further casualties.

On the 7th of June, 1863, Lieutenant Andel received a commission as first lieutenant of Company C, which was endorsed in red ink: "For gallant conduct in the actions before Vicksburg, Mississippi."

During the Yazoo expedition the Twelfth Missouri Regiment was detailed to do duty on the so-called Mosquito fleet as artillery. Lieutenant Andel had occasion to act as "officer of the deck" several times. Later on he was ordered to report to Gen. Peter Joseph Osterhaus as aid-de-camp, in which capacity he served until his regiment was mustered out before Atlanta, Georgia, in September, 1864. May 16, 1864, Lieutenant Andel was commissioned captain of Company D, but never commanded that company. He took part in all the battles and skirmishes in which the Twelfth Missouri Regiment participated except from May

22, 1863, to the end of August of the same year, during which time he was at home under surgical treatment. During the coal miners' strike in 1894, Company A, Belleville guards, were organized for the protection of life and property and Casimir Andel was unanimously elected their captain, although not present at the citizens' meeting.

During the railroad strike in 1877, Captain Andel's Company A did service from July 23d to August 8th, partly in East St. Louis and partly in Belleville.

After the strike the Eleventh Regiment, Illinois National Guards, was organized, and Captain Andel was elected colonel, although not an applicant and not present at the officers' meeting.

On March 1st, 1894, Company D, Fourth Regiment, was organized and Colonel Andel was elected captain, although not a member and not wishing the position. He refused at first, but was finally persuaded by Col. Hugh Bayle, then assistant adjutant-general of the state, to accept with the condition, however, that his resignation would be accepted any time after three months. When the time came, Company D was ordered to Carterville and Mounds, and, of course, the Captain could not resign. He did so, however, on March 1st, 1895, having served just one year in the Fourth Illinois National Guard Regiment, quitting military life for good, as he then thought.

But now came the war with Spain. Governor Tanner offered Colonel Andel command of the Fourth Illinois Regiment, and the Colonel's patriotism would not permit him to refuse. He accepted and left a few days later with his regiment for Cuba, as he then thought. His original orders were to report to General Shafter, at Tampa; this order was changed, however, when the regiment reached Albany, Georgia, orders from war department directed the fourth Illinois to Jacksonville, Florida, to report to General Lawton. General Lawton was superseded by General Arnold when the regiment arrived, to whom Colonel Andel reported. He had a very poor camping ground assigned, but tried to make the best of it by ditching and elevating the low places. His men went to work with a will and created one of the prettiest camping grounds in the vicinity in a very short time.

Colonel Andel went with his regiment to Savannah, Georgia, and remained until November 17th, 1898, when he resigned, the war being virtually over and his presence being needed more at home than in the field.

Before he left his regiment, to which he was very much attached, he secured the colonelcy of the same for Lieut.-Col. Ebner Swift, of the Ninth Illinois Regiment, a distinguished officer of the United States Army, who had seen actual service in the field. Upon his return home Colonel Andel took charge of the First National Bank of Belleville, Illinois, whose cashier he has been for a quarter of a century.

EBEN SWIFT.

Colonel Eben Swift, who was the second and last commander of this regiment during its history as a part of the United States Volunteer Army, was born in Texas, his father at the time holding a commission as major in the United States service.

He was appointed by General Grant as a cadet-at-large to the Military Academy, at West Point, from which he graduated in 1876, and was assigned to the Fifth United States Cavalry as a second lieutenant. In January, 1878, was appointed regimental adjutant, and acted in this capacity until 1887; was promoted to first lieutenant in October, 1884, and to that of captain in December, 1893.

In May, 1898, he entered the United States volunteer service as a major in the Seventh Illinois, and in July he was promoted to lieutenant-colonel of the Ninth Illinois, and in November of the same year was commissioned colonel of the Fourth Illinois.

Prior to his entering the volunteer service, he took part in the field in Wyoming, Idaho, Nebraska and Colorado, in the movements again the Sioux, Cheyenne, Bannock, Nez Perces and Ute Indians, up to and including the year 1879; and in frontier garrison service to the year 1887. From this date up to 1890 he filled the position of aid-de-camp on the staff of Gen. Wesley Merritt; engaging in field and garrison duty in Oklahoma and Indian Territory to 1893, and as assistant instructor in Military Art in the United States Infantry and Cavalry School at Fort Leavenworth, Kansas, to 1897, when he was placed on duty with the Illinois National Guards, where he rendered efficient service up to the date of his muster into the volunteer service of the United States.

HARRY S. PARKER.

Captain Harry S. Parker is a son of Richland county, Illinois, having been born therein on the 3d of January, 1871. During the year following, his parents moved with their family to Effingham, his present home, where he pursued the elementary branches in the city public schools, but before completing the course of study laid down in these schools, he sought the larger sphere of education in the Oakdale school at Leavenworth, Kansas, and later attended night school in his home city, while the days he spent working in the shops of the Vandalia Railraad; also attended Austin College for a time and studied law with the

Wood Bros. of Effingham,—doing office work at the time; also spent one year in the Kent Law School of Chicago, Illinois. In February, 1896, he was admitted to the Bar, and June 1, of the same year, opened a law office in the city of his childhood. He became a charter member of Company G, Fourth Illinois National Guards, in the early part of 1892, as a private, being made first sergeant in May, and was discharged in September, of the same year, in order to attend school. Reenlisted in June, 1893, and was made sergeant major of the Third Battalion and on Thanksgiving day of the same year was commissioned a captain and made regimental adjutant. During his military career he has served under Colonels R. M. Smith and J. B. Washburn in the Illinois National Guards, and after being mustered into the United States service, with the regiment on May 20, 1898, under Colonels Casimir Andel and Eben Swift, mustered out with the regiment, under the last named, at Augusta, Georgia, May 2, 1899, having spent almost one year as a United States volunteer.

FIRST BATTALION.

BEGINNING APRIL 4, 1899.

The suspense under which we had been resting, or trying to rest submissively and patiently, was broken on the morning of April 4th, about 1 o'clock in the morning, when we received orders to be ready with all our belongings, which, in this land of souvenir gathering, had grown to no small proportions, including tentage and cooking apparatus. It need scarcely be said that the boys responded to this order with an eagerness and alacrity that did not always characterize them when the call to fatigue, drill or dress parade went echoing down the streets of our camp. Accordingly, every man was on the move by 4:30 o'clock, getting that part of the regimental menagerie belonging to this battalion and the many other articles of more or less usefulness and importance to the soldier who is out in defense of his country's flag and honor, into condition for evacuation of camp at Buena Vista, and our initial march on the "Home, Sweet Home" trip.

Having answered the familiar call of "soupy, soupy, soupy," at 5:30 o'clock, at 6 the wagon train began to make its appearance on the scene and very soon willing hands, moved by gladdened hearts, were stowing away tents, trunks and boxes, in fact, about everything that a soldier thinks he needs as a necessary baggage equipage, in the large land ships of Uncle Sam's army, and about 9 the driver's yell and snap of whip opened the throttle of his four-muled power motor and the long train moved out on the old military road, over which Spain had so recently moved her war equipments for a similar purpose, to its destination at the dock on Havana bay, where our valuables were placed on lighters and towed out into the harbor, stowed away on the steamer that was to bear us on our homeward journey. As soon as the wagon train had gotten out of the way, our battalion was formed into line, equipped in light marching order and the commanding voice of Major Bennet was heard in those old familiar words that never sounded better, "battalion attention," and every fellow straightened up to his best proportions, awaiting the next command that started our feet, in unison with our minds, on the long desired march toward our "own beloved home." The march of six and one half kilometers over the military road to the quaint, old city of Havana, was made without accident, or even incident of unusual note, except the limestone dust from the pike that rose in clouds and was driven about us and into our faces by the strong breeze that fanned us, under the heat of the tropical April sun. Near noon we filed in through the iron gates opening to the commodious sheds in connection with the San Jose docks where our now weary feet first tread on Cuban territory twelve weeks previous, and truly the shade and refreshing breeze from the bay were welcome friends.

After some four and one half hours of rest and waiting the bugle call aroused us, and our packs and guns were soon in place on sturdy shoulders and we were moving with quick step on the two United States tugs that had just run alongside the docks to carry us out on the bay near the remains of the fated Maine, where the Whitney, a steamer of the Plant Line, dressed in war paint, lay at anchor awaiting her priceless cargo. She is a ship of medium size, sidewheeler, a fact that almost made some of the boys sick as they thought how easily she would rock and toss to the rolling waves that began to rise and fall, in their imagination, until their crested heads threatened to pass over us. Disapprovals of her as a boat unworthy of such a cargo, were not unfrequently heard as we approached her and took in her dimensions and exterior appearance, but on entering her hull these remarks and gibes gave way to expressions of approval and surprise at her commodious and cleanly quarters, so different from the great transport that carried us into this port; yet, perhaps in this, only because we were not so numerous a quantity in comparison to the space to be occupied, for it was not known to many of us up to this time that Company C was dropped out to accompany the Second Battalion, which marched into the dock sheds, weary and dust stained, just before our departure and whose wagon train was being unloaded as we took our departure from the docks. It was therefore the honor of Companies L, F and D to accompany headquarters and our efficient band; also we had the pleasure of the company of J. A. Hardin, second lieutenant of Company D, First North Carolina Volunteer Infantry, of Reidsville, North Carolina, who had been on detached duty to the Tenth United States Infantry and who was assigned to our regiment for return to his own regiment at Savannah. Also Clark M. Carr, first lieutenant Company L, Ninth Illinois Volunteer Infantry, of Galesburg, was assigned to this regiment for transportation on his way to Washington, answering an order looking to a position in the regular army.

On board the Whitney, we found her appointments for the accommodation of soldiers not the equal of those of the Mobile, but which lack was fully overcome by our more roomy quarters and the liberties accorded to us, for we were excluded only from the dining room and middle aft deck, which was assigned to headquarters. But we had not been aboard long until the "pipe" was heard on many lips. "Well, we are doomed to stay in the harbor all night, for the commissary stores are not here yet, and we can't leave after sundown."

This heart-saddening rumor grew out of the fact that it was nearing that time, and by harbor laws no vessel bound for another port could leave after that hour. But our ship's commander was a man who well knew how to meet such emergencies, and accordingly about that hour weighed anchor for the start. Just as the sun, like a great ball of fire, was slooping down behind a covering of fleecy clouds, as if to hide himself from the scene, made so grandly beautiful by his mellowed rays, our boat moved alongside the United States steamer Resolute, which fired for us a parting salute, and out under the frowning walls of old Morro into the open sea we steamed, just three months, lacking one day, from the time of our entrance. Nothing eventful occurred save seasickness that got hold of some of our boys almost at the thought of being on the ocean, until the morning of Wednesday. While the captain and purser of our boat, the colonel, staff and line officers were regaling themselves at the morning feast, when a sudden racket on the hurricane deck attracted the eyes of all at the table to the skylight above, revealing to the experienced officers that something was not moving smoothly, and at once the officer of the day and guard were hastily despatched to the scene to learn the cause and give what assistance was necessary. It turned out that a couple of the boys who wore red and white stripes on their pants and do the blowing for the regiment, were discussing the propriety of settling a slight difference between them in a hand-to-hand set-to. The officer of the day granted them full permission to do so, but requested them to get off the boat, lest they should accidentally knock someone overboard. This

SUNSET FROM THE MAINE, CUBA.

seemed to cool their blood or something else, and in an hour or two they were aiding in a concert on the aft deck of the officers' apartment.

By 9 o'clock the ship was tossing and swaying considerable to the motion of the water, that was dancing to a strong breeze from the Florida coast, having passed Key West light at 5 A. M., and aside from the crew that did not wish something to settle his stomach, or even go farther, was the exception to the rule; even the chaplain, after several hours' fight against the inevitable, "heaved up Jonah," keeping his state room, as did many others during the day. About 5:30 on Thursday morning we sighted a light house far in our front and at 6:00 we were in sight of land which proved to be Egmont Key, the beginning of a chain of islands lying off Tampa and forming a kind of breast water to the main land. After a few hours a tug ran along side and we were informed that we would soon be visited by a lighter, that would carry our belongings to the above island, where they would be disinfected, and we would be quarantined three days prior to going to Port Tampa. The work of unloading continued until after dark, when the last of our companies were landed by a tug and sought out quarters in the tents erected by their comrades who were perhaps unfortunate enough to get off the boat ahead of them. While the voyage was to us tedious, owing to the very low speed of the boat, there were other discomfitures and inconveniences met with in landing and getting adjusted in our quarters that seemed entirely inexcusable, owing to a lack of facilities to unload the lighters at the docks, where one entire load and part of another remained during the night, to be caught in one of those terrible down pours of rain that are so well known to the soldier that has spent any time in the sand-clad state of Florida. During the day, amid storm and rain, the unloading of lighters went slowly on, while a gang of government employees were busily engaged opening trunks, boxes and so forth and subjecting their contents to a fumigating process that consumed hours for each batch submitted to the disinfecting vault. When, as we were here told, the government had at an immense outlay fitted up a large floating disinfecting station and anchored it in Havana bay, in order to expedite the transfer of troops from the island, one wonders at our being brought here where facilities are so meagre.

From the wharf we were marched into a double twilled barbed wire stockade, carrying on its front a kind of "don't you try it" appearance, which indicated to us that within these limitations our days of quarantine were to be spent. During this time Company C and the Second Battalion also came ashore and entered the same quarters, pitching their neighborly tents alongside of ours ready to pass the ordeal with us. One of our men, after expressing his opinion of the whole matter, suggested the propriety of writing a history embodying all the facts, entitled "The Army of Occupation on the Island of Fumigation, or Three Days in Hades." How this embodied the views and feelings of all concerned the writer is not able with certainty to say. And something of an ordeal it was, for along with the inconveniences of landing and want of facilities to care for our private belongings, was that of no place in which to do our cooking. Consequently when the rain began to pour down in torrents on Friday morning with a heavy sea gale, we soon found our fires in a sad plight and our breakfast not much better; all this, with the brevity of rations in some companies, made our "home coming," to say the least, unpleasant. For the wind continued its heavy gale and our tent flies flapped and cracked like the wings of some huge bird struggling to destroy its antagonist or free itself from an unwelcome captor. Yet we are glad to say that in Paul M. Carington, M. D., Surgeon United States Marine Hospital service, and his able corp of assistants, we met with kind, gentlemanly and hospitable treatment, doing all they could to make our stay as agreeable and pleasant as circumstances would admit.

After spending our four days in the quarantine corral, Monday morning, before the dawn of day, the gentle voice of the soldier could be heard in every direction, and the blazing fires at every company's quarters told that the "soup" maker was at his task of preparing an early breakfast, and at 6 personal baggage began to find its way to the dock, and by 7:30 both battalions were aboard the fine little river steamer Margaret, of the Plant system, and a three hours' ride on a calm sea brought us alongside of the commodious docks at Port Tampa, Florida, where disembarkation and re-loading of men and baggage was hurried up in true American style, which put us in readiness on a train of three sections for our trip to Savannah. At 3:10 the wheels were in motion, rolling us over the sandy, wooded plains and ridges, and among the swamps and lakes of Florida, at a rate that made us feel that we were on some well equiped road in Illinois, save its lack of smoothness. Night threw her sable curtains gently about us after a hundred-mile run and we settled down for our rest.

Soon after leaving Waycross, just over the border line in Georgia, the gray dawn became visible, soon followed by the silver bars that shot up the sky from the sun that still hid his face below the horizon, opening to our view the still level, pine-clad plains with their many marshy tracts, similar to that which was hid from us by the gentle dropping of the pall of night. Soon after sun-up we crossed the broad, clear Savannah river, on which several small boats, occupied by four or six negroes, by whom they were being pulled down its liquid pathway, yet nothing about the scene could indicate their mission or their destination. Another eventful thing occurred during this run of between four and five hundred miles. At High Springs, about 9:30 P. M., Colonel Wrenn, general superintendent of the Plant system of transportation, who was the guest of Colonel Swift on this trip, took him and his staff to the hotel for dinner. As we took seats about the neatly-spread tables that reminded one of home, our waiter stood gazing in a kind of blank, astonished way upon the scene, the very picture of antiquation or a slightly back number of his occupation. But no sooner was he addressed by one of the hungry company than his eyes flashed as that of one of his color only could, and the prompt reply that came from his broad mouth at once awakened our curiosisy, which was soon formed into a chorus of suppressed laughter that increased into almost uproarious bursts as one after another his pert, witty and philosophical replies came with promptness in answer to questions propounded, or as explanations of, or comments on, the "viands," as he called them, with which he was regaling us in no sleepy fashion. All of which plainly told that he was of the stamp of Booker T. Washington, or, perhaps, Frederick Douglass. By common consent it was voted that it was worth more than the meal cost us (we being Colonel Wrenn's guests) to enjoy the rich, spicy wit of the man who, on passing the first dish, nicely-fried, juicy steak, remarked that they had "other viands coming," and they came in profusion. Returning to the train, we tried to hustle the porter out of his easy-going way to get our berths ready for a good night's rest, which we realized on the following morning had been ours. We had not proceeded far after our morning lnnch when *the* incident of the trip occurred that aroused the indignation of about every man on board. We suddenly came to a halt at Southover Junction, with our train headed in another direction than that of Savannah, which led Colonel Wrenn to hasten to the head of the train to learn the cause, only to return in a few minutes to inform us that our destination was changed to Augusta, Georgia, and bid us good-bye. This not only called for a change in our course, like Israel at the borders of the promised land, but also to part company with Lieutenant J. A. Hilden, whose destination was Savannah.

At the end of a run of about three hours we found ourselves passing around the city of Augusta on a serpent-like track that seemed to follow the streets in its wanderings to the northwest, for a distance of some five miles, when we side-tracked, unloaded and were soon wending our way up a long incline to the top of a large sand hill, "Monte Sano," west of the city, where we found in camp MacKenzie tents, mess-shacks and other conveniences constituting a good camp awaiting us, into which we entered and began in true earnestness the unpacking and arranging of our varied articles so essential to the comfort and gratification of an American soldier of "occupation." While sorely disappointed over not getting into Savannah, we find Augusta a beautiful city of some fifty thousand inhabitants, located in the beautiful and fertile valley of the Savannah river, a city well laid out and of modern date in its improvements.

ISAAC NEWTON WILSON.

Isaac Newton Wilson, first lieutenant Company L, was born at Olney, Illinois, January 30, 1876, attended the Olney public school until 1892, when he entered the Western Military Academy at Alton, Illinois, and attended that

school until the close of the term of 1895, when he graduated. Returning to Olney he was active in the formation of Company L, Fourth Regiment State Guards. On the call for troops for the war with Spain he was first lieutenant of Company L, and was with the company until October, 1898, when he was seized with Durgue fever and on the advice of his physician he resigned his commission, which was accepted and he was honorably discharged on the 29th day of October, 1898, with the brevet rank of captain. He immediately returned to Olney to recuperate his health and in the month of December of that year he went to New York City, and entered the wholesale commission house of Francis McMulkin & Company.

HOMER C. COEN.

Homer C. Coen, the subject of this sketch, was born near Olney, Illinois, June 27, 1879, spending the first ten years of his life on the farm where he was born. In May, 1895, he enlisted in Company L, Fourth Illinois National Guard, and in June of the same year was promoted to the position of corporal, continuing as such until the old company was discharged; and when, on the 23d of April, 1896, the new company, bearing the same letter, was formed, he joined it, receiving the appointment to the position of first sergeant.

When the call of April 26, 1898, for volunteers came he was in attendance at school, in the University of Illinois, where he held the position of corporal in the company of cadets, composed of students, he having formerly completed the course of study in the high school of Olney, Illinois, from which he was a graduate. His company heeding the call, entered Camp Tanner at Springfield, where three days later he joined them and was mustered into the service of the United States. On the 8th of November, 1898, he was commissioned second lieutenant of the company at Savannah, Georgia, which he held until May 2, 1899, when with his comrades he was mustered out at Augusta, Georgia.

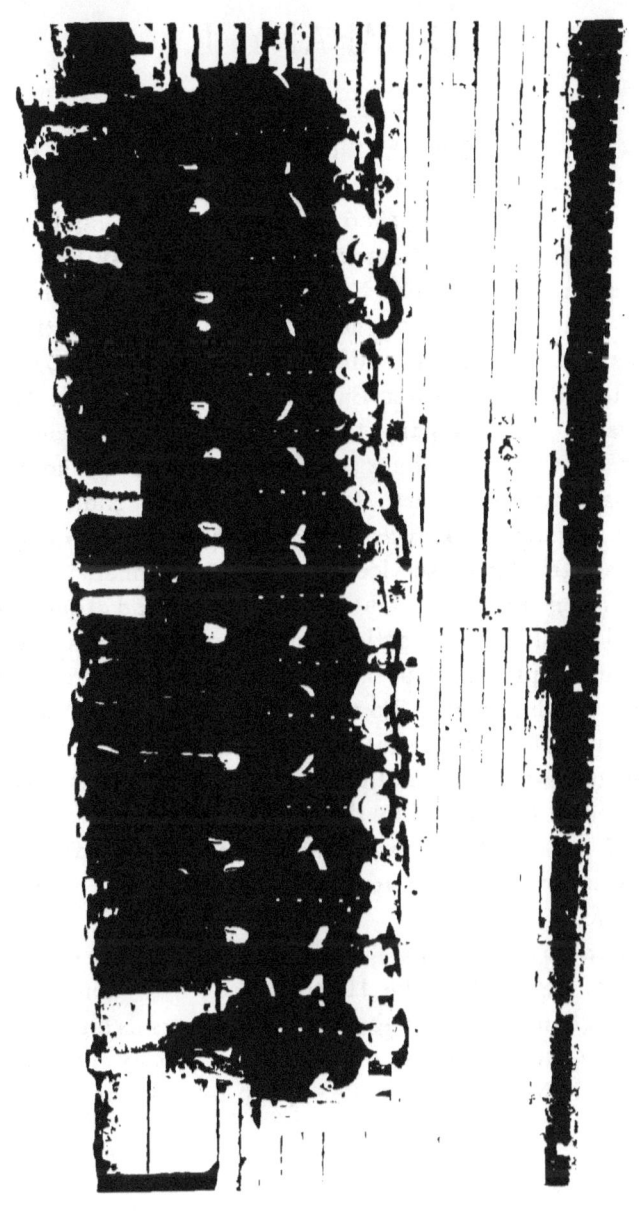

COMPANY L.

Company L, Fourth Illinois, was organized as a Guard company at Olney, and sworn into the service of the state of Illinois on April 24, 1896, by Lieutenant-Colonel Washburn, with Franz Muench, captain; I. N. Wilson, first lieutenant, and Rolla N. Hensley, second lieutenant. The company was assigned to the Second Battalion, commanded by Major McWilliams, and in 1897 was transferred to the First Battalion, commanded by Major Bennet. The company took part in the state encampment of 1896-97, where it was known as "The Kid" Company of the Fourth. After the destruction of the Maine, Company L was probably the first company of the state to offer its services to Governor Tanner. Intense enthusiasm prevailed among the boys, and they were drilled in all kinds of tactics, with marches in heavy order, and, in compliance with orders, the company was recruited to one hundred men, who were drilled until called out.

The call came about 1 A. M. on the morning of the never-to-be-forgotten 26th of April, and the news was announced to the people by the blowing of whistles and ringing of bells. The town was in a frenzy of excitement when the company left at 8:30 P. M. for Camp Tanner, via P. D. & E.

Arriving at Camp Tanner at 11 A. M., on the 27th, we were assigned to the Holstein barn with Company G, of Effingham, where we took up our quarters as high-graded stock. Company L, as every other company, took extra men with them so as to have enough to pass the examination, and as it was cold and raw, quite a little suffering was caused by the scarcity of blankets, we having but eighty-seven for one hundred and twenty-five men; but as the days wore on the numbers decreased, as many were sent home as were undesirable, and others being homesick and tired of the army ways at the start; but only two of the old guards failed to try and pass the examination. Lieutenant Wilson was sent home for more men, and on May 10 returned with ten recruits.

At last, on the 16th of May, the company was examined physically, and many were the heart-broken boys who failed to pass the examination, and when the time came for them to part from their more fortunate comrades many broke down and cried. Company L, with an aggregate of eighty-one men and three officers, was sworn into the service of the United States with the remainder of the First Battalion, at 4 P. M. on the afternoon of the 19th of May, the Second and Third being mustered in on the 20th.

On the evening of the 25th of May, orders were received to go to Tampa, and on the evening of the 26th, the regiment was started on its triumphant tour through the south. Unfortunately, at Waycross, Georgia, orders were received, ordering us to Jacksonville, where we arrived on the 29th. Here we were assigned to the Second Brigade, Second Division, Seventh Army Corps, and brigaded with the First Wisconsin and Fiftieth Iowa, commanded by Brigadier-General Bancroft. Under general recruiting orders, Corporal Robinson was sent home with Lieutenant Schrader, of Company D, to recruit twenty-five men for Company L, who were enlisted at Olney, on June 21, reporting at Jacksonville, June 25, 1898. From July 3 to July 11, Company L was detailed on provost duty, and encamped at camp "Hobo," in East Jacksonville. On August 10, camp was changed from Springfield to Panama, as the Fourth had been assigned to the Second Birgade, Third Division, with the First South Carolina and Sixth Missouri, commanded by General Barkley.

Captain Muench was placed in command of the First Battalion from August 25 to September 16, when returned and sent home on a sick leave, September 19. Lieutenant Wilson being in command of the company. Here were spent the most miserable days of our army experience, with half the company on the sick report, and seventeen down with typhoid fever in the Third Division hospital, and some furloughed; a few only were left able for duty. Twenty-four out of a total strength of one hundred and six were all Company L could muster for the grand review before General Alger, when it took a whole battalion to make a company, and where the regiment passed a mere wreck of what had been the healthiest in the service.

Of all our sick only one succumbed to the fever, Bugler Louis Lomelino, of Springfield, Illinois, who died at Third Division hospital, September 29, 1898, beloved by every boy in the company, for a better fellow, a truer soldier, or a braver soldier never gave his life for his country. On the 26th of September the regiment was ordered on provost, and Company L assigned to station number three, corner of Duvall and Palmetto streets, where they stayed until the Seventh Army Corps was ordered to Savannah, preparatory to embarking for Cuba. While on provost the regiment was assigned to Second Brigade, First Division, with Second South Carolina and Ninth Illinois.

On October 22d, the regiment was ordered on provost in Savannah, and was the first regiment to meet the people of that place, Company L being assigned to station number six, corner Barnard and Huntington streets, where amid a people in love with the military, and endowed by nature with hospitality, the boys lived a life of the blessed, and in return amused the people by tossing negroes skyward in a blanket (and once in a while a comrade lately returned from a furlough). Never will the boys forget the Thanksgiving dinner of 1898, when Southern hospitality proved too much even for a Northern soldier's appetite, and Company L left the table hopelessly defeated. First Lieutenant Wilson resigned while stationed here, October 29. On November 14, First Sergeant Homer Coen was appointed and commissioned second lieutenant. On November 26 the regiment was relieved from provost duty, and went into Camp Onward, near Dale avenue. Here athletics took the lead and Company L's foot-ball team defeated Company M's by a score of ten to nothing.

Camp life was the same old routine of drills, marches and parades, but at last, on January 3d, the regiment embarked with the Ninth Illinois on the United States transport Mobile, and no regiment ever left Savannah leaving behind so many friends or was accorded a more loving farewell than the Fourth. The Mobile reached Havana on the 5th, and on the 6th the First Battalion marched out to Camp Columbia and established camp. Here in a strange country, among strange people, the boys enjoyed themselves for three months, but hailed with joy the order to leave, April 3d, and on the evening of the 4th, just as the United States steamship Resolute was firing the evening gun, and the band playing the Star Spangled Banner, the First Battalion, on board the Plant Line steamer Whitney, steamed out of Havana Harbor, bound for Tampa, Florida, where we arrived on the 6th, and were unloaded and detained three days on the United States Quarantine Station, Egmont Key, the dreariest place God ever created. The First and Second Battalions left Egmont Key on the morning of the 10th, and were loaded on the Mobile & Ohio cars at Port Tampa and taken to Camp MacKenzie, Augusta, Georgia, where we arrived April 11th. Here we were encamped until mus'ered out, May 2d, when Company L returned to Olney, Illinois, as a body and, arriving there on the 4th, were received by the entire population of the city, and feasted in a royal manner. Many have been the ties formed within the last year, and may our comradeship be as warm as that which characterizes the veterans of 1861 and 1865.

COMPANY L ROSTER.

Those not otherwise mentioned were mustered into the United States service May 19, 1898, and mustered out May 2, 1899. The figures following the name indicate age·

FRANZ MUENCH, Captain, 37, Olney, Ill., merchant.
I. N. WILSON, First Lieutenant, 22, Olney, Ill., merchant; resigned Oct. 29, 1898.
ROLLA HENSLEY, Second Lieutenant, 22, Olney, Ill., clerk; promoted First Lieutenant, Nov. 12, 1898.
HOMER COEN, First Sergeant, 18, Onley, Ill., student; promoted Second Lieutenant, Nov. 14, 1898.

SERGEANTS.

John J. Horner, 20, Olney, Ill., merchant; appointed First Sergeant, Nov. 14, 1898; discharged Jan. 23, 1899.
Elbert Rowland, 20, Olney, Ill., student; appointed First Sergeant, Jan. 23, 1899.
Marshall Wallis, 20, Olney, Ill., student; reduced to ranks Sept. 10, 1898; discharged Nov. 3, 1898.
George Temple, 21, Olney, Ill., express agent; appointed Q. M. Sergeant, Nov. 1; relieved Apr. 8, 1899.

CORPORALS.

Rolla Dean, 20, Olney, Ill., carpenter; appointed artificer June 1, 1898; discharged March 31, 1899.

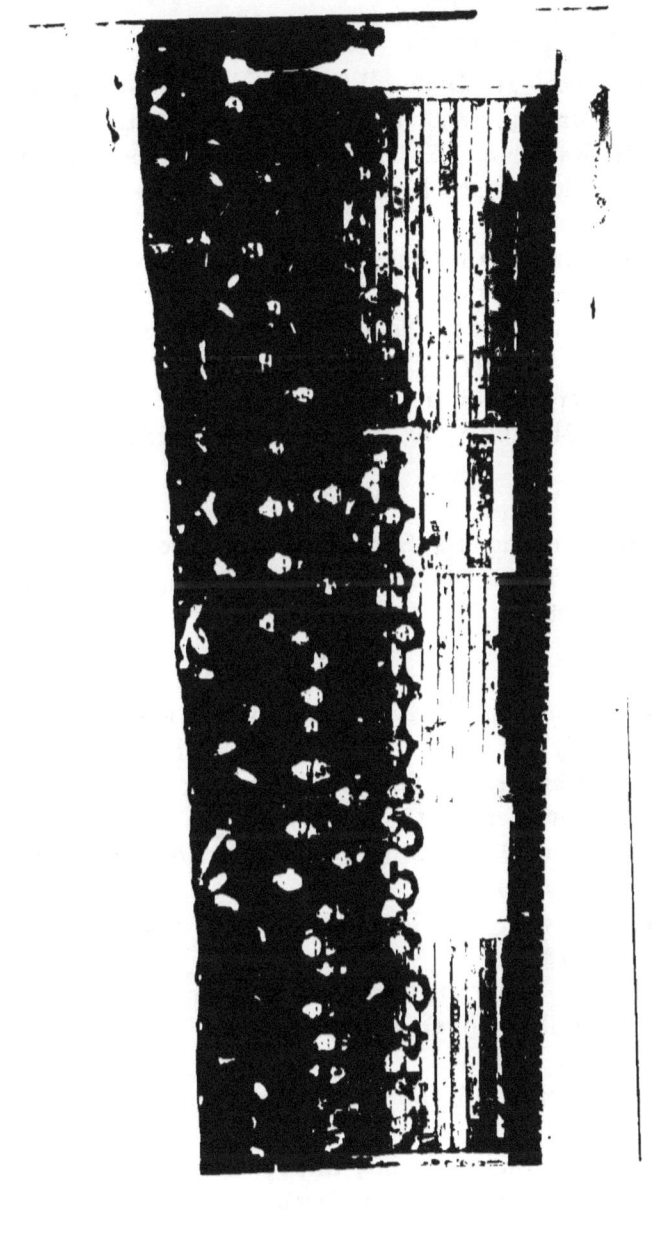

Roy Jones, 21, Olney, Ill., plasterer; appointed Corp., May 19, 1898; appointed Sergt., Sept. 10, 1898.
Oscar Kaufman, 20, Olney, Ill., clerk; appointed Q. M. Sergt. Apr. 8, 1898; appointed Sergt., Feb. 1, 1899.
Lynn Barnard, 18, Olney, Ill., student: appointed Sergt., Dec. 1, 1898.
Ross Hensley, 25, Olney, Ill., express agent; appointed Q. M. Sergt., May 18, 1898; relieved as Q. M. Sergt., Nov. 1, 1898.
William McKnight, 20, Ingraham, Ill., student.

MUSICIAN.

Louis Lomelino, 19, Springfield, Ill., bookkeeper. Died at Third Div. Hosp., Jacksonville, Fla., Sept. 29, 1898.

PRIVATES.

Allen, James, 34, Olney, Ill., railroader; appointed Corp., July 13, 1898.
Arnold, Charles, 26, Olney, Ill., farmer; appointed Wagoner, Feb. 1, 1899.
Arnold, John D., 25, Olney, Ill., farmer; discharged March 24, 1899.
Arnold, Martin, 24, Olney, Ill., farmer; discharged March 1, 1899.
Barckman, Isaac, 21, Olney, Ill., farmer.
Barlow, Ralph, 19, Olney, Ill., student; appointed Corp., Feb. 1, 1899.
Beck, Clarence, 26, Olney, Ill., clerk; discharged Nov. 19, 1898.
Behymer, Alvin, 30, Noble, Ill., railroader.
Black, David, 28, Calhoun, farmer; transferred to Hosp. Corps, June 10, 1898.

Busunder, Ralph, 20, Clay City, farmer; transferred to First Ill. Vol. Cav., June 9, 1898.
Byer, John, 20, Olney, Ill., student; appointed Corp., June 13, 1898; discharged March 15, 1899.
Byers, Lyman, 18, Olney, Ill., student; discharged Sept. 16, 1898.
Christy, Earnest, 19, Olney, Ill., merchant; appointed Corp., Sept. 10, 1898.
Coen, John O., 31, Olney, Ill., farmer; appointed Corp., Dec. 1, 1898.
Cope, Omer, 28, Olney, Ill., brickmason.
Coventry, Clinton C., 23, Olney, Ill., teacher; appointed Corp., Dec. 1, 1898.
Duvall, Edward J., 23, Olney, Ill., laborer.
Eckenrode, James A., 22, Olney, Ill., merchant.
Edmiston, Clarence, 20, Olney, Ill., student; discharged Feb. 3, 1899.
Evans, Pearl, 27, Noble, Ill., railroader.
Ewing, Walter, 22, Evansville, Ind., embalmer; transferred to Hosp. Corps, June 10, 1898.
Fishback, Clyde, 18, Olney, Ill., student; discharged Sept. 12, 1898.
Fleming, George, 19, Olney, Ill., student; appointed Corp., March 24, 1899.
Frey, Edward, 32, Collinville, Ill., farmer.
Genoway, Theodore, 23, Passport, Ill., farmer.
Gordon, Charles, 19, Sumner, Ill., baker, discharged Jan. 24, 1899.
Gross, Edward O., 23, Olney, Ill., clerk.
Guess, Alma, 19, Sumner, Ill., painter.
Harlan, Andrew, 24, Sumner, Ill., laborer; dishonorably discharged Dec. 27, 1898.
Harlan, Samuel, 20, Sumner, Ill., laborer.

Harmon, Cameron, 22, Ingraham, Ill., farmer; discharged Apr. 4, 1899.
Harmon, Harry, 24, Olney, Ill., laborer.
Hans, Rutherford, 21, Parkersburg, Ill., laborer; appointed Corp., July 13, 1899.
Heath, Thomas, 23, Claremont, Ill., clerk.
Heim, John, 24, Olney, Ill., plasterer.
Iaun, Alexander, 24, Olney., Ill., butcher.
Kaser, Jacob, 21, Olney, Ill., shoemaker.
Kinkade, John, 28, Olney, Ill., farmer; discharged Apr. 4, 1899.
Kinkade, Robert, 32, Olney, Ill., Farmer.
Kitch, Roy L., 22, Cairo, Ill., Clerk.
Laws, Almon, 23, Sumner, Ill., Painter.
Laws, Frederick, 20, Sumner, Ill., Stock Buyer.
Locke, Harry, 18, Olney, Ill., Farmer.
McCawley, Barnard, 18, Clay City, Ill., Laborer.
Mather, William T., 22, Olney, Ill., Barber.
Newson, Amos, 25, Olney, Ill., Farmer.
Nickerson, Charles, 18, Olney, Ill., Student; appointed Corp., May 19, 1898.
Pampe, Louis, 22, Parkersburg, Farmer.
Patterson, William, 23, Parkersburg, Farmer.
Petty, Roy, 20, Sumner, Ill., Engineer.
Ridgley, Archibald, 19, Olney, Ill., Student.
Richey, George, 19, Olney, Ill., Farmer.
Robinson, Richard, 21, Olney, Ill., Clerk; appointed Corp. July 13, 1898; discharged Nov. 3, 1898.
Rose, Thomas, 18, Clay City, Ill., Laborer; appointed Musician, Nov. 6, 1898.
St. John, Paul, 18, Olney, Ill., Student; appointed Corp. May 19, 1898.
Seibold, Frank, 19, Olney, Ill., Student; discharged March 13, 1899.

Rhode, Earl S., 20, Olney, Ill., Jurist; appointed Corp. July 13, 1898.
Houston, Jasper, 36, Ingraham, Ill., Farmer.
Teney, Harry, 20, Olney, Ill., Laborer.
Terhune, William, 30, Sumner, Ill., Farmer; appointed Chief Cook, Feb. 1.
Van Scyoc, Shannon, 28, Sumner, Ill., Clerk.
Wallis, Edward, 18, Olney, Ill., Student; discharged Nov. 3, 1898.
Wallis, Robert, 18, Olney, Ill., Student; appointed Corp. July 1, 1898; discharged Nov. 3, 1898.
Webb, John, 20, Olney, Ill., Farmer.
Weir, Benjamin, 18, Olney, Ill., Printer.
Weston, Adam, 19, Olney, Ill., Farmer.
Wharf, Eugene, 19, Olney, Ill., Student; discharged Feb. 15, 1899.
Wood, Medford, 23, Olney, Ill., Laborer.
Zook, Arthur, 18, Olney, Ill., Mechanic.

RECRUITS ENLISTED JUNE 21, 1898.

Balding, Henry, 21, Samsville, Ill., Farmer.
Barnard, Stephen, 24, Orleans, Ind., Farmer.
Christy, Clinton, 22, Olney, Ill., Printer.
Colvin, Peter, 21, Olney, Ill., Printer.
Cutter, Harry, 18 Olney, Ill., Painter.
Donnells, Gilbert, 23, Newling, Ind., Farmer; discharged Nov. 27, 1898.
Fleener, George, 26, Wakefield, Farmer.
Gharst, John, 23, Claremont, Farmer; discharged Dec. 28, 1898.
Johnson, George, 21, Sumner, Ill., Hostler.
Linxwiler, Clarence, 20, Sumner, Ill., Laborer.
Loughmiller, Bunn, 26, Hancock, Ind., Farmer.
Mattingly, Charles, 18, Olney, Ill., Farmer.

McGuire, Cree, 22, Carmi, Ill., Farmer.
Miller, George, 29, Wakefield, Ill., Farmer.
Moore, Otis, 23, Calhoun, Ill., Farmer.
O'Kean, Charles, 37, Olney, Ill., Laborer.
Patterson, Arthur, 24, Grayville, Ill., bookkeeper; appointed corporal, Sept. 10, 1898.
Runyen, Burt, 20, Olney, Ill., Brickmason.
Roberts, Frank, 24, Sumner, Ill., Farmer.
Simon, John, 24, Claremont, Ill., Farmer.
Sloan, Frank, 25, Clay City, Ill., Cooper.
Sutherland, Clay, 18, Sumner, Ill., Farmer.
Sumner, Henry, 33, Sumner, Ill., Engineer.
Williamson, Roland, 21, Calhoun, Ill., Laborer.
Wright, Frank, 25, Calhoun, Ill., Laborer.
Houser, Rolla, 21, Berryville, Ill., Farmer; enlisted at Jacksonville, Fla., Aug., 1898.
Musgrove, Virgil, 23, Claremont, Ill., Farmer; enlisted at Jacksonville, Fla., Aug., 1898.
All not otherwise mentioned as discharged were mustered out on May 2, 1899, at Augusta, Ga.

N. P. PAVEY.

Captain N. P. Pavey, whose portrait is here given, is twenty-four years of age. In 1890 he entered the Western Military Academy, and in 1892 was appointed first lieutenant and adjutant, and graduated from that institution as captain in 1894.

He was specialy recommended to President Cleveland for appointment in the United States Army, by Capt. Jesse M. Lee, United States Army Inspector of Military Academies.

Organized a company at Mt. Vernon, Illinois, which

was mustered into the Illinois National Guards as Company D, Sixth Infantry, and was elected captain by acclamation, June 17, 1896.

The company was afterward transferred to the Fourth Infantry, to be designated Company F. In the relation he volunteered his services to the United States, and entered Camp Tanner at Springfield, Illinois, April 26, 1898, and was with the Fourth Illinois Volunteer Infantry in said service, until it was mustered out at Camp McKenzie, Augusta, Georgia, May 2d, 1899.

Captain Pavey is the youngest of three sons of General C. W. Pavey, ex-auditor of the state, and at present special examiner, Department of Justice.

WILBUR E. SATTERFIELD.

Lieut. Wilbur E. Satterfield was born near Mt. Vernon, Jefferson county, Illinois, March 31, 1871. He completed his education in the Mt. Vernon high school. June 1, 1896, he was mustered into Company F, Fourth Illinois National Guards, as a private, and soon after was appointed first sergeant of the company; volunteered his services to the United States on the 24th of April, 1898, and on the 17th of May, of the same year, was mustered into the United States volunteer service. In this capacity he held the position of first sergeant until March 27, 1899, when he was appointed second lieutenant, receiving his commission April 17, of same year; and as such was mustered out at Augusta, Georgia, with his company on the 2d of May, 1899.

COMPANY F.

A company of militia had been talked of in Mt. Vernon for a year or more, the result of which was the organization of a company that was sworn into the military service of the state on the evening of June 17, 1896, Colonel Washburn of the Fourth Regiment officiating. This company with its fifty-three enlisted men was designated as Company D, Sixth Regiment Illinois National Guards. An election was held the same evening, which resulted in the election of N. P. Pavey, captain; T. P. Shanahan, first lieutenant; and W. H. Woodworth, second lieutenant. Arms and equipment did not arrive until about two weeks later. It being such a short time till the annual encampment and all the members, with very few exceptions, being unacquainted with military matters, we drilled about three hours six nights in the week until July 25, when we went into camp at Springfield, where the company, though the youngest in camp, made a very creditable showing.

The Sixth Regiment being from the northern part of the state, the officials took the first opportunity to transfer our company to a command nearer home, which was done by an order issued from the adjutant-general's office about August 10, 1896, transferring us to the Fourth Regiment and designating the organization as Company F, where it has since remained.

Lieutenant Woodworth resigned in November, 1896, he being succeeded by Corporal F. J. Baldwin. Lieutenant Shanahan resigned in February, 1897, and was succeeded by Sergeant Edwin M. Dufur. Lieutenant Baldwin resigned in June, 1897, and was succeeded by Sergeant Pearl Legge. Lieutenant Baldwin was the last of our officers to resign, there being no other change in the officers till March, 1899, when Lieutenant Dufur was relieved from the service, the company being in Cuba at the time. Lieutenant Legge was appointed to fill the vacancy caused by Lieutenant Dufur's leaving the service and First Sergeant W. E. Satterfield was appointed to fill the vacancy caused by Lieutenant Legge's promotion.

But, to return to a narrative of the company's history. Soon after returning from camp in 1896 it was decided to hold drills once a week, which custom was continued up to the time of entering the volunteer service in the Spanish-American war. Company F went to the annual encampment again on July 21, 1897, and during the week's tour of duty we took part in the military parade at the dedication of the Logan monument in Chicago, July 26. After returning home nothing of importance occurred until early in the winter when the Cuban trouble began to attract attention. The stirring events occurring there were, of course, watched by all Americans and the members of our company were no exception to the rule. The daily papers were closely watched and when it was announced that the government at Washington had set a time when Spain must have either conquered the people of the Island or withdraw, the war began to grow still more interesting. It was only a short time till the members of our company began to talk of "going to Cuba" and some of the more visionary ones doubtless saw themselves winning fame and glory upon many hotly contested battle-fields in the Queen of the Antilles. The day-dreamers, however, were aroused from their lethargy on February 16, 1898, when the news of the awful work in Havana Harbor, the night before, cast a gloom over our country. Then it was that the boys began

to realize that our "going to Cuba" would probably be a
reality within the next few months. On April 23, 1898,
our company was asked whether it would tender its services to the national government in the coming war. A
meeting was held the next afternoon. Although it was
Sunday the hall was crowded with patriotic citizens who
were anxious to be present upon the occasion which was of
so much importance to the members of our company. The
roll was called with the request that those who would enlist should answer to their names and step forward. It was
only a matter of a few moments when every one in the
ranks had signified their willingness to serve their country
in time of need. This action was approved by a hearty
cheer from the spectators. There were five or six members of the company, however, who, for various reasons,
did not make their appearance at the meeting that afternoon and, of course, did not enlist.

Late on the night of April 25, 1898, orders were received directing Company F to report at Springfield, so the
boys knew what it meant when they heard "assembly"
sounding at the armory the next morning. As each man
reported he was directed to return home and don his uniform
at once, as it was thought that we could get away that
afternoon. Transportation was not arranged, though,
till the next morning. Assembling at the armory at 6
o'clock the morning of the 27th, we marched to the station
headed by the Mt. Vernon Military Band and followed by
nearly the entire population of our city. The events of
the next few moments will be long remembered by hundreds
of eye-witnesses and participants. Some knew what war
meant—others did not; the knowledge of some along these
lines had been acquired by actual experience—that of
others had been learned at father's knee or gleaned from
school-books. But regardless of all this, war, with all its

horrors, appeared more real to many of our friends and relatives that morning than it had ever seemed before. With the God-speeds of friends and the tears of those nearer, our train started at 6:20 A. M. for Springfield—a date long to be remembered.

Nothing of importance occurred until Litchfield was reached, where Company K joined us. We arrived at Springfield about 11 A. M. and in the course of half an hour the cars had been switched into the state fair grounds, where we unloaded and were soon among the multitude of patriotic sons of Illinois who had preceded us. Company F was quartered in the Polled Angus stock barn, together with Companies B and C, which were already comfortably located, the former being up-stairs and the other two on the ground floor. Our company, on arrival at Springfield, contained sixty-six enlisted men. Within a week or two Captain Pavey returned to Mt. Vernon, where he enlisted eight more men, who joined the company about May 11. This date, however, was preceded by an occurrence that will long be remembered by many of the boys. We were soundly sleeping a few nights previous, when, upon being aroused, it seemed that all the noise and noise-making apparatus had been turned loose in Camp Tanner. After rubbing our eyes for a few moments and wondering what it all meant, some one was heard to say that Dewey had completely annihilated the Spanish fleet at Manila. The celebration was kept up for some time, when the noise finally ceased, and quiet reigned supreme once more. Of the seventy-four enlisted men reporting for examination in Company F, ten were rejected. It was a sore disappointment to some of them. After the examination several men came into the company from various sources. Two were received from the Second Regiment, two from the Seventh, four from Company C, of the Fourth, and two enlisted with the company at Camp Tanner. The day we were mustered into the national service a member of the hospital corps was sent to be sworn in with our company. Previously having the required number, this made one too many, so it became necessary to drop out one of our own members. This was remedied by one of the boys voluntarily offering to return home. Company F was then, on the afternoon of May 19, 1898, sworn into the national service. The members of the company returned to their quarters declaring that their days of "tin soldiering" had passed. Early in the evening of May 25 our regiment received orders to proceed to Tampa. Part of the night was spent in writing to the folks at home, while another part was devoted to an entirely different occupation. Many of the boys, believing that all is fair in love and war, and knowing the regard the average American has for relics of war, began, after the lights were out, looking for such blouses as were yet adorned with buttons in order that he might become possessed thereof. The next morning some of the buttons were gone from nearly all of the blouses and all from some of them.

We were up early the morning of May 26, and by 5:00 o'clock were ready to board the cars. It was a weary wait, however, as Company F. consisting of eighty-three enlisted men, did not go aboard until three o'clock in the afternoon. Company F together with the remainder of the First Battalion was on the last section of the special, until East St. Louis was reached, when we took the lead the rest of the way. Belleville was reached about 11:00 P. M., where several of the home folks were patiently awaiting our arrival. This city being the home of Colonel Andel, it had been the intention to have a parade there, but owing to the lateness of the hour this was dispensed with, and after stopping an hour, we again resumed our journey. It was cheering indeed to see the many ways devised by the people in the little towns through which we passed, in order to give vent to their patriotic enthusiasm. The arrival of the train was announced by the blowing of whistles and tremenduous cheering.

While in Cairo, Illinois, the writer was sitting by a comrade whose travels, up to this time, had probably not been very extensive. This young man was intently gazing upon the placid Mississippi when, upon turning around, he said, "I wouldn't take two hundred dollars for what I've seen already." At Jackson, Tennessee, we were entertained by some Jacksonian youths who greeted us by saying: "Us Southern people don't like you 'Nawthen' people." This indeed seemed rather strange and some of the boys began thinking we had got in the wrong pew by coming south. Happy to say all such thoughts as these were dispelled long before we reached Jacksonville.

But, before leaving Tennessee, the writer desires to relate a little incident that happened while a passenger train was passing ours which was on a switch. A passenger in one of the coaches yelled out as he went by: "Where you from?" when one of our boys replied: "We're from Mt. Vernon," not stopping to think that possibly the questioner had never heard of Mt. Vernon and maybe did not know what state it is in.

The people of Albany, Georgia, will always hold a warm place in the memory of many soldiers for their kind treatment. Upon arriving there we found an abundant supply of refreshments awaiting us, consisting of sandwiches, cake, cream puffs, light rolls, lemonade, Georgia biscuits, cigars, cigarettes and tobacco.

Jacksonville was reached at 3:00 A. M., May 29, after being on the road about sixty hours. The camp was located in a section of Jacksonville known as Springfield, and until the formal name of "Cuba Libre" was adopted it was known as Camp Springfield. The boys doubtless remember the many stories that were soon put into circulation regarding the camp and its location. One report had it that the camp was located in a cemetery where two thousand five hundred yellow fever victims had been buried, and that it was positively against the law to dig into the earth at all, for fear of stirring up fever germs. Many of the new arrivals believed these stories at first, and it was quite a while before they ventured to dig small trenches around their tents in order to carry off the rain.

Had it not been for the story tellers, camp life at times would have been monotonous in the extreme. There was one story that went the rounds at old Camp Springfield which the writer believes will bear repeating here. This is the story: All persons having knowledge of military matters and regulations remember that it is the duty of the guard stationed at the guard house to call, "Turn out the guard" and at the same time announcing the rank of the officer, when one entitled to the compliment is seen approaching guard headquarters. One day a New Jersey boy who was walking his post in a military manner at the guard house saw the brigadier-general coming. Being a stranger to military matters and becoming somewhat confused, he gave vent to the following expression: "Here comes the head guy! Turn out the push!"

About three weeks after arriving at Jacksonville, the companies in the volunteer army were increased to one hundred and three enlisted men. Sergt. C. U. Stull was selected as the recruiting officer for Company F. He seturned home and in the course of three days had succeeded in enlisting twenty men, all of which, with the exception of two, volunteered from Mt. Vernon, there being eighteen from our city and two from Belleville.

Camp Springfield was occupied until about August 10, when the regiment removed to a new camp at Panama Park. This, indeed, proved a bad move for the regiment, for within two weeks typhoid fever began to claim its victims and by the end of the first week of September not half of the command was fit for duty. This was a sad time for the Fourth Illinois, as well as for the other regiments located at Panama Park. Then, too, many a home in the North land was overshadowed by gloom upon the receipt of intelligence that death had claimed a loved one. Although Company F had many in the hospital at this time, it was hoped that the company would emerge from the dark period with no vacant places but this was not to be. At 7:15 P. M., Wednesday, September 14, 1898, occurred the death of our beloved comrade, Private John Bert Reid.

> Another soul had wended its way
> To the realms of joy above
> Where all are free from sorrow and pain,
> And dwell in peace and love.

The next evening the members of our company, heartbroken and sad, followed the remains to the terminal station in Jacksonville; a salute was fired, taps were sounded and a hero had gone from our ranks.

It would be difficult to predict what the final result would have been had the regiment remained in the fever stricken camp, but in compliance with an order issued about September 22, the entire regiment removed into the city of Jacksonville, where it did provost duty during the remainder of our stay there.

Companies M, F and K were stationed at provost station No. 4, which was located in the eastern part of the city, not far from Fairfield. Company M left this station sometime later and Company K also left us about two weeks before we went to Savannah. The troops at provost station No. 4 had charge of the street car line, a saloon in the neighborhood and some stands near the camps in Fairfield. On October 23, Company F, together with three other companies of the regiment, received orders to proceed to Savannah and in pursuance to such orders, began packing our belongings and making preparations to leave for our new location. After the tents were down and packed, the information was received that it had been decided not to send us till the next day, so we marched down to provost headquarters to spend the night. Several of those who had a sufficient quantity of the coin of the realm contributed part of it in payment for a bed for the night. With many of them, this was the first time they had slept in a bed since leaving home. The boys spent October 24 in seeing the sights of Jacksonville for the last time. Company F left provost headquarters at 9 o'clock that night and marched to the terminal station, where, after waiting about two hours, we were loaded into two very poor cars. The cars were equipped with short slat seats and more than two-thirds of the windows had been broken out, so that the prospect for a pleasant trip to Savannah seemed rather out of the question. Major Bennett, who was acting provost marshal at the time, however, informed the railroad officials that he would not allow men under his command to ride in such cars, while Dr. Galbraith informed them that they would be responsible for the health of the men who rode in such cars. The objection made by our two officers proving successful, we were soon comfortably situated in two nice coaches. The train pulled out of Jacksonville at 12:30 A. M., October 15, arriving at Savannah about 9:15 A. M., covering the distance of one hundred and seventy-eight miles in about nine hours. The trip was without incident.

Company F occupied provost station No. 4, which was afterward changed to No. 5. The camp was on Bull street just south of Extension Park. Savannah, without doubt, has some of the kindest people on earth within its limits. We were very tired and hungry on arriving at our new camp and not having the cooking apparatus in good working order the prospects for supper were rather gloomy. Imagine our surprise and joy when a servant of a lady living near by was seen approaching us with an abundant supply of sandwiches and butter. Pretty soon another lady sent over a big boiler of coffee with cream and sugar, so that we did not fare so badly after all.

Our boys will always recall with pleasure the events of Thanksgiving day, November 24. In the afternoon six large tables were constructed and placed in our company street. This work had scarcely been completed when our neighbors began to arrive with such articles as would tickle the palate of an epicure. The ungainly appearance of the rough pine tables was soon lost in their covering of snow white linen, while the decorations of pink and white crysanthemums completed a picture which only an artist could paint. The arrangement of the tables was completed about 4 o'clock, when the company fell in and marched to the rear of the tables where we halted long enough for several camera owners to photograph the scene. The two ranks of the company then separated and marched down either side of the tables until each man came opposite a plate, when the command "Seats" was given. Under each plate was found a daintily folded napkin and a beautiful button-hole boquet.

When seated the boys laid aside the little rules they had learned at mother's table in years gone by, and proceeded in the most comfortable way to supply the wants of the inner man. That this was done to the entire satisfaction of all concerned goes without saying. After all had finished a speech was called for, and Private Combs responded in a few well chosen words, in which he thanked the people of the vicinity for their hospitality. When the tables were cleared and the dishes washed, it was discovered that we had left twenty pies, four turkeys, ten pounds of celery, six pounds of butter and two gallons of potato salad, which were disposed of for dinner the next day.

For several days there had been talk of our regiment being removed from provost duty, as we had then been policemen for more than two months. Our boys had hoped that this talk would prove unfounded, for we were located in a most excellent community and had made many friends there. As a result of this it was with no little regret that, on November 29, Company F left its pleasant surroundings and went into regimental camp. Company H, Third Nebraska, relieved us. Only a little more than four weeks had been spent in regimental camp when, on Sunday, January 1, the Fourth Illinois received orders to proceed to Cuba. The Ninth Illinois received orders at the same time and both regiments went on the transport Mobile. We began packing early Monday morning and the wagons commenced hauling our baggage to the wharf at noon. The Ninth went on board the vessel Monday evening while we remained in camp. Having all our bedding packed and it being rather cool, not many of us slept much. We were, of course, up early the next morning and after disposing of a rather limited breakfast and cleaning up the quarters, we fell in and marched to the wharf. The assignment of quarters was a rather slow task and it was not until 10:25 A. M. when Company F marched on board, where we soon relieved ourselves of our load and went above to get a parting look at the wharves of Savannah and bid good-bye to the many friends who had come to see the start. Our quarters, by the way, were on the third deck, so that it was necessary to go down three flights of stairs to get to them. At 11:15 A. M. Tuesday, January 3, the Mobile was loosed from her moorings and amid the cheers of the hundreds of people who were on the different wharves along the river the twenty-five hundred men on board began the journey to Cuba.

A short distance down the river we passed the Roumania, with the Second South Carolina on board, and which followed a few minutes later. About half way down the river our tug released its ropes and bade us good-bye. The Roumania kept in sight until we got out to sea a short distance, when she disappeared behind us. By 2 o'clock we, for the first time in our lives, were out of sight of land and also out beyond the boundaries of the United States. A little later many of the boys began showing the effects of their first voyage at sea. Along the railing on either side of the upper deck there was a solid row of the boys intently engaged in "feeding the fish." To those who were not similarly affected it seemed rather laughable, and disregarding the seriousness of the affair we well ones comforted the unlucky boys as best we could by giving vent to such expressions as "Fall in to vomit," "Feed the fish," or upon seeing some one approach the railing some one would shout, "You're next." The ocean Tuesday afternoon was smooth, but that night the wind increased and the rolling sea caused the troubles of many on board to grow.

The next morning the upper deck was crowded with those who were anxious to see the first rays of sunlight break over the deep. The light on St. Anastasia island, St. Augustine, was sighted about 7 o'clock, but no land was visible. Soon after noon the coast of Florida came in sight and several land marks were passed, among which were Palm Beach, one of Florida's winter resorts, a wrecked schooner and a lighthouse. The lights of Miami came into view about 10 P. M. That was the last sign of life we saw in the United States.

Members of the crew had informed us that we would reach Havana about noon Thursday, and as a result the deck was crowded early in the day with those who were anxious to get a first glimpse of the Cuban coast. About 11:30 land was sighted several miles east of Havana, and soon we were close enough to get a good view of the country near the ocean. Gloomy Morro appeared about 1:30 P. M., and soon the blowing of whistles and the shouting of people along the wharves announced our entrance into far-famed Havana harbor. Probably the first and most gratifying sight to all of us on entering the harbor was the Stars and Stripes floating over Morro and over the buildings of the city.

The Mobile tied up at 2 P. M., Thursday, January 5, after a voyage of about fifty hours. We remained on board that night, going ashore the next morning and leaving for our new camp in the afternoon. Thursday night we had the pleasure of seeing the searchlights of our war vessels as they swept the harbor. After going ashore we were not allowed to go beyond the limits of the sheds; but even within these narrow limits the new arrivals saw many things that were new to them, among which was a Spanish orderly who had been sent to accompany an American officer to the wharf. This being our first sight of a Spanish soldier, some of our readers can imagine how we gathered around him to get a good look at one of the servants of the boy king of Spain. Then the odd-looking drays of Havana began making their appearance on the driveway. Soon after our small dinner of hard tack, corned beef, baked beans and black coffee had been consumed, the smokers began to make the acquaintance of Cuban cigars and cigarettes. On account of the low prices of cigars, it was no trouble for the boys to obtain genuine "Havana fillers."

In passing through the business streets to our new camp, we were enthusiastically cheered by the business men and pedestrians. Cuban flags and the Stars and Stripes were to be seen everywhere, and in passing the English consul's residence the old gentleman was seen diligently waving a British flag and an American banner. After one of the hottest marches we had enjoyed since leaving home, our new camp was reached. The location, like all others, was an ideal one, and it was only a few days until we were again settled down to the ordinary routine of camp life.

On February 19 our brigade, as well as most other brigades of the Seventh Army Corps, started on a nine days' march to Guines, a town of probably ten thousand population, located about thirty miles southeast of Havana. On account of want of space the writer will not attempt to describe this trip, but suffice it to say it will long be remembered by those who took part in it.

About the middle of March the regiments of the Seventh Army Corps began receiving orders to return to the United States to be mustered out. The receipt of such orders was always the signal for wild demonstrations. Our yelling time came Monday, April 3, but as circumstances alter cases, the boys of our regiment were not given the opportunity to join in a grand chorus of cheers such as some of the other regiments had done in the past. Orders came Monday afternoon and the companies were lined up in their respective streets at different times to listen to the reading of the good news. Those who had been anticipating a trip to Montauk Point or Camp Meade, Pennsylvania, were somewhat disappointed, but nevertheless all were glad to know that our service in Cuba would soon be at an end and knowing the rainy season would not find us on the island. Tuesday morning the boys were lined up, and after disposing of a hastily prepared breakfast, they finished packing their belongings and took the tents down. The wagons drove in, the baggage was loaded, and it was soon on its way to the wharf.

We, the First Battalion, band and headquarters, left the old camp at 9:15. While not regretting having to leave for the states, every member of the regiment will doubtless have pleasant memories of this camp, for, besides being camped there longer than at any previous camp, the health of the men was better than at any other camp.

The march to the wharf was a very dusty one, but the thoughts of coming events probably kept the men from complaining. The wharf was reached about noon, and after waiting for the baggage to be loaded we went aboard two government tugs and were taken out to the Plant line steamer Whitney. At 6 o'clock the mouth of the harbor was left behind, and we got our last glimpse of the rugged walls of Morro. The vessel not being fitted for regular transport service, there were no berths except the staterooms, and of course these were not for common soldiers, so the boys scattered over the decks and available places, reminding one of the steerage apartment of an emigrant steamer. The lights of Key West were sighted at 5 o'clock Wednesday morning. A short time before noon we struck a rough sea and several cases of sea-sickness followed. That night, however, was the roughest time we experienced on the water. The wind almost blew a gale, which made it quite laughable to see some of the uninitiated sons of Illinois try to walk the deck and keep their feet. In attempting to do so one would give a short exhibition of a cake walk, closely followed by figures unknown to any dancing professor, ancient or modern. At 6:45 A. M. Thursday, the

Whitney anchored off the quarantine station on Egmont Island, twenty-five miles southwest of Tampa, and in the afternoon, by means of lighters and tugs, succeeded in getting ashore.

After arriving on the wharf the companies were lined up and marched past one of the fumigating plants, where we were relieved of our blanket bag and blanket roll, being allowed to take no equipment to the camp except gun, belt, bayonet, canteen and haversack. Egmont is one of the group of islands at the mouth of Tampa bay. It is composed of sand, is half a mile wide and two miles long. Besides the quarantine station, a lighthouse is also located here.

After three days of very close confinement in quarantine, the First and Second Battalions of our regiment left Egmont Key Monday morning, April 10, aboard the Plant line steamboat Margaret, for Tampa, where we landed about 2 o'clock. About 3 o'clock the first section of our train left Port Tampa over the Plant system. The night passed without incident and we were rejoicing over the fact that Savannah would soon be reached, thus ending a very tiresome journey. Then many of the boys, especially those who had a best girl awaiting them, had commenced to prepare for the pleasant meeting, when, at a junction three miles from the city, hope and happy anticipation were shattered when the news came that we were not going to Savannah at all; instead, Augusta was to be our destination. The boys, like true soldiers, soon forget these troubles and were making the best of it. At Yamassee, South Carolina, our train was switched from the Plant system to the Charleston & West Carolina, over which we entered Augusta at 1:25 in the afternoon, making the journey of five hundred and forty-seven miles from Port Tampa in about twenty-two hours.

The members of Company F were given the physical examination April 17, which all troops were required to pass before being mustered out. Our arms were turned in at the arsenal at Augusta on the morning of April 27, just one year after leaving home for the war.

On Tuesday morning May 2, 1899, with the rest of the Fourth Illinois Volunteer Infantry, Company F passed into history. The regiment was mustered out by noon. Company F being on the first section of the special train, left Augusta about 4 o'clock in the afternoon. A short distance out of Augusta it was learned that a wreck had occurred near Atlanta which necessitated our going by way of Smithville, Georgia. This made our train late and we did not arrive in Atlanta until six o'clock the next morning. After an hour's stay in Atlanta the train started for Chattanooga, where it arrived at 11:00 A. M. To this city, however, our route led through Dalton, and Marietta, Georgia, two places made historic by General Sherman's army while on its march to the sea. Near Chattanooga we had the pleasure of seeing Lookout Mountain and Missionary Ridge. Chattanooga was left behind about noon and Nashville was reached a few minutes after six o'clock. At 7:35 we left Nashville. Company F arrived at home at 9:30 on the morning of May 4, 1899, after having been away just a year and a week. The approach of our train was announced by the firing of a cannon which was located in the yards of the Mt. Vernon Car Manufacturing Company. The Mt. Vernon Military Band and hundreds of our friends and relatives had gathered at the station to welcome us home again. The company, or those of us who had not been hurried off home by our over-joyed relatives, fell in and, headed by the band and followed by the High School Cadets and Coleman Post G. A. R., marched to the public square where, after a few short addresses, the company was disbanded. The next evening a sumptuous banquet was tendered the company by our citizens in the rooms of the Mt. Vernon Collegiate Institute, which rooms, by the way, had formerly been our armory and it was also in these rooms we had volunteered for the war a little more than a year before. After the banquet, the company adjourned to the Opera House, where a public reception was tendered us. Hon. C. H. Patton delivered an address of welcome, which was responded to in behalf of the company by Capt. N. P. Pavey, he being followed in a few words by Arthur T. French, who gave a short sketch of the company's travels. So ends our story.

ARTHUR T. FRENCH.

ROSTER, COMPANY F.

PAVEY, NEIL P., Captain, Mt. Vernon, Ill.
DUFUR, EDMUND M., First Lieutenant, Mt. Vernon, Ill.
LEGGE, PEARL, Second Lieutenant, Mt. Vernon, Ill.; promoted to First Lieutenant, vice Dufur dismissed.

SERGEANTS.

Satterfield, William, First Sergeant, Mt. Vernon, Ill.; promoted to Second Lieutenant, vice Legge promoted.
Patton, Otto C., Quartermaster Sergeant, Mt. Vernon, Ill.
Rice, James, Mt. Vernon, Ill.
McCurdy, Charles, Mt. Vernon, Ill.
Stull, Charles U., Mt. Vernon, Ill.

CORPORALS.

Gibson, Edgar, Mt. Vernon, Ill.; promoted to Serg't.
Hinman, Earl, Mt. Vernon, Ill.; promoted to Serg't.
Stearns, Will E., Mt. Vernon, Ill.; reduced to ranks.

COMPANY F.

Brandon, Henry J., Mt. Vernon, Ill.
Pasley, Chan, Mt. Vernon, Ill.
Lorton, Ernest A., 106 East Second street, Alton, Ill.
Brooks, Charles, Mt. Vernon, Ill.
Cotton, Sam C., Mt. Vernon, Ill.
Stanley, David, Chicago, Ill.; reduced to ranks.
Sergeant, William H., Chicago, Ill.; reduced to ranks.
Bayless, Cromwell, Mt. Vernon, Ill.
Dunley, T. S., Marlow, Ill.
Cooper, Thomas, Mt. Vernon, Ill.; reduced at ranks at his own request.

MUSICIANS.

Wolf, Alfred B., Mt. Vernon, Ill.
Swift, Alva, Mt. Vernon, Ill.
Polk, Albert H., Artificer, Mt. Vernon, Ill.
Hunter, Edward, Wagoner, Mt. Vernon, Ill.

PRIVATES.

Anderson, William H., Mt. Vernon, Ill.
Atkinson, John V., McLeansboro, Ill.
Boswell, Fred F., Mt. Vernon, Ill.; promoted to Corp.
Benton, Henry M., Mt. Vernon, Ill.
Bishop, Jesse, Mt. Vernon, Ill.
Bowling, Jacob M., Carbondale, Ill.
Cooper, Richard L., Mt. Vernon, Ill.
Combs, Earnest E., Mulberry Grove, Ill.
Craig, Robert, Kinmundy, Ill.
Craig, Charles W., Kinmundy, Ill.
Cox, Samuel W., Spring Garden, Ill.
Dimmick, Pearl, Mt. Vernon, Ill.
Dewey, Edgar A., Mt. Vernon, Ill.
Daulton, Alonzo, Mt. Vernon, Ill.
Easley, Oscar, Mt. Vernon, Ill.; promoted to Corp.

Ellis, Lawrence, Wayne City, Ill.
Estes, Charles L., Mt. Vernon, Ill.
Ellington, Charles, Mt. Vernon, Ill.
French, Arthur T., Mt. Vernon, Ill.
Goodrich, Frank, Mt. Vernon, Ill.; promoted to Corp.
Gilbert, W. Gus, Mt. Vernon, Ill.; promoted to Corp.
Harris, William T., Fitzgerald, Ill.
Heiserman, Frank R., Mt. Vernon, Ill.
Herman, Fred W., Jr., Mt. Vernon, Ill.; Company Tailor.
Holland, James M., Dahlgreen, Ill.
Hastings, Charles W., Makanda, Ill.
Jenkins, John M., Carbondale, Ill.
Johnson, William, Newman, Ill.
Koons, Joseph, Mt. Vernon, Ill.
Karn, Earnest E., Belle River, Ill.; promoted to Corp.
Laird, Orley E., Mt. Vernon, Ill.
Legge, Charles, Mt. Vernon, Ill.
Morgan, George W., Mt. Vernon, Ill.; promoted to Corp.
Moyer, Frank, Mt. Vernon, Ill.; promoted to Corp.
Malone, Cal., Mt. Vernon, Ill.
Muir, Ed E., Mt. Vernon, Ill.
Moore, Edgar T., Mt. Vernon, Ill.
Mooney, Earnest V., Dayton, Ohio; promoted to Corp.
Owens, Ed H., Mt. Vernon, Ill.
Pierson, John, Mt. Vernon, Ill.
Palmer, Charles, Mt. Vernon, Ill.
Reid, Bert, Mt. Vernon, Ill.; died Sept. 14, 1898.
Redburn, Clarence H., Mt. Vernon, Ill.
Redman, William, Mt. Vernon, Ill.
Reece, James L., Mt. Vernon, Ill.
Stephenson, Charles, Mt. Vernon, Ill; promoted to Corp.
Sprouse, John A., Mt. Vernon, Ill.
Spies, John R., Mt. Vernon, Ill.
Stanfield, Charles H., Buck Creek, Ind.

Trotter, Dohn C. O., Mt. Vernon, Ill.
Traver, Carl, Clinton, Iowa.
Wise, Joe, Mt. Vernon, Ill.
Wilbanks, Crawford B., Mt. Vernon, Ill.
Wood, John P., Dahlgren, Ill.
Wilford, Webster, Marion, Ill.
Whitsell, George O., Mt. Vernon, Ill.

RECRUITS.

Artzinga, Edward, Belleville, Ill.
Brougher, Austin L., Obdyke, Ill.
Beagles, Ambrose, Mt. Vernon, Ill.
Dewey, Charles L., Mt. Vernon, Ill.
Garrison, Harry L., Mt. Vernon, Ill.
Garrison, Jasper, Mt. Vernon, Ill.
Ketcham, Charles W., Mt. Vernon, Ill.
May, John R., Enfield, Ill.
Marks, Emerry A., Flint, Ill.
Maloney, John T., Jr., Mt. Vernon, Ill.
McMurray, John, Belleville, Ill.
Mason, Noel W., Mt. Vernon, Ill.
Oldham, Ned B., Mt. Vernon, Ill.
Rivers, Ferdinand R., Mt. Vernon, Ill.
Reece, Jesse A., Marlow, Ill.
Sowers, Lemuel, Marlow, Ill.
Solomon, Harris B., Mt. Vernon, Ill.
Sursa, Samuel, Mt. Vernon, Ill.
Threlkeld, Edward W., Mt. Vernon, Ill.
West, Bert, Mt. Vernon, Ill.
Woody, John W., Mattoon, Ky.

Corporal Henry J. Brandon was transferred to the Signal Corps, a short time before leaving Savannah, Georgia.

Corporal Edward Gibson and Earl Hinman were promoted to sergeants while in Cuba.

After weeks of waiting and repeated efforts we regret that a roster so incomplete has to be inserted.

FERDINAND J. SCHRADER.

Capt. Ferdinand J. Schrader, born December 7, 1870, at Belleville, Illinois, attended city public school, graduated therefrom in 1886, and accepted a position as clerk with the St. Clair Title Office, examiners of land titles, with which firm he is still connected. When Company D, Fourth Illinois National Guard, was organized, March 1, 1894, he enlisted in its ranks as a private; soon after he was appointed corporal and then sergeant, and before he was in the service six months he was made first sergeant of said company. On March 25, 1895, he was elected second lieutenant of the company and served in that capacity until July 23, 1897, when he was elected first lieutenant. When, on April 26, 1898, the company volunteered its service to the United States, and left for Springfield, Illinois, he felt it his duty to go, leaving his young wife, whom he had married less than a year before, dangerously ill, with a baby but a few days old, and was mustered into the United States service on May 19, 1898, as the first lieutenant of Company D, Fourth Illinois Volunteer Infantry. His sense of duty and pride kept him in the service until his company was mustered out at Augusta, Georgia, May 2, 1899. Upon the resignation of the captain of the company at Jacksonville, Florida, in July, 1898, Lieutenant Schrader was recommended by the colonel of the regiment as his successor and on July 15, 1898, he was

Co. D.

Lieut. M. R. Hilgard.   2d Lieut. W. C. Andel.

commissioned as such by Governor Tanner. In the capacity of captain he served until the final muster out of his company, at Augusta, Georgia, May 2, 1899.

EDWARD ABEND, Jr.

Lieut. Edward Abend, Jr., was born in Belleville, Illinois, February 5, 1871, and where his home has been during these twenty-eight years of his life. He graduated from the public schools of this city when seventeen years of age, when he entered the employ of the Gas & Electric Light Company of his home town as collector and bookkeeper, which position he held until November, 1897, when he was elected secretary and treasurer of the Western Brewing Company, which he filled until the call for troops in the American-Spanish war, which call he answered.

In the year 1894 he organized Company D, Fourth Illinois Volunteers, which organization was sworn in on the first of March, 1894, he entering its ranks as a private. On April 14th, of the same year, he was appointed corporal, and on July 3d received the appointment of second sergeant. March 2, 1896, he was made first sergeant, which position he filled until July 23, 1897, when he was commissioned second lieutenant. On the first call for volunteers in the late war, his company volunteered in a body, and he was mustered into the United States volunteer service May 19, 1898, bearing the same rank, that of second lieutenant.

Capt. E. P. Rogers, of this company, having resigned his commission in the army July 15, 1898, and First Lieut. F. J. Schrader having been duly commissioned to fill the vacancy, Lieut. Abend was advanced to the rank of first lieutenant, which position he held until November 10, 1898, when he tendered his resignation; returning to his native city, he at once resumed his position as secretary and treasurer of the Western Brewing Company.

MILOSH R. HILGARD.

Milosh R. Hilgard was born in 1870, and makes the business of plumber his occupation. He entered the United States service with his company, bearing a commission of second lieutenant, in which capacity he served until the time of First Lieutenant Abend's resignation, some months prior to the removal of the regiment to Havana, Cuba, when he was advanced to the position of first lieutenant, serving in this capacity until the company was released from the volunteer service by muster out.

WILLIAM CASIMIR ANDEL.

William Casimir Andel was born in Belleville, Illinois, on the 30th day of June, twenty-two years ago.

He spent several years at the public school, of this city and then attended the Missouri Military Academy, of Mexico, Missouri, from which he graduated with honor in 1895. He secured a position in the office of the Belleville Stove Works after returning to his native city and attended commercial college in the evenings. In July, 1895, he with his brother, George, joined Company D, Fourth Regiment Illinois National Guards, with which they went to Springfield in 1898 to be mustered into the United States service to fight the Spaniards. Both the Andel boys remained privates, until August 8, when W. C. Andel was made

Corporal, though their father was now their colonel and had the power to promote them; he showed no partiality even to his own sons. Late in the summer and fall, when the companies were much reduced by the illness of the men, Corporal Andel had double duty to do—being for a while the only corporal in the service of Company D. He also acted sergeant. Owing to his splendid constitution he was none the worse for the overwork in spite of the dangerous climate of the southern states during the summer months. For his faithfulness to duty, and interest in his work he was commissioned second lieutenant of Company D on the 18th of November, 1898, filling the vacancy caused by the promotion of Lieutenant Hilgard to first lieutenant, taking the place of First Lieutenant Abend, resigned.

On January 3, 1899, the Fourth regiment sailed for Cuba, and both Lieutenant Andel and his brother, though the latter had been dangerously ill in Jacksonville, Florida, went with them; the latter afterwards got an honorable discharge and came home the last of January. Lieutenant Andel served in Cuba with his regiment until it returned to the United States in April, and was mustered out of the service in Augusta, Georgia, on May 2, 1899. He returned to his home with his company, and accepted his old position, which was kept open for him.

After repeated efforts we find ourselves at the press, without an historic fact from Company D, which must not be construed as indicating a non-history-producing organization.

COMPANY D ROSTER

When not otherwise stated, mustered in, May 19, 1898,. and mustered out, May 2, 1899.

SCHRADER, FERD J., Captain, Belleville, Ill.
HILGARD, MILOSH R., First Lieutenant, Belleville, Ill.
ANDEL, WILLIAM C., Second Lieutenant, Belleville, Ill.

SERGEANTS.

Hutchinson, William, Belleville, Ill.; enrolled as Serg't; appointed First Sergeant, August 5, 1898.
Barnikol, Walter, Belleville, Ill.; mustered in as Corporal; promoted to Serg't. Nov. 26, 1898; appointed Quartermaster Sergeant, March 2, 1899.
Knoble, Adolph G., Belleville, Ill.; mustered in as Sergeant; acting First Sergeant October 16 to November 5, 1898.
Link, Charles, Belleville, Ill.; mustered in as Quartermaster Sergeant; relieved by Q. M. Serg't Barnikol, March 2, 1899.

CORPORALS.

Koener, Kent K., Belleville, Ill.; mustered in as Corporal; appointed Serg't September 22, 1898. On provost guard in August.
Rhein, Walter L., Belleville, Ill.; mustered in as Corporal; on duty as Acting Serg't., October 15 to November 16, 1898.
Adam, Otto, Belleville, Ill.; appointed Corporal July 8, 1898.
Burk, Edmund, Belleville, Ill.; appointed Corporal July 8, 1898.

Merz, Arthur G., Belleville, Ill.; appointed Corporal Sept. 22, 1898.
Koska, Robert, Belleville, Ill.; appointed Corporal Nov. 26, 1898.
Wilderman, Eugene, Belleville, Ill.; appointed Corporal Nov. 26, 1898.

COOK.

Shaefer, William R., Belleville, Ill.; appointed Cook Aug. 29, 1898; reduced to private at his own request, Nov. 26, 1898; promoted cook March 11, 1899.

ARTIFICER.

Seifert, William F., Belleville, Ill.; appointed Artificer June 1, 1898.

MUSICIAN.

McElhannon, Robert C., Nashville, Ill.; appointed Musician Aug. 2, 1898.

WAGONER.

Wallace, William O., Lebanon, Ill.; enlisted June 16, 1898; appointed wagoner, Sept. 2, 1898.

PRIVATES.

Brandmeier, Fred, Belleville, Ill.; on duty as colonel's orderly June 4 to Sept. 8, 1898; on permanent detail at provost headquarters from Oct. 19 to Oct. 27, 1898.
Badgley, Calvin I., Belleville, Ill.
Bonville, William F., Belleville, Ill.
Besse, Robert W., Belleville, Ill.; on duty as cook from May 21 to Aug. 29, 1898.
Burk, William P., Belleville, Ill.

Braun, John A., Jr., Belleville, Ill.; enlisted June 16, 1898.
Carter, Charles, Jr., Freeburg, Ill.
Chenot, Benjamin L., Belleville, Ill.; on duty with regimental quartermaster, June 8 to June 12, 1898.
Callihan, Ollie P.; orderly at brigade headquarters Sept. 16 to Oct. 18, 1898.
Greener, Joseph, East St. Louis, Ill.; on duty as Armorer, with ordnance department repair shops, July 9, 1898, to April 11, 1899.
Harris, M. Lesler, Belleville, Ill.
Hughes, James, Belleville, Ill.
Hoppe, William M., Belleville, Ill.; orderly and clerk at brigade headquarters from Aug. 8, 1888, to Apr. 3, 1899; on duty at regimental headquarters from Apr. 8, 1899.
Homberg, William H., Belleville, Ill.; on duty with Regimental Band from May 21 to June 26, 1898.
Hubert, Charles, Belleville, Ill.
Harden, Elmer E., Belleville, Ill.; enlisted June 23, 1898.
Hess, William G., Belleville, Ill.; enlisted June 17, 1898.
Herman, Theodore F., Belleville, Ill.; enlisted June 17, 1898; on permanent detail at provost headquarters from Oct. 27 to Dec. 23, 1898.
Klass, Fred, Belleville, Ill.; appointed Cook Jan. 12, 1899; reduced to private at own request, Mch. 3, 1899; on provost guard in Augusta, Ga., from Apr. 16, 1899.
Koerner, William K., Belleville, Ill.
Kohl, Jr., Julius J., Belleville, Ill.; enlisted June 17, 1898.
Krause, John W., Belleville, Ill.; enlisted June 16, 1898; appointed Company Tailor Dec. 25, 1898.
Lord, George W., East St. Louis, Ill.; enlisted June 24, 1898.
McDougal, D. Grant.

Merker, Samuel A., Belleville, Ill.
Miller, Philip, Belleville, Ill.; on duty as Wagoner from Sept. 15 to Dec. 8, 1898.
Maurer, John, Belleville, Ill.; enlisted June 16, 1898.
Munie, Michael L., Belleville, Ill.
Meder, Arthur J., Belleville, Ill.; enlisted June 16, 1898.
Preston, Lester C., Irving, Kans.
Paul, Joseph A., Belleville, Ill.
Rhein, Walter, Belleville, Ill.
Renecke, Fred, Belleville, Ill.
Radersheimer, Henry E., Belleville, Ill.; enlisted June 17, 1898.
Smith, Leon G., Belleville, Ill.
Smith, Robert M., Belleville, Ill.
Scahill, Edwin I., Belleville, Ill.
Sarlouis, John.
Thomas, Charles E., Belleville, Ill.; detailed as courier to General Lee July 4, 1898; and detached—mounted messenger; detached for duty at Seventh Army Corps April 3, 1899. Returned to company April 18, 1899.
Totsch, Charles N., Belleville, Ill.; acting corporal from Oct. 15 to Nov. 25, 1898.
Tischbein, George, Belleville, Ill.; enlisted June 25, 1898.
Ward, William H., Belleville, Ill.
West, Benjamin J., Belleville, Ill.
Wunderle, Gustavos, Belleville, Ill.; on duty at regimental stables June 5 to 11, 1898.
Wolf, Walter J., Lebanon, Ill.; on provost guard in Augusta, Ga., from April 16 to April —, 1899.

RESIGNATIONS.

Rogers, Capt. Eddy P., Belleville, Ill.; resignation accepted to date from July 15, 1898.

FOURTH ILLINOIS. 85

Abend, Edward, Jr., First Lieutenant, Belleville, Ill.; resignation accepted to bear date of Nov. 9, 1898.

DISCHARGED FOR DISABILITY.

Harman, J. Albert, Private, Belleville, Ill., discharged Sept. 7, 1898. Honest and faithful service. Character good.

Waugelin, Louis E., Corporal, Belleville, Ill.; made Corporal July 8, 1898. Discharged Oct. 13, 1898. Service honest and faithful. Character good.

Wasmann, Edgar E., Private, Belleville, Ill.; enlisted June 16, 1898. Discharged Nov. 7, 1898. Service honest and faithful. Character good.

Schroeder, Elmer, Private, Belleville, Ill.; discharged Nov. 17, 1898. Service honest and faithful. Character good.

Schroeder, Adolph G., Private, Belleville, Ill.; discharged Dec. 2, 1898. Service honest and faithful. Character good.

DISCHARGED BY ORDER TO ACCEPT COMMISSION.

Hilgard, Milosh R., First Sergeant, Belleville, Ill.; discharged Aug. 4, 1898, to accept second lieutenancy of same company.

Andel, William C., Corporal, Belleville, Ill.; discharged Nov. 22, 1898, to accept commission as second lieutenant of same company.

DISCHARGED BY ORDER.

Niemyer, Arthur, Corporal, Belleville, Ill.; discharged Sept. 15, 1898.

Ropiequet, Richard W., Sergeant, Belleville, Ill.; mustered in as private, on regimental recruiting service, from June 11, to 29, 1898. Clerk of regimental com-

mander July 9 to Sept. 18, 1898. Made Sergeant
Aug. 5, 1898. Discharged per telegram Sept. 17,
1898.

Betz, Charles W., Sergeant, Belleville, Ill.; discharged per
telegram Oct. 11, 1898.

Bartel, Fred J., Private, Belleville, Ill.; discharged per telegram Oct. 29, 1898.

McConaughy, Malcom M., Corporal, Belleville, Ill.; made
corporal July 8, 1898. Acting sergeant Oct. 15 to
30, 1898. Discharged Oct. 30, 1898, per telegram.

Wise, Walter A., Corporal, Belleville, Ill. On duty with
regimental band from June 17, 1898. Reduced to
ranks July 6, 1898; restored a corporal, Aug. 5,
1898; discharged by telegram Oct. 30, 1898.

Bonean, William C., Private, Belleville, Ill.; discharged
by telegram Oct. 30, 1898.

Hay, Eugene J., Private, Belleville, Ill; discharged by telegram Oct. 30, 1898.

Hilgard, Richard W., Private, Belleville, Ill.; discharged
per telegram Oct. 30, 1898.

Miller, Fred G., Private, Belleville, Ill.; discharged per
telegram Oct. 30, 1898.

Englemann, Otto B., Private, Belleville, Ill.; enlisted June
16, 1898; discharged per telegram Nov. 9, 1898.

Feucht, Otto H., Private, Belleville, Ill.; on duty as corporal Oct. 15 to Nov. 19, 1898; discharged per telegram Nov. 17, 1898.

Needles, Homer, Private, Belleville, Ill.; acting Corporal
Oct. 15 to Nov. 17, 1898; discharged per telegram
Dec. 14, 1898.

Schnittker, William T., Musician, Belleville, Ill.; detailed
as Musician June 6, 1898, and appointed Musician
Aug. 2, 1898; discharged per telegram Dec. 15,
1898.

Poirot, Edwin J., Private, Belleville, Ill.; enlisted June 17, 1898; discharged per telegram Jan. 2, 1899.
McCullough, Robert J., Private, Belleville, Ill.; discharged per telegram Jan. 2, 1899.
Barnett, Henry J., Private, Winamac, Ind.; discharged at U. S. General Hospital at Ft. Myers, Va., June 17, 1898.
Andel, George K., Private, Belleville, Ill.; discharged Jan. 17, 1899.
McCullough, Ralph E., Private, Belleville, Ill.; enlisted June 23, 1898; discharged Jan. 17, 1899.
Wooters, Major, Sergeant, Belleville, Ill.; discharged Jan. 21, 1899.
Hoerr, Adolph J., Private, Belleville, Ill.; discharged Jan. 21, 1899.
Strauss, Carl, Corporal, Belleville, Ill.; acting Corporal from Oct. 15 to Nov. 25, 1898; promoted Corporal Nov. 26, 1898; discharged Feb. 11, 1899.
Erwen, Peter, Private, Belleville, Ill.; on duty at regimental stables July 24 to Sept. 27, 1898; orderly to regimental commander Sept. 8, 1898, to February 13, 1899; discharged Feb. 13, 1899.
Hill, William B., Private, Belleville, Ill.; enlisted June 16, 1898; discharged Feb. 13, 1899.
Ward, Edgar A., Private, Belleville, Ill., discharged Feb. 14, 1899.
Baker, George E., Private, Belleville, Ill., discharged Feb. 16, 1899.
Mills, William N., Private, Lebanon, Ill.; enlisted June 16, 1898; discharged March 8, 1899.
Lind, William C., Private, Belleville, Ill.; discharged March 22, 1899.
Rogers, Robert D., Private, Belleville, Ill.; discharged March 17, 1899.

TRANSFERS.

Dickerson, Edward W., Private, on duty at regimental hospital from May 24 to June 9, 1898; transferred to Hospital Corps, U. S. Army, June 10, 1898.

Goelitz, Hugo G., Corporal, Belleville, Ill.; appointed corporal July 8, 1898; on duty at regimental headquarters as clerk July 7 to 27, 1898; clerk at division headquarters July 27 to August 9, 1898; clerk at regimental headquarters Aug. 10 to Nov. 22, 1898; transferred to Hospital Corps, U. S. Army, Nov. 30, 1898.

Merck, Fred, Corporal, Belleville, Ill.; on duty at regimental bakery July 27 to September 26, 1898; transferred as first-class private to U. S. Volunteer Signal Corps, December 14, 1898.

DIED OF DISEASE.

Metzger, Fred P., Private, Belleville, Ill.; enlisted June 23, 1898; died Sept. 19, 1898, at Belleville, Ill.

Archibald, George, Jr., Private, Belleville, Ill.; enlisted June 16, 1898; died Oct 13, 1898, at Third Division Hospital, Seventh Army Corps.

Wise, Otto J., Private, Belleville, Ill.; died Nov. 3, 1898, at Belleville, Ill.

COMPANY C.

Company C organized at Carbondale, Illinois. On the night of April 24, 1898, Captain Barton received orders to report with his command to Col. James Washburn at the fair grounds in Springfield, April 26, 1898. Was mustered

CAPT. E. E. BARTON.

into the United States volunteer service by Captain Roberts May 19, 1898. On the 26th of May the command left Springfield under orders to report to General Shafter at Tampa, Florida, but at Albany, Georgia, orders were changed to Jacksonville, Florida, arriving there May 29, 1898, about 2 o'clock A. M.

At day break the order was given to fall in, or rather fall out of the cars and then fall in. On this trip Company C had two sleepers, which made it very pleasant. After eating a light breakfast of canned beef, hard tack and coffee, Company C, along with the regiment, was marched around through the sand drain up into regimental front in the woods, and here rested until about 2 o'clock P. M., when camp was pitched. August 10, 1898, the command marched to Panama Park, about three miles north of the first camp. Previous to this move the company had been recruited up to one hundred and three enlisted men. Panama Park was where the regiment had so much sickness. In Company C, with a strength of one hundred and five men, at one time there were only six privates, two corporals and the captain for duty, the rest either being sick in hospital quarters or on a furlough.

Matters kept growing worse until September 25, 1898, when General Lee issued orders for the regiment to proceed to the city of Jacksonville for provost guard duty, and Company C was assigned to station No. 2 at General Lee's headquarters. On October 24 the company moved to Savannah, Georgia, and was assigned to station No. 2, Irish Park. Moved from provost station about two miles into the country on November 28, to Camp Onward, Georgia. Received orders January 2, 1899, to proceed to Havana, Cuba. Broke up camp the morning of January 3, and marched through the streets of Savannah to the wharf and embarked on the transport "Mobile" for Cuba. Arrived in Havana harbor January 5, disembarked and marched through Havana out to Camp Columbia January 7, a distance of about five miles. Left Camp Columbia February 16 for practice march to Guines, Cuba; arrived February 21. Passed in review before General Gomez February 23. Started on return trip to camp February 24, arriving in camp February 27. Left Camp Columbia for Havana April 4; embarked on transport "Yarmouth" for Egmont Key April 4, arrived April 5, disembarked and went into quarantine at United States detention camp April 6. Embarked on steamer for Port Tampa April 10, arriving same date; thence by rail to Augusta, Georgia, arriving April 11. Mustered out of service May 2, 1899, at Augusta, Georgia.

On the evening of March 16, 1899, Colonel Swift ordered Captain Barton to report to him with the company. The colonel then presented him a handsome sword, the gift of the company, with a few words to the captain. Among other things the colonel said: "The position of captain is the hardest in the army to fill and still hold the respect and admiration of his men and his colonel. I am pleased to present this sword to a man who has successfully filled that office."

COMPANY C ROSTER.

E. E. BARTON, Captain, Carbondale, Ill.
THOMAS F. LOUDON, First Lieutenant, Carbondale, Ill.
HORACE F. TEETER, Second Lieutenant, Carbondale, Ill.

SERGEANTS.

Oliver P. Robinson, First Sergeant; enrolled as private, mustered in as Corporal, appointed Sergeant Oct. 1, 1898; appointed First Sergeant Dec. 26.
William E. Davis, Quartermaster Sergeant, Marion, Ill.; mustered in as Corporal, appointed Quartermaster Sergeant Feb. 11, 1899.

Barton, Richard H., Carbondale, Ill., mustered in as Sergeant
Thompson, Ward E., Carbondale, Ill., mustered in as Sergeant
June, Marvin A., Cairo, Ill., mustered in as Corporal, appointed Sergeant July 26, 1898.
Hemphill, Walter, Carbondale, Ill., mustered in as Corporal, appointed Sergeant Feb. 9, 1899.

CORPORALS.

Taylor, Charles H., Carbondale, Ill., appointed Corporal July 26, 1898
Dixon, Claude M., Carbondale, Ill., appointed Corporal July 26, 1898.
Loudon, Oliver P., Carbondale, Ill., appointed Corporal July 26, 1898
Hord, Robert G., Carbondale, Ill., appointed Corporal July 26, 1898
Boulden, William G., Carbondale, Ill., appointed Corporal December 15, 1898
Knight, John C., Marion, Ill., appointed Corporal Dec. 15, 1898
Hunter, Floyd, Marion, Ill., appointed Corporal Jan. 11, 1899
Kedin, Carl F., Chicago, Ill., appointed Corporal Jan. 11, 1899
Walker, Ben A., Carbondale, Ill., appointed Corporal March 26, 1899
Byron, Joseph E., Galesburg, Ill., appointed Corporal April 7, 1899
Grant, Ernest R., Carbondale, Ill., appointed Corporal April 7, 1899
Ashley, Charles H., Carbondale, Ill., appointed Corporal April 7, 1899

Parrish, John, Makanda, Ill.; appointed Corporal April 7, 1899.

MUSICIAN.

Conner, Benjamin, Carbondale, Ill.

ARTIFICER.

Doolin, John A., Carbondale, Ill.; appointed Artificer Sept. 2, 1898.

PRIVATES.

Anderson, Charles E., Carterville, Ill.
Baker, Marcus, Cottage Home, Ill.
Baker, Fred G., Meade, Ill.
Bricker, George, Carbondale, Ill.
Bailey, Thomas C., Makanda, Ill.
Boyce, Donald, Murphysboro, Ill.
Barringer, Joseph X., Fredonia, Ill.
Cline, Harry X., Marion, Ill.
Childers, William, Carbondale, Ill.
Cole, Warren A., East St. Louis, Ill.
Cowan, Charles A., Carbondale, Ill.
Crowell, Frank, Carbondale, Ill.
Crowell, Joseph, Carbondale, Ill.
Cunningham, Ross H., Marion, Ill.
Dixon, Harry E., Carbondale, Ill.
Davis, Daniel W., Marion, Ill.
Dickson, Edward, Carbondale, Ill.
Daily, John H., Pinckneyville, Ill.
Deck, William A., Makanda, Ill.
Dever, Charles L., Metropolis, Ill.
Etherton, Loren E., Makanda, Ill.
Elliott, Frank, Carbondale, Ill.
French, William, Pinckneyville, Ill. This man holds the

record of the company, never having been on the sick list.

Gher, Thomas F., Makanda, Ill.
Guill, Robert C., McLeansboro, Ill.
Gallaway, Charles, Norris City, Ill.
Hayden, Kenneth, Carbondale, Ill.
Hendrickson, Willis, Sparta, Ill.
Hinchcliff, Samuel V., Carbondale, Ill.
Hinchcliff, Ernest A., Carbondale, Ill.
Holiday, Walter C., Murphysboro, Ill.
Hartwell, Charles K., New Dennison, Ill.
Hawkins, Dwight J., Carbondale, Ill.
Henley, George W., Makanda, Ill.
Jeter, Robert H., Marion, Ill.
Jones, Frank I., Pinckneyville, Ill.
Kays, John E., Thompsonville, Ill.
Kirkpatrick, Carl, Virden, Ill.
Knight, James S., Thompsonville, Ill.
Knight, William, Marion, Ill.
King, Harry A., Eddyville, Ill.
Montgomery, Augustin B., Du Quoin, Ill.
McMillan, John F., Carterville, Ill.
Nolan, James F., San Francisco, Cal.
North, Lee Roy, Cottage Home, Ill.
Nauman, Fred L., Carbondale, Ill.
Otis, John, Jersey City, N. J.
Ogden, John, Carbondale, Ill.
Pursell, Perry P., Pinckneyville, Ill.
Rodman, Harry C., Du Quoin, Ill.
Smith, Edward H., Carbondale, Ill.
Strauch, Ernest A., Pinckneyville, Ill.
Stanley, Rupert A., Makanda, Ill.
Sands, John A., Masters, Ill.
Sanders, David R., Progress, Ill.

96   HISTORY OF THE

Sowers, John W., Murphysboro, Ill.
Thompson, William, Carbondale, Ill.
Taylor, Charles R., Carbondale, Ill.
Turman, Alfred, Carbondale, Ill.
Toler, William I., Carbondale, Ill.
Tinsley, Sod, Pinckneyville, Ill.
Waters, Thomas B., Marion, Ill.

DISCHARGED.

William W. Biggs, Carbondale, Aug. 22, 1898.
Thomas M. Otrich, Anna, Sept. 4, 1898.
Louis H. Kaha, Cairo, Oct. 15, 1898.
Charles R. Stuart, Cairo, Oct. 30, 1898.
Edward E. Miller, Makanda, Dec. 25, 1898.
Chas. D. M. Renfro, Carbondale, Dec. 19, 1898.
Frederick L. Jones, Murphysboro, Jan. 1, 1899.
Homer E. Mills, Makanda, Jan. 1, 1899.
James M. Scurlock, Jr., Carbondale, Jan. 26, 1899.
Charles R. Slade, Woodlawn, Feb. 3, 1899.
John B. Bristol, Cairo, Feb. 4, 1899.
James W. Stephens, Marion, Feb. 6, 1899.
Elbert L. Damron, Progress, Feb. 6, 1899.
William L. Ellis, Murphysboro, Feb. 13, 1899.
Ephraim Hagler, Makanda, Feb. 13, 1899.
Elliott L. Morton, Paris, Feb. 18, 1899.

TRANSFERRED.

Carl Baker, Mead, hospital corps, June 10, 1898.
Percy C. Linck, Robinson, hospital corps, June 10, 1898.
Harry L. Stites, Cairo, hospital corps, June 10, 1898.
Horace Sorrels, Hope, Kansas, signal corps, December 3, 1898.
Stanley R. Sharts, Marion, engineer corps, December 25, 1898.

THE HOME RECEPTION.

As was anticipated by the friends of Company C, the home coming was not in compact form—some of the men residing at Cairo, some at Makanda and other points—therefore the date of reception was fixed for Tuesday evening, May 9. Ample preparations were made by the citizens of Carbondale. As is usual in this city, the general public received the committees with open hearts and hands. The proprietors of the opera house generously tendered the free use of that comfortable and commodious building. The new proprietor of the Newell House threw open wide the doors from basement to attic without a cent of charge. The electric railway gratuitously furnished all desired lights. Of provisions of every character there was enough and to spare, all contributed by our generous people.

The entertainment at the opera house was a grand success. The program was elaborate and well rendered. Capt. S. Walker presided. The short address introducing the soldiers to the public did credit to the old veteran. It was a burst of eloquence and pathos that will be long remembered by those present. Judge Barr, in his address of welcome, added to his reputation as an orator. The only fault was that he did not occupy more time. He paid eloquent tribute to the returned soldiers, lauded the men in the field and fully endorsed the acts of President McKinley in his conduct of the war. The songs, recitations, etc., were of a high order. Grear's Concert Band, of Murphysboro, certainly the best musical organization in southern Illinois, gave the finishing touches to the occasion and gave the public a grand specimen of the talent our sister city has gathered together and of which she is justly proud. And here we desire to say that this fine band contributed financially to the reception by making a charge for services but little in excess of expenses incurred in transit between the two cities.

At the banquet plates were laid for one hundred. Eighty soldiers sat down and were amply supplied with the very best the good ladies of our city could prepare for them. The mothers, sisters and cousins waited on the tables. And the boys enjoyed it all. When the soldiers had finished, then the relatives and friends again and again filled the tables until not less than three hundred had participated.

A social reunion and dance closed the festivities. All who so desired participated. Not until dawn announced that the night had passed did the merry, happy girls and boys cease their enjoyment. It was a joyous occasion and a full tide of happiness had sway throughout.

May we not suggest to the boys of Company C that they form an organization and hold annual reunions? Our people would be glad to meet them at least once a year and entertain them as they deserve.

EDWARD J. LANG.

Maj. Edward J. Lang, born at Paris, Illinois, April 10, 1867, graduated Paris High school, 1885, thoroughly mastered the trade of carpentry and joiner and was foreman for a number of leading contractors in Paris, and other cities, and followed the business of contractor and builder up to July, 1897. Was appointed instructor of woodworking in Illinois Institution for the Deaf and Dumb and continued in this occupation until call of the President for volunteers. Joined Company H, Fourth Regiment, Illinois National Guard, April 20, 1887, appointed corporal and sergeant. Elected second lieutenant and first lieutenant.

Became captain of company September 3, 1890. Elected major Fourth Regiment, Illinois National Guard, May 10, 1893, and re-elected May 10, 1897. Answered call for volunteers April 26, and was commissioned major of Fourth Illinois Infantry by Governor Tanner May 20, 1897. Served with regiment at Camp Tanner; Springfield, Illinois; Jacksonville, Florida; Savannah, Georgia; and Havana,

MAJOR E. J. LANG.

Cuba, and mustered out with regiment at Augusta, Georgia, May 2, 1899. Served with regiment at Cairo, Illinois, in railroad strike of 1894. Was in command of five companies of Fourth Illinois National Guard at railroad strike in Chicago for eleven days, 1894.

The Second Battalion, Fourth Regiment Infantry, Illinois Volunteers, formerly Second Battalion, Fourth Regiment, Illinois National Guard, was mustered into the United States Volunteer Army on the 20th day of May, 1898. The battalion, as mustered in then, was practically the same as in the National Guard, although there was a slight addition to the personnel of the enlisted men, but the officers were the same as in the Illinois National Guard. Before leaving Camp Tanner, Springfield, Illinois, for the place of rendezvous, the regiment was recruited to the minimum fighting strength, or eighty-one enlisted men and three officers. But later, on June 10, 1898, orders were received from the War Department to recruit up to the maximum fighting strength of one hundred and six men and three officers. This was done under the supervision of Capt. H. S. Parker and a detail of one man from each company, with headquarters at Effingham, Illinois. By June 27, 1898, the battalion numbered one hundred and six men to each company.

The composition of the battalion at the time of muster in was as follows:

Major—Edward J. Lang, commanding.
Adjutant—First Lieutenant H. J. White.
Sergeant-Major—Sergeant Harry E. Shutt.
Quartermaster-Sergeant—Sergeant Lew Myers.
Trumpeter-Sergeant—Sergeant Coma Fragden.

The companies were officered in the following order:

COMPANY G.

Captain—C. E. Ryman.
First Lieutenant—John Burr.
Second Lieutenant—John Wright.

Company I.

Captain—Samuel S. Houston.
First Lieutenant—E. P. Clayton.
Second Lieutenant—P. P. Stout.

Company K.

Captain—David Davis, Jr.
First Lieutenant—George L. Zink, Jr.
Second Lieutenant—William F. LaForce.

Company B.

Captain—E. W. Hersh.
First Lieutenant—W. A. Howell.
Second Lieutenant—Lyman Harris.

According to the United States organization, the battalion sergeant-major, quartermaster-sergeant and trumpeter-sergeant are simply details instead of extra sergeants, and accordingly these three "non-coms" joined a company. Sergeant Shutt was subsequently detailed as sergeant-major and acted as such up to the time of his promotion.

There were several changes among the officers, and are as follow:

On February 1, 1899, Capt. David Davis, Jr., resigned, leaving a vacancy in the captaincy of Company K. Second Lieutenant LaForce also resigned, leaving a vacancy there. First Lieut. George L. Zink was made captain. Sergeant Seamen was made first lieutenant and Sergeant Rose second lieutenant. Sergeant-Major Shutt, on November 1, 1898, was made second lieutenant of Company H, this leaving a vacancy as sergeant-major. Sergt. F. S. Barker, of Company B, was made sergeant-major to fill this vacancy.

Another change made in the personnel of the officers was when Captain E. W. Hersh of Company B resigned, on February 18. First Lieutenant W. A. Howell was commissioned as captain, Second Lieutenant Lyman Harris as first lieutenant and sergeant, Major F. S. Barker as second lieutenant. This left another vacancy as sergeant-major and Sergeant Charles Clark of Company I was appointed to fill this vacancy. On February 1, Lieutenant H. J. White, battalion adjutant, resigned, and his position was filled by a detail of one of the line lieutenants as acting adjutant.

The Second Battalion has always made a fine record for itself in drill and military bearing. Its drill at the time of muster into the United States service was chiefly in battle formation, and by extraordinary hard work prepared itself to meet the enemy, but it never had the opportunity as the protocol was signed while the Fourth Regiment was still on the soil of the United States. But the protocol did not stop the hard work, the regiment kept persistently and gained a degree of proficiency in drills and reviews not surpassed by any other in volunteer service, and when it appeared before our President and that gallant old man, General Wheeler, brought forth the remark by the President,—"That is the best volunteer regiment I have ever seen." The battalion has served with the regiment throughout the service, being in Camp Tanner, Springfield; Camp Cuba Libre, Jacksonville, Florida; Camp Panama Park, Panama Park, Florida; Camp Onward, Savannah, Georgia, and Camp Columbia, Cuba. The battalion movements up to the time of leaving Cuba for the United States have been identical with those of the regiment.

In the morning of April 4, 1899, at 10 A. M., the two

battalions received orders to embark on the steamship Yarmouth for transportation to the United States.

Soon after "the general" was sounded and tents were struck, and in less than an hour the battalion was ready for the hot wearisome march from Camp Columbia to the San Jose wharf in Havana, a distance of about five and one-half miles. This distance was covered by 4:00 P. M., and soon after the wagon train began arriving with

TRANSPORT YARMOUTH.

camp equipage and baggage, and it was then loaded on the transport. As the loading was not completed by 5:00 o'clock, the ship steamed out in the ocean and anchored off Morro Castle and the rest of the baggage was brought out on a lighter and put on board our ship. This work was finished by 8:00 P. M., and the ship immediately weighed anchor and started for Egmont Key quarantine station.

Soon after the lighter parted company with us, an incident occurred that, for the time, caused some little flurry of excitement. The bedding in one of the forward state rooms took fire, and the captain at once deciding to take no chances, ordered the boat turned to the shore. But the discipline of the crew and the self control of the soldiers having knowledge of it, prevailed, and it was soon extinguished, having done but little damage. Yarmouth at once turned her prow to the north, proudly riding the gentle billows.

As seems common in the case of soldiers, sea-sickness

SEASICK.

began to manifest itself, but it was reserved for the following day to see just how it could get in its work to the discomfort of about two-thirds of our men, many of whom became very impolite and spit (?) on the floor, while some who tried to act in well bred style made the most miserable botch of it. The fellow that never experiences it don't know how good one feels after he recovers from this dreaded affliction, and can poke fun at the other fellow who has not yet got beyond the period when he wants to walk, have the boat sink, or is willing to die,—just "any old thing" other than that which drafts so heavily on his attention, and his stomach also, at times. After a ride continuing less than twenty-four hours we found ourselves viewing the setting sun off Millet Key, the island on which the Florida state quarantine is located, twenty-five miles out the bay from Port Tampa, when the boat's captain reported, and the ship was moved off a short distance and anchored to await the dawning of another day, while many of us sought our resting place on the deck and wrapped our blankets about us only to realize we were in a climate several degrees colder than where we spent the night before, for north wind seemed to be coming off an iceberg or some other refrigerator plant.

Soon after the dawn of day on the sixth, the early riser could see a ship approaching from the south, which on reaching our port side we discovered was crowded with bluecoats, who later proved to be our comrades on the sleepy Whitney, which had left Havana harbor some three hours in advance of us.

After considerable "red tape" delay and a busy day of unloading the freight of our vessels, during which time a severe storm had arisen, making the bay quite rough, we were taken off by a tug and landed on Egmont Key, which is certainly a well-chosen point for a quarantine, *i. e.*, if the desire to keep those quartered there from entering the state, for its dreariness would produce almost any disease desired. Here Companies D and B found quarters in tents ready awaiting "folk of their ilk," while the rest of us pitched the tents we brought with us from Cuba.

The scenes without our canvas cottages, viewed by the light of oil lamps placed at intervals throughout the camp, and the growling, hissing wind from off the sea that flapped our tents, growing colder and colder, was about as cheerless as any picture we had looked upon in our soldier life. True, the white sand of which the island is composed reminded us, though faintly, of the snow-clad earth of our

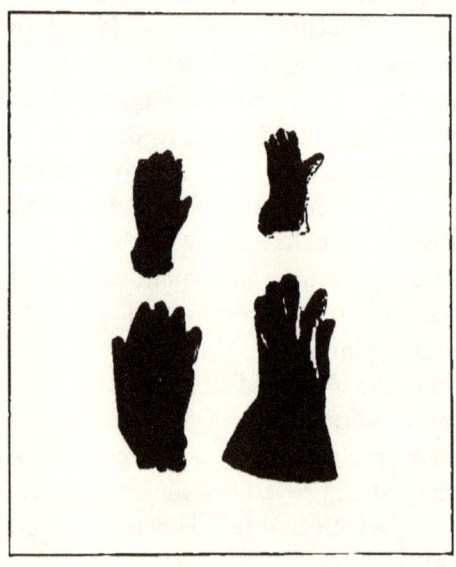

BEFORE AND AFTER FUMIGATION.

own state. Yet it lacked the cheer attending the fall and glitter of those beautiful crystals of our "far off northland."

But, as if to add to our grief and chagrin, on the following morning we found ourselves wet from the rain that sifted through our tents during the night, while the surgeon in charge forbid our going to the beach, not one hundred yards distant, with all our longing to gather shells. All this seemed not only arbitrarily inconsistent to us, but no less displeasing. Still more, at roll-call our sergeants read an order from our commander forbidding any man, under penalty of ten days' extra quarantine, to leave the grounds enclosed by the double barbed-wire fence, strong and high. We didn't kick to the colonel about it, knowing he was only conforming to quarantine regulations, yet it seemed they feared we would inocculate the sand on the seashore, or the worthless growths on this more worthless little hump in the sea. Here, also, we went through all the horrors of fumigation during the three long, wearisome days of our stay on Egmont Key. The anxiety to part company with this inhospitable sand bank was not less than that which was felt in reference to getting away from the more lovely land of Cuba. But the work of the disinfecting of our stuff was completed, and the evening of the 9th settled upon us to find all our baggage on board the little Margaret, that was to steam us up the bay to Port Tampa, while all in camp sank into the usual quiet under a clear sky.

Monday morning witnessed the unusual activity that ordinarily attends the moving of a camp; but the labor was much reduced on this occasion, since we were not to move our tentage.

At an early hour the last of our movables was put on board and we soon followed. When the little ship, on which we were so closely packed as to find little more than standing room, loosed her lines and started for our next transfer point, where we landed about 11 A. M., and by 4 P. M. we were moving out of Port Tampa on the third section of a train booked for Savannah, Georgia. But the unexpected and undesired again occurred, for the next day, when almost in sight of our desired destination, we were run out another road and brought to Augusta, Georgia, where we found in Camp McKensie well-fitted quarters awaiting us, where we began, as a regiment, the last of our camp housekeeping experience, which culminated with our being mustered out of the United States service, with the remainder of our regiment, on the 2d of May, 1899, and the same day started for our respective homes.

COMPANY G ROSTER.

The following we copy from a roster published soon after the company entered the United States service:

CLAUD E. RYMAN, Captain, Effingham, Ill.
JOHN BURR, First Lieutenant, Effingham, Ill.
JOHN R. WRIGHT, Second Lieutenant, Effingham, Ill.
JOHN C. HUTCHINGS, First Sergeant, Effingham, Ill.
JOSEPH H. HICKMAN, Quartermaster Sergeant, Effingham, Ill.

SERGEANTS.

Roy E. Seltz, Effingham, Ill.
Frank E. Worthington, Effingham, Ill.
George H. Harvey, Effingham, Ill.
French E. McElroy, Effingham, Ill.

CORPORALS.

Isaac N. Cook, Effingham, Ill.
Clyde E. Pfeifer, Effingham, Ill.
Charles F. Thomas, Effingham, Ill.
Arthur L. Abraham, Watson, Ill.
William J. Cook, Patoka, Ill.
John H. Dial, Altamont, Ill.
Haden Shouse, Effingham, Ill.
Charles F. Gravenhoust, Effingham, Ill.

James W. Davis, Fredricksburg, Ind.
Abbie B. Switzer, Farina, Ill.
Edward C. Donaldson, Edgewood, Ill.

MUSICIANS.

William N. Schneider, Effingham, Ill.
Schuyler R. Parrill, Farina, Ill.

ARTIFICER.

Samuel N. Mefford, Knoxville, Tenn.

WAGONER.

Freeman Shouse, Effingham, Ill.

PRIVATES.

Alexander, Stephen T., Effingham, Ill.
Anderson, William D., Effingham, Ill.
Austin, Calvin P., Effingham, Ill.
Baughman, Charles A., Effingham, Ill.
Ballenger, Reuben, Effingham, Ill.
Barnes, Rodney, Effingham, Ill.
Bascom, Francis M., Farina, Ill.
Bourland, Alexander B., Effingham, Ill.
Brooks, Charles, Effingham, Ill.
Carman, William H., Effingham, Ill.
Case, Harry R., Farina, Ill.
Claypool, Fred A., Edgewood, Ill.
Cook, John R., Patoka, Ill.
Cronk, John A., Watson, Ill.
Cronk, James A., Watson, Ill.
Currie, Arthur, Brubaker, Ill.
Crist, Charles E., Alma, Ill.
Caldwell, Bert W., Effingham, Ill.
Denind, David U., Effingham, Ill.

Doobs, Charles, Louisville, Ill.
Dial, Silas M., Altamont, Ill.
Dunlap, Thomas G., Shumway, Ill.
Edwards, John A. L., Edgewood, Ill.
Ervin, Verna, Louisville, Ill.
Edmunds, George, Alma, Ill.
Ensign, Otis L., Altamont, Ill.
Faucher, Charles B., Altamont, Ill.
Gehl, Nicholas A., Casey, Ill.
Gosslee, Paul, Effingham, Ill.
Gossett, Jess A., Casey, Ill.
Gossett, Robert A., Casey, Ill.
Hall, William, Watson, Ill.
Harris, George W., Effiingham, Ill.
Harvey, George E., Effingham, Ill.
Hall, William, Watson, Ill.
Harris, George W., Effingham, Ill.
Harvey, George E., Effingham, Ill.
Hill, Homer H., Mason, Ill.
Hilton, James M., Montrose, Ill.
Hunter, Walter E., Effingham, Ill.
Hutchings, Joseph A., Effingham, Ill.
Hastings, Joseph, Effingham, Ill.
Hanawalt, John O., Effingham, Ill.
Headler, Alfred R., Alma, Ill.
Headlee, Myron C., Alma, Ill.
Ingram, Isaac D., Brubaker, Ill.
Kœster, George, Effingham, Ill.
Loy, Elam S., Watson, Ill.
Liechty, John, Effingham, Ill.
Mason, Arthur L., Watson, Ill.
McNeil, Samuel H. H., Alma, Ill.
McNeil, John R., Alma, Ill.
Needham, William G., Montrose, Ill.

Needham, Oscar, Montrose, Ill.
Newbanks, Wade F., Effingham, Ill.
O'Connell, Daniel J., Effingham, Ill.
Overbeck, Frank B., Effingham, Ill.
Padgett, George E., Effingham, Ill.
Pifer, Theodore E., Altamont, Ill.
Hoe, Alfred L., Effingham, Ill.
Poor, William W., Effingham, Ill.
Record, Walter H., Watson, Ill.
Ross, Andrew I., Alma, Ill.
Roberts, Lewis H., Effingham, Ill.
Robertson, George C., Effingham, Ill.
Richardson, Richard, Louisville, Ill.
Richardson, Thomas, Louisville, Ill.
Sale, Junius A., Effingham, Ill.
Scott, Lennie R., Montrose, Ill.
Shenefield, Martin, Altamont, Ill.
Schilling, Charles M., Altamont, Ill.
Smith, John M., Effingham, Ill.
Smith, Irwin W., Farina, Ill.
Sprinkle, William J., Watson, Ill.
Starner, Clarence G., Effingham, Ill.
Shreffler, Arthur, Alma, Ill.
Thompson, Arthur, Shumway, Ill.
Titzell, Harry E., Farina, Ill.
Upton, Daniel N., Effingham, Ill.
Vaughn, William T.
Walker, John H., Altamont, Ill.
Wallace, Byron, Effingham, Ill.
Welker, John F., Avena, Ill.
Williams, Otho S., Effingham, Ill.
Williams, Kirk A., Alma, Ill.
Wood, William I., Watson, Ill.

E. P. CLAYTON.

Lieutenant E. P. Clayton was born in Farina, Illinois, December 29, 1867, moved with his parents to Vandalia in 1871, where he still resides. In 1886, he joined the Illinois National Guard, casting his lot in with Company I, of his adopted city, and in 1890, was appointed corporal. In 1892, he was elected first lieutenant of the company, which rank he held until in 1893, when he resigned, and gave himself up entirely to civilian life for about one year. But his military spirit was only dormant, for when in 1894, the great railroad strike at Mounds, Illinois, gave occasion for the Governor to call out the Illinois National Guard, he revolunteered and was appointed first sergeant, which position he filled until July 17, 1897, when he was by the vote of his comrades again called to the position of first lieutenant.

On the breaking out of war between our nation and that of Spain, he, with Company I, promptly reported for duty at the capitol of our state, on April 26, 1898, and with it was mustered into the United States Volunteer service, on the 20th day of May following. Was appointed ordnance officer, on the 17th of August, and also filled the position of regimental adjutant most of the time until December 21, when he was relieved from duty in both positions, to allow of his complying with special order No. 175 Head Quarters first division seventh army corps by which he was appointed provost marshal of first division seventh army corps, which position he filled until relieved by special order No. 72 Head Quarters seventh army corps dated at Havana, Cuba, April 3, 1899, that he might return to his regiment in view of its leaving for the States on that date.

On arriving at Augusta, Georgia, he was placed in

charge of a detail of sixty men to do provost guard duty in that city, in which capacity he served until mustered out on the 2d of May, 1899.

Lieutenant Clayton seems to have felt the importance of that truth so tersely stated in Holy Writ, viz: "It is not good that man should live alone." Hence he accordingly took to himself a helpmate in the person of Miss Anna Gerche on October 8, 1893, and is now the happy parent of a daughter born to them June 6, 1895.

COMPANY I.

Company "I" was mustered into service in June, 1884. Their first captain being Jerome G. Wills with H. J. Gouchneour and Benjamin Martin as lieutenants. Captain Wills served one year and was succeeded by Capt. J. B. Washburn August 15, 1885, who remained with the company until April 12, 1887, when he resigned, and remained out of the company until February, 1888, when he was again elected captain and remained as their commander until elected lieutenant-colonel in 1892. Capt. George Andrews was then elected as captain and resigned in May, 1884, when Capt. S. S. Houston was elected and served up to the present time, and through the Spanish war. Company "I" did duty in almost every railroad and coal miner strike since 1884. Were at East St. Louis, Chicago, Cairo, Centralia and several coal mine strikes in the southern part of the state.

The days immediately preceding the 26th of April, 1898, while our nation was waiting in breathless suspense for the war drums, alarm, were hours of anxiety for the mothers, fathers, brothers and sisters and friends of the members of Company I, and of doubt, debate and excited enthusiasm among the boys. Hour after hour the ears were strained to catch the peals of the fire bell, and night after night was passed in restless slumber. When at last the tocsin sounded, the boys responded in eager hurry and enthusiasm. Amid scenes of intense excitement they gathered at the Armory, and with nervous, trembling hands, prepared their accoutrements, in readiness for instant departure. Mean-

NON-COMMISSIONED OFFICERS, COMPANY I.

time the news had gone through the surrounding country and towns. Like the Revolutionary fathers of old, the people forsook the plow in the furrow and gathered at the point of central interest in the city of Vandalia. When the boys were ready to move a tremendous crowd was in attendance from the country and neighboring towns, to bid them God-speed and wish them a safe return. A most eloquent and patriotic as well as hopeful address was delivered by Hon. J. J. Brown, which aroused the patriotism and enthusiasm of his auditors to a high degree. Other excellent speeches were delivered by several citizens.

At last, after bidding relatives, family and friends a fond farewell, the boys marched proudly away to the station and aboard the cars amid the cheers and tears of the assembled thousands. On the way to Springfield they were greeted at the numerous towns and villages by exhibitions of the patriotic ardor of their fellow countrymen, who had not witnessed such a scene under such circumstances in a generation of time.

The company landed in Springfield on the the 27th day of April, and marched directly to the State fair grounds, afterwards known as Camp Tanner, and were quartered in a cattle barn with Company K, of Litchfield, and Company D, of Belleville. Now began a long siege of patient endurance, unrelieved by many incidents of humor, pleasure or comfort. It was only the eager expectation with which the boys looked forward to the period of action that made the weeks from the 27th of April to the 20th of May endurable.

Companies K, I and D were a little more than ordinarily unfortunate in being so crowded. The room in the barn was not adequate for the accommodation of so many men. We slept six in a stall, with sometimes one or two crowded at the feet of the other men. It is doubtful if so many animals were ever before crowded into those stalls, and we believe there never will be again, for if the humane society is seized with the "expansion" fever, it may hover its protecting wing over the soldier animals also. We here learned what it meant to be the "pivot" man, with five under a blanket, when we had the latter desirable article. The state was "short" on almost everything when the troops were called to Springfield, which fact made it necessary for the boys to call upon the folks at home for necessary bedding. Company I did not call upon its friends in Vandalia in vain. The wants of the boys were no sooner known than they were promptly and abundantly fulfilled, and soon the boys were in possession of a generous supply of blankets, quilts and comforts. An almost criminal disregard of the needs and health of the troops was shown by the state administration in failing to provide even the necessities in anything like a sufficient manner.

We were about as short on "grub" as on bedding. The first few days the ration consisted mostly of steak broiled over the fire and black coffee and some very fair bread. I said coffee. We always doubted its being genuine, and suspicioned that it was doctored in a manner and for the purpose of conducing toward the order of Springfield. Much indignation was felt among the boys at the attempts of the Springfield people to secure the mustering out of the troops in that city, despite the benefits of travel pay the boys might receive. Their zeal is not surprising when it is understood that retail dealers could buy coffee in one-hundred-pound lots for eight cents less per pound than could the state of Illinois of Springfield dealers in amounts of one ton.

As to the beef, well, it had evidently seen "service." "Goodie" one of our most prolific wits, used to say that you couldn't stick a fork into the gravy. The potatoes had been through the "flood," while the rice—victim of the cooks—rattled as it went its course.

Despite these unpleasantries there was nothing but good humored criticism of the arrangements and fare. We were all too eager to see service and too much excited as well as inexperienced to appreciate the culpable negligence of the state authorities. It is proper to say here that our condition was much better than that of the cavalrymen and the Seventh infantrymen.

Company I made rapid progress in military efficiency under its excellent officers. On the guard lines the company was "stiff," or accommodating just as circumstances demanded. It contained a set of fellows capable of understanding and appreciating situations and acting with original, independent judgment when instructions did not "fit the case." As an instance of this Gov. Tanner was one night halted by Si Bullington. In answer to the challange the governor replied, Governor Tanner, and started across, but Si again halted him. "Why," said the governor, "its all right, I'm Governor Tanner, I'm in command here." But Si stuck to his instructions as close as the Yankee peace commissioners did in the terms of the protocol. "But, my boy," said the governor, "I'm Governor Tanner." "I don't give a cuss," said Si, "if you're the shade of Julius Cæsar, you can't get across this post." The governor chuckled and moved on. But, if in reply to the challange, "friend with a bottle" was given, few Company I men had the heart to keep a brother out. There was a hole on the west side well known and remembered by all Company I men. That hole was a literal bonanza to the sentinel who was lucky enough to possess it and a boon friend of the adventurous, fun-loving boys, who liked Springfield society. Well sheltered, in the hollow by-trees, on two sides, it was comparatively secure from the observation of over curious officers. Here Walt Pollard was stationed one evening, about sundown, just at the time the "noctural animals" began to prowl. Walt, as is well known, has a capacious and a varied appetite. As pies, cakes, cookies, candy, cigars and other stuff was acceptable to him he did a good business. Nearly four regiments of soldiers stole furtively through that hole. The camp looked about as deserted as a church house during a week-day prayer meeting, while Springfield was hilarious. Walter was enterprising and expressed a desire to take that hole south with him. All were sorry that he could not get the "consent of the officers" for Walter's generosity was abounding. We felt quite sure that he would have loaned it to us to go on guard with in return for a "pretty rifle" during guard mounting.

But, for military form we (sometimes) had a strict regard. As guard mount was in the evening we were instructed to halt all persons seen on or near our posts during the night. Nothing was said about proceedings in daylight. So when day arrived we still adhered rigidly to our instructions and halted everything in sight. We could see guard relief coming when it was still a half mile away. But if we had been sitting or reclining, on its appearance we calmly resumed pacing our posts. When we thought it was about the regulation distance away we were suddenly startled—wheel quickly about, bring our rifles to a charge bayonets and shout, in stentorian tones, "Halt! who's there? answer, "Corporal with the Relief." "Advance! Corporal of the Relief, and be recognized." Talk about red tape! and strange to say no "He of the shoulder straps" corrected us. Nevertheless on the several dress parade reviews and on the Sunday inspection of Governor Tanner, Company I acquitted itself well, demonstrating that it was second to no company in the regiment, and deserved the honor of carrying the regimental colors which it had won at the previous annual encampment for its superiority as a military organization.

Lewis Brown was the first company barber. That is a fact not difficult to remember. It is one of the first that occurs to one who attempts to narrate the history of the company. It is, however, a painful recollection reminding one forcibly of the proceeding of the Indian squaws in pulling the hair out of the heads of white men whom the tribe adopts, Lewis after his own fashion converted us to red brothers. He began operation in Springfield nor ceased till we were mustered out. He became, however, a very creditable hand with the razor.

These are the principal incidents up to the time of muster in. On the physical examination Company I was specially unfortunate. It lost more men than any other in the regiment—in all twenty-one. This reduced the number below the necessary limit. The deficit was made up with men drawn from the surplus of other companies. The disappointment of the rejected men was keen and distressing. Several of them shed tears when they left the grounds to return home. Some of them afterward succeeded in enlisting when the companies were recruited up to one hundred and nine men, and lived to repent their folly as they called it. Considering the humble duty performed by our company, and its limited field of operations, and the seeming greedless sacrifice of its members, it is not to be wondered at that some, forgetting the conditions prevailing at the time of their enlistment, cursed themselves for fools. Some civilians, forgetting likewise, were disposed to look with a sort of patronizing pity for the mind on him who was patriotic enough to forsake the pursuit of money getting, and offer his life and liberty for the cause of humanity at his country's call. Not long after returning home this spring a young lady stated that while a great many very good kind of fellows had enlisted what they called, at home, THE boys, that is, the upper crust (I suppose these were sons of well-to-do fathers, who had climbed to the top from the bottom of the ladder by hard work—the respectable lads of leisure who dress in fine clothes, part their hair in the middle, go away to college, take the girls buggy-riding and to the dances, tip their hats to the old ladies, turn up their dainty smellers at the laboring man, and who never earned a dollar in their lives) had not gone to the front. I replied, "When a fellow gets too infernally nice to fight for his country, he had better be shot or put in an asylum for the helpless and feeble, for he is absolutely a burden to society."

Let it be remembered that it was predicted that our armies would meet with disaster on land and sea in the first engagements; that the attitude of Germany, France, Russia and other great powers was in doubt; that some even predicted that a foreign foe would land on our shores; that our brilliant series of unbroken victories was entirely unforeseen and unexpected, and that a bloody struggle was expected by all.

When we look back at contemporary conditions we can better understand the wisdom and the lofty patriotism that inspired men to enlist. They weren't excited fools, by any means. This is a pardonable digression, I believe, since the soldiers have been the victims of their own censure and the patronizing pity of others who also forgot the conditions which prompted the boys to take the step they did, and despite many declarations to the contrary, I firmly believe that if a call were to be made to-day, that every soldier in the late war would promptly enlist, if convinced that his services were needed.

On the failure of many to pass the examination, depended the opportunity of others of us to get into the service. Their misfortune was our blessing. "It's an ill wind that blows nobody good." We have cause to this day to congratulate ourselves on having been associated with such an agreeable, intelligent, sociable and manly set of fellows as were the boys of Company I, and with such considerate, gentlemanly and brotherly fellows as our officers. We are very thankful that we were not compelled to serve under a set of supercillious, bumptious, overbearing ignoramuses, who knew nothing in military science and life to appreciate but their uniforms, who believed themselves little Napoleons, ready to spring into full flower, and we untrained paddies. We love a leader, like Houston or Clayton, but a driver we hate.

Accordingly, the date of muster in found us ready and eager. It was a solemn scene, when on the 20th of May, 1898, we lifted our right hands and solemnly swore to faithfully serve our country for two years. Tears stood in the eyes of many as they realized the solemnity and portent of the step they were taking. But these feelings were soon relieved by playfully bantering others who had not yet been mustered in—calling them "tin soldiers," and the like, and referring to themselves as "old veterans."

A feeling of tension existed during the time that intervened from the date of muster in until we were ordered to proceed to the front. Deep satisfaction prevailed when we were at last ordered to proceed to Tampa, Florida. The well ones ceased their quarrelling and the "sick ones stopped crying for quinine and pills," and all busied themselves in packing up. There were no heart-rending scenes at our departure. Most of our friends had been to see and visit us in camp. So that when we received our orders an air of strict attention to plain business prevailed. A great many, however, snatched a few brief moments to pen a line to friends at home. One little lady was faithful to the last, however. Roll Suerley was the envy of every man in the company. One of the prettiest little lasses that it has ever been our lot to see was there to bid him a last farewell. He fondly pressed a farewell kiss on her ruby lips as the train moved away nor heeded the taunts of his envious comrades. We knew right then that Roll would make a good soldier. He had both courage and an inspiration.

We marched aboard the cars at 1:15, but it was not until towards 4 P. M. that we begun to travel toward the sunny south land. Our fellow countrymen unwearied by many previous and similar occasions cheered us on our way. At Girard the ladies of the Woman's Relief Corps met us at the train and supplied us with sandwiches and coffee. We had but little beside "hoss" and hard tack to eat on our way down aside from what we got at our numerous stops and thus had occasion to remember the kindness of the ladies with deep gratitude. At Belleville, the home of Colonel Andel, the people were lavish in their generous good will. They provided us with nearly half a car load of good things but sorry to say the enlisted men never saw any of it. The officers and commissary men got the whole "cheese." It wasn't the only occasion when they seemed to think that they were the whole army and the sole object of the praise, admiration, gratitude and beneficence of their fellow countrymen. But the good and generous citizens of Belleville have our sincere thanks for all that.

On the 27th day of May we crossed the Ohio river, once the dividing line of deadly foes, and whose banks and bordering forests had rung to the echoes of hostile cannon, and plunged into the forests of western Kentucky. Our journey through "Dixie" was fraught with especial interest to most of us. Few had ever before been south of the

Ohio, and were alive to study the soil, climate, industrial conditions and above all the people of this renowned section of our country. We had heard much of them, and looked to see the people turn from us with averted looks and unfriendly glance; but we traveled on, and on meeting with nothing but hospitable receptions, kindly interest and good will, and by the time we reached Jacksonville we concluded that the "South" was a myth; that there was no "North," no "South," but that the whole land was our own dear country, with one " cause, one flag and one heart." Everywhere we were greeted with the same patriotic enthusiasm, generous good will and hospitality with which our own friends bade us farewell. At Fulton, Kentucky; Jackson, Tennessee; Holly Springs, Mississippi; Waycross, Americus and Albany, Georgia, large crowds of enthusiastic people greeted us. At the last named place the people served us handsomely. Cigars, lemonade, coffee and sandwiches were provided. Though the First Battalion absorbed most of the supply, ours came in for substantial recognition, although the citizens expressed regret of their ignorance of more to follow, which occasioned the limited supply of provisions. Words cannot express our gratitude toward, and appreciation of, the southern people. What we had heard of the hospitality of the south was more than realized.

A number of us took occasion to shake hands with and talk to as many old Confederate veterans as possible. When we told them that the gray-haired "boys" at home sent them tidings of good will, tears trickled down their furrowed, grizzled faces. At Fulton, Kentucky, one large, fine looking old soldier questioned me with "Where you all from?" "Illinois," said I, with pardonable pride. "Well," said he, "you ought to be good fighters then, for your daddies fit us mighty hard." We appreciate that remark, for if we have nothing else to brag about we can boast that we are the sons of our daddies—the boys of '61.

The southern scenery and industrial conditions interested us much, particularly the agricultural implements and appliances. Herman Smith, after closely studying the various styles of mule harness, remarked that he guessed he would send home for a lot of twine string and start a harness shop. While passing through one of the small towns on this trip, Alma Smith was struck in the eye by a stone thrown by some unknown person, but supposed to be a "coon." The injury seemed permanent, for at last accounts the sight was nearly gone. This was one of the most distressing occurrences of the trip.

We arrived in Jacksonville the 29th of May, tired and hungry. Tired of everything, particularly cold beans and "canned hoss." One man—private Geo. Cheeney—was laid up with rheumatism and had to be carried from the train on a stretcher. The trouble was contracted on guard at Camp Tanner. He was later taken to the division hospital but was soon out again. He was the first Company I man to report to the hospital.

By evening of the 29th our tents were up after much labor and tedious inconvenience in procuring them. We were soon ready for business and found that it wasn't going to be long in coming our way and wearing a most serious aspect. We had not then heard of Gen. W. H. Bancroft, but it wasn't long 'til we thought nothing for even a moment of any other man in the United States. The general was soon the subject of general thought and conversation. He haunted our thoughts by day and our dreams by night.

In common with many others we thought we had little to learn, but under the critical, efficient hand of General Bancroft we soon found that we didn't even know when, where and how to salute. In coming from the hydrant with a bucket of water one morning "Tubby" Aderholt neglected that important function in acknowledging the early morning presence of the general, whereupon the latter promptly halted him, commanded him to drop his bucket, salute and keep his hand going in pump handle fashion for ten minutes. After that if the General was within a quarter of a mile Tubby kept his weather eye on him and saluted if he even looked in Tubby's direction.

The General also had an eye for martial bearing and appearance, as Ira Snyder found to his chagrin. The General once commanded him to stand "straight" in line.

John Ira did his best but did not satisfy the critical eye of the officer. Said he, after several vain attempts by Ira, "are you knock-kneed?" "Slightly," said John Ira. The General was no less a stickler for punctuality than for other important details. The officers and men of Company I will not soon forget the row he raised over a five minute delay in getting breakfast, due to a failure of the cookshack guard to awaken the relief. But we all learned to appreciate and respect General Bancroft. He was the making of the regiment.

When we first went to Jacksonville some alarm was felt over the presence of prowling Spanish assassins said by the sensation-loving press to be in the country, waylaying soldiers on the guard lines, poisoning drinking water, etc. "Goodie" Griffith, in wandering about the guard lines, accidently stumbled onto Cliff Sweet. Cliff—new at the business—was greatly alarmed. He gave the challenge in trembling accents, sighed deeply when the answer was given, and answered in a relieved tone of pleasant surprise, "Oh! is that you, Goodie?"

Before long we had abundant opportunity to work off our nervousness on the stump patches which were entirely too numerous to permit any indulgence of ideas of soldierly leisure. Anyhow the "Florida Sand and Improvement Co." proved a blessing to Florida. The labor we boys expended on stumps and ditches, and the money we left in Jacksonville so far improved conditions that a great number of dwelling houses are going up on the site of our old camp ground. We suppose the owners of these sites got the work done at greatly reduced rates. We understood that "nigger" labor in the long run wasn't cheap, which fact prevented a rapid development of resources.

The sergeants and corporals thought that those were the "times that tried men's souls." They could scarcely ever finish a job without going two or three times down the line to rustle up the detail which had gradually evaporated under the hot sun, on the pretext of getting drinks or attending to other very imperative duties. (Boys, you know what.) The boys soon had many friends among the ladies of Jacksonville. So deep were some of the ties and so vivid some of their tender experiences, that memory will be annihilated ere they cease to remember with mixed emotions their fair friends of the sunny sands of Florida. So great was the fascination these southern dames exercised over the Yankee boys that the risks run by the gallant boys in getting across the guard lines were amazing. One of the most dauntless of these devoted gallants was Thomas F. Pantry. It would have taken triple guard lines, and three lines of yelping terriers and three of bull dogs to keep intrepid Tom in camp when the spirit of the "divine passion" animated him. Consequently Tom had the privilege of lying in the guard house and indulging in day dreams of his lady love, or philosophizing on the wisdom of his action as he cut poles or built bridges as an extra duty man. Tom was very popular with Sergeant Adams in the latter capacity 'til his ardor begun to cool, as the result of much trial and tribulation. Tom could give most of the boys pointers on night skirmishing tactics if he couldn't on those in the drill regulations. Tom, however, had the gift of originality. He used to undress, go to bed and apparently to sleep in order to deceive his eagle-eyed duty-devoted corporal,. Charles Smith. After the others had begun to snore, wily Tom would lift the flap of the tent, roll out on the ground, dress and hie himself away to his waiting lady love. The stumps were a great obstacle to safe running after night. So Tom, one day, surveyed a route through the stumps for the night run. But " the best laid plans of mice and men gang aft a glee." That night a double guard line was on. He passed the first line in safety by dint of crawling about one hundred yards on each side of the line. But a double guard was on. Just as Tom was congratulating himself, up rose the shadowy form of a sentinel. That made Tom eager and enthusiastic for a foot race. He touched his shank ponies into a gallop and with much confidence dashed down the premeditated path. " Pride goeth before a fall." The guard headed him off. He bobbed in and out among the stumps like a scared rabbit, but soon came in contact with a gigantic stump which brought him to earth with rather a sudden stop and huge grunt. The guard hauled him in promptly. After this experience the gallant Tom concluded that it was useless to expend any effort in laying plans since extemporaneous ones were as good as any in a stump patch. He would have grubbed stumps with alacrity and pleasure in the *right place* after that.

The liveliest skirmish in which any of us ever participated occurred when the graybacks struck camp. When it was first rumored that the old confederate seam squirrel had invaded our quarters, a small panic seized many. Lively hunts at once ensued. It was amusing to see the rigorous, drastic measures to which the boys resorted in order to get rid of them. Salt, vinegar, kerosene and everything that would kill a louse were put into huge caldrons of boiling water and his louseship treated to the first, last and only bath of his life. The first victims felt considerably mortified and humiliated but we gradually became reconciled to our unavoidable circumstances and derived consolation from the knowledge that all good soldiers had to make the acquaintance of graybacks. But it was a credit to the boys the way they fought the pests and gallantly contended with them for the undisputed possession of every square inch of their soil of which we kept always a good supply in Jacksonville. But the boys did not like to be reminded in a public way of the presence of these little would-be comrades of the soldier boys. The editor of the Jacksonville Times Union and Citizen told them about it once and ate his words the next day to save his measly skin and his office from the hands of the angry boys. The devil take Jacksonville is the earnest prayer of every good soldier of Company I. There was an abundance of dirt, a paucity of bath tubs and a good supply of scheming sharks. The merchants could give pointers to any traveling fake that ever lifted his voice in behalf of brass goods and cheap shoddy.

While it only fell to the lot of Company I to pursue a very sober and humble path of duty, yet its career was not devoid of incidents perhaps trifling in themselves yet of considerable interest and excitement to the boys at the time of their occurrence, particularly to those who participated in them. Those who assisted at different times to vary the monotony were Wm. T. Bailey and Herman Smith, when they one morning came to blows over a can of milk. But few blows were passed, yet they were cool and earnest. James McLaren and Ed Fellwock also furnished us a lively scene one evening, as did also Mabry and Benjamin Sunday.

Another morning, immediately on return from drill, we were excited by the report that a Company I man had shot himself. It proved that Alma Smith while "fooling" with a pistol that was loaded accidentally fired a ball through the calf of his leg. (The bullet wounded two calves.) The wound was quite painful but not serious. After a few weeks on crutches, he was as fit as ever. This was the only Company I man wounded by a bullet during the whole Spanish-American war. Other companies can, however, show a better record than this. The crutches involved the temporary possessor in a skirmish over the right to a certain portion of the tent with private Geo. Cheeney. The dispute became so serious that the crutches for a time threatened to take action in the matter. The question was finally referred the captain, who settled it in a very decisive way by consigning the sticks to the top of the mess shack, where there was an abundance of room. Quarrels sometimes make better friends, as this occurrence served to demonstrate. We never heard, however, whether Mabry and Sunday ever became good friends or not. Mabry was as devilish a tease as ever walked on two legs. He used to be a thorn in Ben's side, constantly irritating and provoking him. They had enough squabbles to make them as loving and tender as brothers, but no one ever discovered anything "soft" about "Mab," although a better fellow to his friends didn't exist. The way he worked a certain lieutenant was a matter of considerable amusement. He showed himself to be a good judge of human nature and an expert in blarneying.

About the most exciting incident that befell us was while on provost in Fairfield. The event occurred at Flynn's saloon, while under the guardianship of Corp. John

D. Haughawout, in charge of a detail of three men composed of Tom Branman, ——— and Geo. Cheeney. While the last named was on guard in front of the store a negro came up the street reporting that a soldier had attacked him, drawing a pistol. The corporal was notified and the two men proceeded down the street to look for the belligerant soldier. The negro was also along for the purpose of identifying him. They soon came across three soldiers proceeding toward the saloon. Before getting close enough for identification, as it was quite dark, the negro charged that one of the soldiers was the one that had assaulted and attempted to rob him. Being a southerner the soldier wasn't inclined to tolerate any such unfounded charge, particularly as he had imbibed a little too freely. So he started for Mr. "Coon." We interposed and succeeded in getting him quiet and starting them for camp. When they got to the saloon, however, they stopped for another drink, an eye closer, I suppose. The "coon" followed them in and renewed the charge. The soldier and his comrades had by this time taken on too much to remain calm. So they declared their willingness to fight anybody and everything, while protesting earnestly that they weren't looking for trouble. They very dramatically threw off their hats, shirts and started to remove their trousers also, all the while eloquently, if not elegantly, declaiming on the injustice done them and their chivalrous desire and intention to annihilate the whole darkey population. Meantime the news spread through the negro quarter and soon about fifty or sixty sable gentlemen were on the scene bent on the protection of their dusky brother and were armed with canes, some of which could hardly have been designed merely for walking sticks. One drew a pistol, but was immediately arrested, but released on promise of good behavior. Meantime the situation was growing worse, negroes were rapidly gathering from all directions, while the excited boys were growing more and more quarrelsome. We were threatened with "coons" on one side and with drunk and enraged soldiers on the other. We finally cleared the barroom of the offending presence of the darkeys, induced the belligerents to rehabilitate themselves and started them for camp. We afterward heard that they were followed and fired upon by a negro, presumably the one who was so offensively aggressive. While this scene was transpiring, an individual laboring under considerable excitement, partly artificial, had burst in on our camp with an excited story of the gravity of the situation. A large detail was quickly fallen in and doubled-quicked to our rescue. When it arrived all was "quiet on the Potomac."

This saloon was the scene of more trouble than almost all the rest of the district included. It was a cheap grog shop and grocery store combined, where the lowest quality of "rot gut" was dispensed to the colored patrons. Bad whisky and bad "niggers" are a dangerous combination to any community.

At another time, while on guard there, a North Carolinian came in with a badly injured head, the result of a contact with a beer bottle in the hand of a colored "heeler." He seemed to be seriously hurt, and suffered great pain. His subsequent fate we did not learn.

George W. Cheeney was also a participant in another row with a Texan, on board a street car. The latter was "tipsy," and became quite profane and obscene in his language, which was very offensive to the ladies present. The conductor finally ordered the car stopped and the offender bounced. As the instructions of the street car guards placed them under the orders of the conductor, he proceeded to fulfill his orders. The Texan, a stalwart fellow, saw the matter in a different light, and proposed to remain through force of might. A struggle ensued, during which, while the rifle being rendered useless by the hold of the Texan, and in the way, was dropped, and the offender pushed off. The rifle having fallen to the ground was reached for by the Texan, but his antagonist got there first. The people, including some officers and soldiers, were greatly excited, and started to interpose to prevent serious trouble. The Texan, however, having regained some sense, immediately surrendered and was marched to camp, all the time indulging in a tirade against street car conductors. His punishment, on court-martial, was made light, owing to the considerate testimony submitted by the guard whom he had attacked.

Ferd Leonard also furnished considerable excitement for the whole regiment one day by pronouncing some fervent and inspired opinions of the colonel in the very presence of that officer. Some thought it necessary to restrain the flow of his eloquence and attempted it in a brutal, inhuman manner. One who did not at first sympathize with the condition of the offender would be driven to a very indignant defense of him at the sight of such cruel, heartless punishment. I must say here that we boys had considerably less regard for those who perpetrated the offence. A little man from the Second Volunteer Cavalry burst into indignant tears and loudly proclaimed his wish for a "six-shooter." I would almost have been willing to take one to have seen him put two more where they ought to have gone. Another officer of the Fourth used to consider it necessary to "buck" and "gag" men in order to discipline them. No one who has any understanding of the character of the volunteer soldier will agree with him as to the necessity of such punishment. It is brutal, fit only to be practiced on unmanageable brutes and the man who does it lacks sense, heart, manhood and honor. He is little better than a brute himself. He demonstrated all this by numerous other acts. This isn't Company I history, but it is history to the members of Company I.

I suppose we boys will not soon forget the hop we took to meet Governor Tanner one night, due to a mistake of the Colonel in reading a telegram. The commanding officer noting the inactivity of the Second Illinois, congratulated himself on stealing a march on its officers. When 11 o'clock arrived and no Governor we were considerably exasperated. We arrived in camp about midnight, hot and tired and dusty. Private Joseph Shuck suffered with a severe attack of the cramps in the muscles of his lower limbs, as a result of the unusual exertion. We almost had trouble with a certain very long, attenuated would-be physician who was exceedingly averse to getting out of his bed to minister to the wants of a sick private. He finally came, under a threat of having him reported. That was about as much professional interest as a great many pill quacks ever evinced in the army.

Although Company I was much more favorably located in the Springfield camp at Jacksonville during the rainy weather, it was with some satisfaction that we settled in the new camp at Panama. It was a more desirable site in every way except for the disadvantage of being so far away from the city. We had moved to escape sickness, which we thought would certainly result from a longer stay in the former camp. We had not long been at Panama, however, before our company was greatly reduced in strength owing to the great inroads of disease. It was not, however, probably due to the last camp. Two good surgeons pronounced the presence of so much fever in the Fourth Illinois to be due to the extreme unhealthfulness of Camp Springfield. But it was the belief of a great many that other causes contributed to bring about this condition, viz.:

the loss of enthusiasm, hope and interest consequent on the termination of hostilities, and the ensuing inactivity and homesickness. This was quite conclusively demonstrated by the comparative condition of companies that had a change of scene and occupation. During the two weeks Company I was on duty in Fairfield, while there was some sickness, the general health of the company was good. On our return to Camp Panama we could muster as many men for morning drill as any other three or four companies in the regiment. But shortly after rejoining the regiment Company I fell a victim to the prevailing conditions and was soon in as lamentable a condition physically as the other companies. In those days it was difficult to muster more than three or four squads for drill or guard duty. Those were times that tried our souls. The quarrels of the officers engendered a restless, dissatisfied, dissenting spirit among the men. Discipline was never at so low an ebb. It seemed the good, hard, earnest labor of General Bancroft and our company officers had been lost. Happily, it was a mistaken notion, as the fine work of the regiment demonstrated later on. Here, at this time, a rather determined effort was made to get rid of the regimental canteen. It was felt that it was the cause of many of our complaints in the rigid administration of the guard line. It was forbidden us to go beyond the limits of the regiment for any purpose without a pass, while venders were kept out of the quarters and stands arbitrarily forced to discontinue business. We felt that this was largely in the interest of the canteen. Indignant at such selfish meanness, we quickly found a way to render the order null and void. The Sixth Missouri and the First and Second South Carolina men were privileged to pass in and out without restraint in order that they might patronize our canteen. So when we desired to go beyond the lines we would walk past a sentinel, perhaps our own "bunkie," and give the password, which was "Sixth Missouri" or "Second South Carolina." If a man acted as if he were going across without giving the word, the guard would call: "Say, you're Sixth Mo., ain't you?" "Yes." "All right; go ahead then."

The movement against the canteen originated with two or three Company I men and a Company A man, who enlisted the sympathy of two or three kindred spirits and started a petition through all the companies requesting the Colonel to abolish the canteen. He had been remonstrated with time and again by his superior officers, all to no avail. In two companies no effort was made to circulate a petition for fear of official vengeance. In some companies as high as eighty to ninety per cent. of the members signed it. In others only thirty to forty per cent., but had the petition been taken through at an earlier date or had all signed it who had in some way and at some time condemned it, not less than ninety per cent. of the whole regiment would have signed it.

When the Colonel learned of the proceedings he threatened to reduce to the ranks every non-commissioned officer who had signed it. It was the desire of some to defy him to do his worst, write him up in the papers, enlist the sympathy of the temperance and church people and arouse popular opinion to such a temper as to make his resignation inevitable. But some were so mortally afraid of the disgrace of being reduced to a private soldier that they made almost frantic appeals for the withholding of the papers from the Colonel. Their wishes were finally heeded, though we have always believed that had we persisted in our former course that beneficial results would have followed despite the fact that it was an unmilitary procedure and would have involved us in trouble and perhaps subjected us to severe punishment. This incident kept the camp in an excited state of mind for several days owing to the numerous and heated arguments that were precipitated. Some very unchristian-like opinions were expressed by both sides.

Another subject of much heated argument was the question of going to Cuba. The partisans of each side were equally pronounced and outspoken in their views. Those who favored the idea, however, were in the minority. But it is probable that if a vote were taken to-day a majority would declare their satisfaction at having gone.

But the most depressing and discouraging feature of life at Camp Panama was the great number of men that fell ill. So many were stricken that even the most healthful experienced a sense of gloom and uncertainty. None knew whose turn it would be next. It would be impossible for the writer in the absence of all notes to mention all those who were seriously ill and those who passed through the "valley of the shadow of death" and lived to tell the story.

We, however, lost by death four men. The first of these was Herman Smith, a jolly, good natured boy who made many original and witty remarks and livened the boys up wherever he was, no matter what transpired. "Harmonica" was usually cheerful and ready to create a laugh. He gave his life to his country and to his God September 24, 1898.

The next to be called was Sergeant Clarence Hall, who answered the last roll call September 27, 1898, three days after comrade Smith had left our ranks. Hall was a man greatly beloved by all the men of his company and deservedly so. As a non-commissioned officer he was efficient, but modest and unassuming. He was considerate and kindly toward those under his direction and control and arrogated to himself no airs of superiority. He was good humored, humorous and a true friend. It will create no envy to say that he was the most popular non-commissioned officer in the company. His case was especially sad, since he left a young and beautiful wife and a little babe. Many were the tears that coursed down the faces of his remaining comrades when the sweet and solemn melody of the bugle summoned him to his last long sleep. May God bless, comfort and protect his sorrowing wife and mother and his fatherless babe.

October 27, 1898, was a day made memorable by the sad and untimely deaths of Patrick Ryan and James McLaren. The former was one of the greatest wits in the company and by his droll stories and Irish wit generally kept his companions in a spirit of great good humor. He was also a true friend, honest and thoroughly reliable. It was never my lot to hear a word spoken in disparagement of Pat Ryan. He was greatly liked by all the boys of his company and his death was a source of deep and profound regret. James McLaren, whose death we were called upon to mourn at the same time, was another hale fellow well met. He was a sharp, shrewd thinker, a jolly fellow who loved a good time and possessed that virtue of virtues in a soldier's eyes, viz: loyalty to friends. To them he was true as steel and was never called upon by them in vain. May the Father of all mercies smile and solace the hearts of the stricken fathers, mothers, brothers, sisters and friends of our dead comrades.

The first Company I man to receive a discharge, because of physical disability, was George Bingaman, with whose misfortune we all sympathized deeply. Then followed, for like reasons, the discharges of James O. Guinn, Henry Wilson, Fletcher Bullington, Harry T. Dungey, Orville C. Bo't, John M. Slichter, Charles O. Toothaker and Rollin D. Snerley, though not in the order named. Some were discharged after we reached Savannah, while others served for a time in Cuba. We lost five men by transfer, viz.: Si Bullington to Indiana Volunteer Cavalry, Edward Hill to United States Hospital Corps, Isaac Hilton to Company G, Cortez W. McKnight to Signal Corps, and Joseph Shuck to Company E.

After the dreary monotony, sickness and death at Camp Panama, the boys of Company I welcomed the change to provost duty at station No. 1, in Jacksonville. As the writer was not with the company during this period of its service, he has had to depend on what has been related to him, and that was not much. It would seem that outside of the necessity of giving numerous shower baths, at which they became experts, the boys met with few exciting adventures worthy of notice.

Akeman related a little story of how he avoided "pinching" a comrade, but the details of it have about escaped my memory. It seems that Peter has a tender, generous heart. He thought to himself, "do as you would be done by." Seeing that the gentleman was laying himself liable to arrest, and being averse to subjecting him to that annoyance and inconvenience, Peter made himself scarce, and allowed the gentleman to escape. It seems that an officer happened to see the proceeding, but appreciating Peter's philanthropy, he connived at the procedure, and secretly reassured him. Peter said it made him "very glad," and I believe myself, the angels must have sung an extra song on the strength of it.

Company I formed a part of the advance guard under Major Bennett, which first took charge of provost work at Savannah, Georgia.

I have heard that the people of Savannah appreciated the advent of the soldiers with feelings of alarm, apprehension and dread. But that the gentlemanly conduct of the boys and the entire ability of the guards to quell all disturbances and control all disorder soon put them at their ease and disposed them to give the boys in blue a hospitable, hearty reception wherever they went. It may safely be said therefore that no small credit for the generous treatment the soldiers received is due those who formed the advance guard and to Company I as a portion of that detail. Our boys won laurels of praise in common with the other companies of the regiment in the great review by President McKinley.

They were royally treated by the citizens of Savannah on Thanksgiving day, and desire here to express their heart-felt gratitude to the people of Savannah for the kindly and generous recognition they received that day. The state of Illinois owes a vote of thanks to the people of Savannah for their generous treatment of the boys of Illinois.

No events of particular importance occurred in Savannah, so far as I could ascertain from the boys. One laughable incident occurred when one night on one of the numerous raids Captain Houston rounded a corner of a house and discerning two shadowy forms in the dark called "halt!" Whereupon a trembling voice replied, "D-d-d-d-don't, don't sh-sh-shoot, Cap, its me." The forms were afterward discovered to be the substantial personalities of Tilen Aderholt and Crowder. But both disclaimed ownership of the voice and have so far succeeded in deceiving themselves that they say and seem to really believe that it was all a joke of the boys' manufacture.

Griffith and Newberry, as well as a few others, paid a good round sum for a night's entertainment but since the fines are devoted to a good cause it is not so good a cause of grief as might be at first inferred. Christmas was a

Capt. S. S. Huston.

1st Lieut E. P. Clayton. 2d Lieut. P. P. Strait.

great day with the Company I boys. They will not soon forget the uproarious, hilarious, jolly time they had that day.

It was not without satisfaction that we received our orders to pack up, preparatory to our departure for Cuba. At least a change was in prospect. As our company marched through the street there were numerous testimonials of the high regard in which the men of Company I were held by the citizens of Savannah. People frequently darted from the ranks of the bystanders to grasp the hands of our boys in a farewell clasp, and wish them God-speed, a pleasant sojourn and a safe return. Some of the devoted sweet hearts of the boys defied the guards at the entrance of the wharf by climbing on army wagons and riding in, in order to bid their young Lochinvars farewell.

Company I fared well in the matter of room on the boat, but some of our men became very sick, notwithstanding, scarcely leaving their bunks from the time of starting to that of landing, and all the time doing their full duty by the fish. We were all deeply touched. The writer was himself too sick to note the condition of many others, but remembers very well the desperate condition of Corporal Hammond.

· After arriving within the harbor of Havana we soon recuperated and became greatly interested in the wonderful land to which we had came. Observing the peculiar method of unloading cattle in vogue, Roy Fogler denominated it a "new brand of jerked beef." So eager did some of the boys come to explore the city of which they had heard so much that they could not wait for the disembarkation of the regiment, but passing the guards they hazarded an independent expedition. These two adventurers were Johnson and Bettner. They hadn't learned nearly all there was to know before they ran afoul of a United States regular, who promptly arrested them and had them incarcerated in a Spanish jail. The next morning, after an interview with Major Harrison, who vindicated their right to be abroad, they were released. Nevertheless they have the distinction of having been the only Company I men to pass a night behind the bars in Cuba. Not that they were the only ones that deserved to, but that they were the only ones that did.

Our first night in camp was distinguished by a rainstorm. Owing to our ignorance of Cuban soil we had failed to properly and adequately stake our tents. Before a great while many of them were down and the unlucky inmates were out wading about in the mud, endeavoring to raise them and drive stakes with any available club in the inky darkness of night.

On several occasions our tents fell in Cuba. One morning, a little while before reveille, the tent of the first squad blew down. Hammond Newberry and Cheeney found about half of their anatomy exposed to the elements. They were compelled to leave their comfortable blankets and dress in the storm. They then endeavored to rouse their comrades, Pollard, Handel, Kimbro and Moffett. Only the latter responded, the others being too comfortable to stir our one second before "get 'em up." With much difficulty and swearing at the sleeping boys under cover the tent was finally raised. Later on the tables were turned and out former luxuriating comrades found themselves in the rain. In vain did they call for our help. We groaned, grunted and finally told them to "chase themselves" in army language. For some time after arriving in Cuba the life of our men was confined to the camp and immediate vicinity, owing to the difficulty of obtaining passes. It took a regular furlough to pass one in safety to the city of Havana, or to Colon cemetery.

But after a time the curiosity of the boys overcame all fears and many were the trips made to Havana with only pure unadulterated nerve for a pass. Mabry and Aderholt were among the initiators of this movement, while Snyder, Fleming, Wright, Johnson and several others weren't far behind. One of these ran onto a regular one day, and, fearing some embarrassing requests, he boldy crossed the street, went up to the sentinel and inquired the way to the post office. He was told and went on his way rejoicing.

Wright, Snyder, Fleming, Spradling and one or two others missed the train returning on one occasion and started to camp on foot. They managed to work upon the sympathies of the various provosts, but finally lost their way and wandered about for some hours in outer darkness. They arrived in camp next morning about 9 o'clock, after having taken a swim, and proceeded leisurely into quarters. They figured that it would not cost any more to miss drill also, and in that they were wise. We never learned just what the trip cost the boys, but from all reports they got their money's worth. They are to be congratulated on their good fortune, for it was seldom on such occasions that the boys got all they were compelled to pay for.

Wright, Fleming and a few others were the participants in a Sunday night lark with some cognac that we all remember pretty well. The former found himself in an unexpected colloquy with "Brother Sam" as he crawled into the back end of his tent, and soon after found himself on the way to the guard-house. But Joe was too full of good spirits to be much depressed.

By far the most important event to the company was the march to Guines. Unfortunately, this was another event the writer missed. About the only occurrence of which we learned that distinguished their experience from that of other companies on the march was the capture by our "snake charmer." Tom Pantry, aided by others, of some very large serpents of the boa constrictor variety. They were thereafter the object of a great deal of interest. Tom soon had them well trained. Many of the nervy and adventurous coiled them around themselves and had their pictures taken. Red Handel was the subject of one of these photos. But it wasn't for any love of notoriety, adventure or snakes that Red submitted himself. It was for an almighty dollar. Red was broke at the time. Knowing Red's antipathy to snakes, some gamester waged him a dollar that he didn't have the nerve to wrap the "big snake" around himself and have his picture taken. One thing he didn't know, and that was Red's attachment to a dollar when he was broke. Red afterward said that he sweat blood, but he wanted that dollar *awful* bad.

It was with some delight that we received orders to pack up preparatory to our return home.

By evening of the first day we were on our way to the transports. Again we suffered all the tortures of sea sickness and were glad enough to arrive off Egneout Key. Here we spent the most disagreeable three days of all our period of service. The dirt and sand and wind were extremely annoying. We ran short of potatoes here, but managed to make up the deficiency. Company K's efficient quartermaster sergeant, "Cap Furz," had marked and branded his potato sacks in an unmistakable manner. But a jack-knife quickly converted the K to an I, when we carried the tubers off the lighter under the very noses of the watchful officers. Some tomato cans were also smuggled through in a sack of spoiled bread and helped materially in filling our vacancies.

During our stay in Augusta, Georgia, we enjoyed more liberty than at any previous time. Indeed, Haman and one or two others moved to town a few days before we left.

Only a few of our men were "pulled" by the Georgia crackers on guard there. Stewart and Bogardus were treated to a night's lodging in the city, as was also Aderholt. What the latter did to the stove and bars in the endeavor to break into a "coon" pen was a plenty. Aderholt had the happy faculty of making the best of every situation. When the fellows "got broke" they instituted some very amusing rag dances as a diversion.

As the time drew near for muster out all was eagerness and enthusiasm. The boys at this time knew more of what was going on officially than at any other time, because of the large number of men detailed from the companies as clerks. Fogler, Haughawont, Whitefort, Short, Foucht and Cheeney were on special duty for some time. Other men who saw special duty at different times during our service were Washburne, Ed Snyder, Si Bullington, Frank Dickson, who was on duty continuously from the time we were mustered in 'til we were mustered out at the regimental and brigade headquarters. He was a very efficient clerk and deservedly popular with the various official staffs. Charles I. Curry, as permanent provost in Jacksonville; William Slichter, Ralph Handel, as canteen clerks, the latter also saw much special duty as permanent provost; Ed Fellwock, permanent provost in Cuba; Hugh E. Kavanaugh, John Kitchen, Jesse Kimbry and William Gilbert and Sergeant Frank Sawler, as special provosts in Augusta, Georgia; Lieutenant Clayton saw special duty as provost marshal and as regimental adjutant for a long period of his service. The token of the esteem in which he was held was mentioned elsewhere. It should be here mentioned that Lieutenant Stout was also the recipient of a sword, the gift of the men of his company at Jacksonville, Florida. If any have not been mentioned in this connectioned, be assured that the neglect was not intentional. This work has been entirely from memory. It would not be at all strange if some things do not therefore appear in the proper connection.

The 5th of May was to us all a day of great rejoicing. We were soon packed, in the morning, and after procuring the little "paper and long green," for which we had patiently (?) waited, we were soon on our way to the waiting cars. A most vexatious delay now occurred. The railway company had made us all sorts of promises, agreeing to have us away by 3:00 P. M., and into the city of Vandalia within twenty-four hours. But, having gotten our money, little did they reck. We were delayed until nearly 6:00 P. M., and did not arrive in Vandalia till some thirty-six hours later. During the delay, some very exciting incidents occurred. Some of the less "nervy" left the train and came up on later trains, but overtook us at Nashville, Tennessee. Klunker was reported to have been badly excited.

The home-coming of the boys was marked with a joy and enthusiasm impossible to describe. The citizens of Fayette county had been kept constantly informed of our movements from the time we left Augusta. In consequence a great crowd of people from all parts of the county were in Vandalia to welcome the men home. Many of them had husbands, brothers or friends in the company who intensified the interest they felt.

The emotions of the boys as the train whistled for the town from which they had marched away over a year before, pen could not convey. Tears of joy were near the surface and the heart throbbed painfully as they anticipated the welcome of the great concourse of their patriotic and appreciative countrymen and greetings of the gray-haired fathers and mothers, the devoted wives and sweethearts, the loving brothers and sisters, the affectionate friends and kindly neighbors.

What they had anticipated was more than realized. The train was welcomed with a tremendous cheer and the lively joyous music of bands. The crush of the assembly forbade any formation of the company as was intended. The boys climbed down into the crowd and into the arms of their relatives and friends. In some the long pent up emotion swept away all barriers and expressed itself in sobs and tears. In others the warm fervent grasp of the hand, the quiet tear and the trembling lip betokened a heart too full for utterance.

After long delay the boys were finally gotten into the Aragon hotel, where an elegant and sumptuous banquet was served. We almost felt that the testimonials of the appreciation and gratitude of the people were more than our humble services deserved. Little had we done, but we were received with all the grace, enthusiasm and devotion that could be extended the grizzled veterans of many a bloody field. As we sat and partook of the elegant viands, and received the gracious smiles and thoughtful attention of noble women and the prettiest girls in the country, we forgot our trials, disappointments and the monotony of camp life and felt that surely we had been more than repaid on that day for all that we had sacrificed. If Father McKinley had then and there appeared and called for volunteers to march into the infernal regions, every kicking, growling grumbler would have sworn his life away. With such noble, devoted, patriotic and beautiful women and girls as this country can boast, it is no wonder our soldiers can "lick" the world. They have both blood and inspiration. God bless the women of America, and particularly the women of Vandalia.

After the banquet a recption was tendered in the

Armory hall. An eloquent, able and touching address of welcome was delivered by Hon. J. J. Brown, and was responded to on behalf of the company by private George W. Cheeney. Other addresses were delivered by ex-Chaplain Todd and Rev. Ned ———, after which the meeting broke up in handshaking. Our deepest gratitude is extended to the people of Vandalia and Fayette county for the apprecaition and gratitude they so ably and substantially expressed.

A reception and banquet under such circumstances involved much work and planning. The arrangements and their execution *could not* have been more perfect. Every want and expense of the boys was anticipated and met. Even passes over the Central R. R. were secured for them, and lodging at the hotels where it was made necessary. We venture to say that of all the receptions that have been tendered returning soldiers not one was more thoroughly enjoyed or enjoyable than the one given at Vandalia. Citizens of Vandalia, kindly accept our most sincere thanks and deepest gratitude.

Boys, we have bade each other, as an organization, good-bye for ever. We were many times discouraged and weary of army life. But as the swift years roll away we will look back upon those months of association and experience with pleasure and satisfaction not unmingled with tinges of regret.

We will miss the camp fire chats, the stories, the songs and the dances. We will miss big, good-natured "Daddy Hammond," the humorous Goodie, the devilish Mabry, droll old Aderholt and Akeman, and last but by no means least, "brother Sam Houston." Yes, we will miss you each and all. But from the "gallery of memory" we trust that we may never be absent, and that each and every image will revive recollections dear and precious, if tinged with sadness.

ROSTER OF COMPANY I.

Houston, S. S., Captain, Vandalia, Ill., Commercial Traveler.
Clayton, E. P., First Lieutenant, Vandalia, Ill., molder.
Stout, P. D., Second Lieutenant, Vandalia, Ill., clerk.

SERGEANTS.

Adams, Thomas E., Vera, Ill., Farmer.
Lawler, J. F., Vandalia, Ill., Butcher.
Clark, Charles A., Vandalia, Ill., Electrician; appointed Sergeant-Major Second Battalion, Fourth Illinois Volunteer Infantry, March 19, 1899.
Hall, C. L., Vandalia, Ill., clerk; died at Third Division Hospital, Seventh Army Corps, Camp Cuba Libre, Jacksonville, Florida, September 27, 1898, of typhoid fever.
Pacatte, Frank, Vandalia, Ill., Laborer.
Jenkins, Ezra L., Vandalia, Ill., Painter; reduced to ranks December 4, 1898.
Hagy, James H., Vandalia, Ill., Laundryman; enrolled as Private, mustered in as Corporal; appointed Sergeant Jan. 1, 1899.
Smith, C. W., Brownstown, Ill., Teacher; enrolled as Private, mustered in as Corporal, appointed Sergeant Jan. 1, 1899.

CORPORALS.

Brown, Lewis, Vandalia, Ill., Laborer.
Hammond, Harry, Vandalia, Ill., Carpenter.
Bullington, J. F., Vandalia, Ill., Teacher; transferred to Second United States Volunteer Cavalry Sept. 8, 1898.
Curry, James T., Vandalia, Ill., Wood-turner.

Sweet, C. W., Vandalia, Ill., Clerk; promoted from Private to Corporal Aug. 1, 1898.
Haughawort J. D., Vandalia, Ill., Teacher; promoted from Private to Corporal Aug. 1, 1898.
Hartman, F. O., Vandalia, Ill., Tinner; promoted from Private to Corporal Aug. 1, 1898.
Carter, Charles R., Vandalia, Ill., Laborer; promoted from Private to Corporal Aug. 1, 1898.
Sturgess, E. B., Vandalia, Ill., student; mustered in June 20, 1898; promoted from Private to Corporal Aug. 1, 1898.
Guinn, James O., Vandalia, Ill., Student; mustered in June 20, 1898; promoted from Private to Corporal Aug. 1, 1898; discharged on disability at Jacksonville, Fla., September 7, 1898.
Mammen, Chas. A., Vera, Ill., Carpenter, promoted from Private to Corporal Feb. 17, 1899.
Moffett, Jesse, Clinton, Ill., Locomotive Fireman, promoted from Private to Corporal Feb. 17, 1899.
Short, John A., Avena, Ill., Merchant, promoted from Private to Corporal, Apr. 20, 1899.
Whitfort, Geo. D., St. Elmo, Ill., Teacher, appointed Wagoner July 1, 1898; promoted to Corporal Apr. 20, 1899.
Brannon, Thos. J., Vandalia, Ill., Laundryman, mustered in June 23, 1898; promoted from Private to Corporal Nov. 2, 1898.

MUSICIANS.

Boyer, Paul K., Vandalia, Ill., Painter, sick in United States General Hospital, Newport News, Va., at date of muster out.
McKnight, F. R., Ramsey, Ill., Telegrapher.

ARTIFICERS.

Manion, H. P., Vandalia, Ill., Teacher, discharged Jan. 28, 1899, from United States General Hospital, Ft. Monroe, Va.

Johnson, F. A., Mulberry Grove, Ill., Farmer, appointed as Artificer, Feb. 20, 1899.

WAGONER.

Foucht, W. A., Shobonier, Ill., Teacher, appointed as Wagoner Apr. 18, 1899.

PRIVATES.

Figures following name indicate age.

Akeman, Peter F., Vandalia, Ill., Farmer.
Aderholt, Tilden, 24, Vernon, Ill., farmer.
Bailey, W. I., 30, Mulberry Grove, Ill., laborer.
Bingaman, George, 20, Vandalia, Ill., clerk; discharged on disability, Aug. 27, 1898, Jacksonville, Fla.
Bogardus, A. D., 18, Clinton, Ill., carpenter.
Bettner, E. J., 23, Vandalia, Ill., printer.
Bass, George W., 22, Watson, Ill., farmer; mustered in June 20, 1898.
Bolt, D. C., 22, Ramsey, Ill., printer; mustered in June 17, 1898; discharged Jan. 13, 1899, by order Secretary of War.
Bullington, F. C., 21, Vandalia, Ill., teacher; mustered in June 18, 1898; discharged Jan. 31, 1899, from U. S. Gen. Hosp., Ft. Monroe, Va.
Courtney, C. S., 25, Ramsey, Ill., printer.
Curry, Charles E., 23, Vandalia, Ill., laborer.
Chandler, Roy, 20, Vandalia, Ill., cigarmaker.
Cheney, George, 23, Saybrook, Ill., teacher.
Cheney, W. H., 20, Saybrook, Ill., student.

Cullom, Charles E., 18, Hagerstown, Ill., student; mustered in June 18, 1898.
Crowder, Charles E., 28, Vernon, Ill., farmer.
Dickson, Frank, 21, Ramsey, Ill., law student; detailed as brigade clerk, Aug. 8, 1898.
Dungey, Harry, 24, Winfield, Kan., hostler; discharged on disability, Aug. 27, 1898.
Dennis, D. D., 28, Chicago, Ill., engineer, mustered in June 18, 1898.
Danbury, W. L., 25, Vernon, Ill., farmer; mustered in June 20, 1898.
Fogler, R. C., 19, St. Elmo, Ill., clerk.
Fogler, H. S., 19, St. Elmo, Ill., miller.
Fleming, C. A., Mulberry Grove, Ill., Farmer, mustered in June 18, 1898.
Fellwock, Edward, Vandalia, Ill., Painter, mustered in June 18, 1898.
German, Wm., Vandalia, Ill., Farmer.
Gilbert, Wm., Chapin, Ill., Farmer.
Griffith, C. L., Vandalia, Ill., Laborer.
Handle, E., Vandalia, Ill., Farmer.
Handle, R., Vandalia, Ill., Blacksmith.
Hill, E. A., Dixon, Ill., Farmer.
Hill, Edward, Effingham, Ill., Laborer, transferred to United States Hospital Corps Sept. 19, 1898.
Hilton, I. N., Montrose, Ill., Farmer, transferred from Company I to Company G, Dec. 28, 1898.
Hollingshead, Jno. R., Vandalia, Ill., Moulder.
Homan, O. H., Lafayette, Ind., Clerk,
Johnson, F. E., Vandalia, Ill., Paper-maker.
Kavanaugh, H. E., Springfield, Ill., Lineman.
Kimbro, Jesse, Smithboro, Ill., Butcher.
Kitchen, John W., Vandalia, Ill., Brick-maker.

Klimper, Charles M., Ramsey, Ill., Clerk; mustered in June 17, 1898.
Leonard, F., Carlyle, Ill., Teamster.
Luther, John F., Vandalia, Ill., Farmer.
Lawler, A. W., Vandalia, Ill., Laborer; mustered in June 23, 1898.
Mabry, E. K., Altamont, Ill., Student.
McLaren, James B., Carlyle, Ill., Laborer; died at Third Division Hospital, Seventh Army Corps, of typhoid fever, at Jacksonville, Fla., Oct., 27, 1898.
Moore, Jno. H., Smithboro, Ill., Farmer.
Minor, Henry, Mulbery Grove, Ill., Laborer; mustered in June 18, 1898.
McKnight, C. W., Ramsey, Ill., Operator; mustered in June 18, 1898. Transferred to United States Volunteer signal corps September 21, 1898.
McKnight, Jas. A., New Philadelphia, Ohio, Miner; mustered in June 17, 1898.
Newberry, Hugh, Knoxville, Tenn., Farmer.
Oldham, Jas. E., Seneca, Mo., Laborer.
Overleese, E. L., Vera, Ill., Farmer.
Pantry, Thos., Dexter, Ill., Laborer; discharged in Cuba April 4, 1899.
Paul, Baker, Petersburg, Ill., Tinner.
Pummill, L. E., Vera, Ill, Farmer.
Pollard, W. O., Vera, Ill., Engineer.
Pittman, D., Brownstown, Ill., Farmer.
Perkins, J. W., Mulbery Grove, Farmer; mustered in June 18, 1898.
Ryan, P. H., Watson, Ill., Laborer; died at First Division Hospital Seventh Army Corps, of Malarial fever, Jacksonville, Fla., Oct. 27, 1898.
Robinson, S. E., Patoka, Ill., Teacher; mustered in June 18, 1898.

Rutledge, J. O., Vandalia, Ill. Teacher; mustered in June 23, 1898.
Surley, R. D., Vera, Ill., Student; discharged march 15, 1899, by order secretary of war.
Sclichter, J. M., Carlyle, Ill., Policeman; discharged Oct., 18, 1898, through commanding officer Fourth Illinois Volunteer Infantry.
Sandy, Benj., Vandalia, Ill., Laborer.
Shuck, Jos., Shelbyville, Ill., Barber; Transferred from Company I to Company E, Jan. 18, 1899.
Smith, Herman, Farina, Ill., Harness-maker; died at Third Division Hospital Seventh Army Corps, Jacksonville, Fla., typhoid fever, Sept. 23, 1898.
Smith, Alma, 20, Brownstown, Ill., Painter.
Stewart, Thos., 24, Vandalia, Ill., Farmer.
Snyder, L. F., 28, Vandalia, Ill., Railroader; mustered in June 20, 1898.
Spraddling, F. E., 21, Mulberry Grove, Farmer; mustered in June 18, 1898.
Snyder, Jno. I., 26, Vandalia, Ill., Banker; mustered in June 20, 1898.
Troyer, D. W., 24, Vera, Ill., Stavejoiner.
Tolbert, T. E., 23, Chapin, Ill., Farmer.
Toothaker, Chas., 26, Effingham, Ill., Engineer; discharged Feb. 16, 1899, from U. S. General Hospital., Ft. Monroe, Va.
Wilson, Henry, 21, Shobonier, Ill., Teacher; discharged on disability, Dec. 3, 1898.
Walker, Walter, 23, Smithboro, Ill., Laborer.
Wright, J. H., 21, Mulberry Grove, Ill., Farmer; mustered in June 18, 1898.
Washburn, A. L., 28, Vandalia, Ill., Jeweler; mustered in June 17, 1898.

Zimmerman, Elmer, 19, Vandalia, Ill., Student; mustered in June 20, 1898.
Blackman, W. J., 21, Paris, Ill., Clerk; transferred to U. S. Hosp. Corps, June 19, 1898.
Hutchinson, M. A., 25, Mulberry Grove, Ill., Laborer; transferred to U. S. Hosp. Corps, June 19, 1898.
Wiley, Warren, 21, Paris, Ill., Salesman; transferred to U. S. Hosp. Corps, June 19, 1898.
All not otherwise distinguished were mustered in at Springfield, Ill., May 20, 1898. All not otherwise referred to as discharged were mustered out at Augusta, Ga., May 2, 1899.

COMPANY K.

ALBERT OWEN SEAMAN.

First Lieut. Albert Owen Seaman was born in Greenville, Illinois, February 7, 1878, and lived there and attended school up to 1894, when he entered Western Military Academy, and attended there during that school year and was promoted to first sergeant and during the spring was placed in charge of the artillery section. The next year he attended Gem City Business College and graduated from there as an authorized expert accountant. At the first call for troops in 1898, he enlisted in the Fourth Illinois and was detailed as battalion sergeant-major First-Battalion, which position he held up to February 1st, when he was made second lieutenant of Company K, and on March 1st he was made first lieutenant of the same company and was mustered out with his company in Augusta, Georgia.

During his time in the army he served on the provost guard under Major Harrison as quartermaster.

PERLEY J. ROSE.

On the 8th of June, 1878, the subject of this sketch, Perley J. Rose, was born; and if the future is to be judged by the past, his is the opening of a useful life. Having graduated from the High School of Litchfield, Illinois, with the class of 1896, he spent the school year of 1896 and 1897 at DePaw University at Greencastle, Indiana.

CAPT. DAVID DAVIS.

CAPT. G. I. ZINK

2D LIEUT. P. J. ROSE.

On September 1, 1897, he was employed by the Big Four railroad as clerk and served in that capacity until April 26, 1898. Enlisted as second sergeant of Company K, Fourth Illinois National Guards, on the 20th of May, 1898, and on March 18, 1899, was promoted to second lieutenant, serving his company as such until mustered out on the 2nd of May, 1899, not having reached his twenty-first year.

HISTORY OF COMPANY K.

Company K was the youngest company in the Illinois National Guard when the organization was called to Springfieln in April, 1898. It was mustered into the state service at Litchfield, by Captain Ewert, on the evening of February 18, just three days after the destruction of the Maine in Havana harbor.

The first officers of the company were Capt. David Davis, First-Lieut. George L. Zink and Second-Lieut. William F. La Force, all of whom entered the service of the United States with the company.

Loss by death: William D. Souter, of Green Cove Springs, Florida, who died of typhoid fever at his home in October, 1898; Charles S. Kingsbury, who died at Third Division Hospital, at Pananca Park, Florida, after a short attack of typhoid; and Corpl. Francis E. Green, who was drowned while bathing in a small stream near Camp Columbia, Havana Province, Cuba. Souter is buried at Green Cove Springs, Florida; Kingsbury at his home in Greenville, Illinois; and Corporal Green is at rest in Elmwood cemetery at Litchfield.

Captain Davis resigned and left the service in February, 1899, and Lieutenant La Force resigned a few days

COMPANY K.

later. Lieutenant Zink was made captain; Serg. A. Owen Seaman, first lieutenant, and Serg. Perley J. Rose, second lieutenant.

ROSTER OF COMPANY K.

DAVIS, DAVID, Captain, Litchfield, Ill.; resigned.
ZINK, GEORGE L., Captain, Litchfield, Ill.
LaFORCE, WILLIAM F., First Lieutenant, Litchfield, Ill.; resigned.
SEAMAN, A. OWEN, First Lieutenant, Greenville, Ill.
ROSE, PERLEY J., Second Lieutenant, Litchfield, Ill.

SERGEANTS.

Simmons, Norton A., First, Litchfield, Ill.
Cripe, Osa, Quartermaster, Girard, Ill.
Foulk, Harry C., Litchfield, Ill.
Schwartz, Adolphus A., Edwardsville, Ill.
Collins, Joseph U., Litchfield, Ill.
George, Robert J., Litchfield, Ill.
Farr, George R., Litchfield, Ill.

CORPORALS.

Machler, Francis P., Litchfield, Ill.
Walters, Nim R., Donnellson, Ill.
Scherer, Luther H., Litchfield, Ill.
Beck, Henry M., Litchfield, Ill.
Stearns, Roy, Litchfield, Ill.
Hughes, Alfred, Taylorville, Ill.
McBrain, Leroy J., Litchfield, Ill.
Stone, Charles U., Middletown, Ill.
Towey, James K., Carlineville, Ill.

Lee, Robert E., Litchfield, Ill.
Grubbs, Harlan P., Litchfield, Ill.
Green, Francis E., Litchfield, Ill.
Cline, Cullen A., Litchfield, Ill.

MUSICIAN.

Tromley, Glen E., Fairfield, Ill.

ARTIFICERS.

Roberts, Richard E., Litchfield, Ill.
Huber, Charles W., Litchfield, Ill.

WAGONER.

Smith, Horace, Litchfield, Ill.

PRIVATES.

Allen, Elmer E., Litchfield, Ill.
Baits, William D., Litchfield, Ill.
Boyd, Guss E., Litchfield, Ill.
Bailey, Allen W., Litchfield, Ill.
Bruce, John T., Litchfield, Ill.
Briggs, Charles W., Litchfield, Ill.
Burns, Francis M., Spring Valley, Ill.
Boatman, Jerry E., Carlineville, Ill.
Campbell, Gilbert, Litchfield, Ill.
Cave, Chauncey L., Litchfield, Ill.
Cole, Frank O.
Cole, Albert.
Cox, William T., Litchfield, Ill.
Coffee, Ollie, Litchfield, Ill.
Cripe, Asa., Girard, Ill.
Dalton, Lin L., Athens, Ill.
Ducrow, George, Irving, Ill.
Davis, Milton E., Hornsby, Ill.

Daub, Harmon, Effingham, Ill.
Ehrhard, Fred W., Litchfield, Ill.
Eichelroth, Henry W., Litchfield, Ill.
Edwards, Amos, Litchfield, Ill.
Edwards, John C., Jr., Litchfield, Ill.
Evans, John, Raymond, Ill.
Finley, William, Litchfield, Ill.
Ferguson, Charles E., Litchfield, Ill.
Froat, Joseph S., Litchfield, Ill.
Freelove, Frank, Litchfield, Ill.
Garrett, John T., Greenville, Ill.
Guiser, James, Kinmundy, Ill.
Gable, Thomas H., Litchfield, Ill.
Harden, William J., New Belin, Ill.
Hartman, Amasa, Middletown, Ill.
Hutchins, Gilbert L., Fairfield, Ill.
Howey, Charles W., Barnett, Ill.
Harbaugh, John J., Litchfield, Ill.
Hanney, James B., Spring Valley, Ill.
Hefley, Charles, Irving, Ill.
Huber, Charles W., Litchfield, Ill.
Jones, Willis, Litchfield, Ill.
Lane, Pearl E., Litchfield, Ill.
Mills, James R., Pana, Ill.
Moynihan, William H., Whitehall, Ill.
Martell, August, Alma, Ill.
Machler, Harry J., Litchfield, Ill.
Mays, Frank, Westfield, Ill.
Mercer, William L., Vera Park, Ill.
Marsh, Frank E., Wagoner, Ill.
Moran, Thomas J., Spring Valley, Ill.
Morlan, Hal J., Fairfield, Ill.
Moncravie, James, Irving, Ill.
Meyers, Edward F., Vandalia, Ill.

Niccum, Chip, Farmersville, Ill.
Nesse, Elliott, Springfield, Ohio.
Newkirk, Cyrus, Effingham, Ill.
Nall, Charles E., Farmersville, Ill.
Owings, Albert C., Litchfield, Ill.
Potter, William, New Athens, Ill.
Pippin, James W., Vandalia, Ill.
Ritchhart, Charles, Middletown, Ill.
Ripley, Benjamin J., Wagoner, Ill.
Roberts, John E., Litchfield, Ill.
Robinson, William, Decatur, Ill.
Sanders, Edgar, Litchfield, Ill.
Schoof, Fritz, Litchfield, Ill.
Seymour, Bert, Waverly, Ill.
Spence, Charles H., Litchfield, Ill.
Stacey, Josiah, Cleveland, Ohio.
Stevenson, William C., Columbus, Ind.
Souter, William D., Jacksonville, Fla.
Tuttle, Harry S., Litchfield, Ill.
Thole, Frank, Litchfield, Ill.
Taulbee, John W., Litchfield, Ill.
Tate, David L., Vandalia, Ill.
Wiley, John C., Girard, Ill.
Williams, Earl, Rockbridge, Ill.
Whitenack, David, Litchfield, Ill.
Whitaker, Louis J., Litchfield, Ill.
Winningham, Claud, Meredosia, Ill.
Windsor, Franklin R., Hornsby, Ill.
Zuber, Henry J., Litchfield, Ill.

The muster out roll of this company having been lost at Augusta, Georgia, by the aid of Captain Davis and others we have been enabled to prepare the above, which, it is believed, contains the names of all who were connected with the organization during its service as United States Volunteers. Yet we were unable to ascertain who were discharged, reduced to ranks or when promoted.

COMPANY B.

E. W. HERSH.

Capt. E. W. Hersh commanded Company B when it was mustered into the United States service, and continued in that capacity until March 18, 1899, when on account of continued ill health he resigned his commission and returned to his home.

Captain Hersh was born at Mt. Vernon, Ohio, January 10, 1866, just when the smoke of battle was clearing away from over our lovely land, occasioned by the civil war.

Removed with his parents to Defiance, Ohio, where the earlier years of his life were spent, and from the High schools of which city he graduated. He is also a graduate of the Chautauqua Literary and Scientific Circle, being a member of the class of 1892.

During the month of February, 1888, he located in Newton, Illinois, and took up the duties of a stenographer and law clerk, during which time also he applied himself to the stndy of law, and was admitted to the bar in the year 1891, when he entered upon the duties of this his chosen profession, in his adopted city of the "sucker" state, where he still resides, holding the position of senior member of the firm of Hersh & Calvin, lawyers and financial agents.

W. A. HOWELL.

Capt. W. A. Howell was born in Shawneetown, Illinois, February 18, 1875, and was educated in the public schools of that city. At the age of fourteen he left school and entered the office of the Gallatin Democrat, where he learned the printer's trade. He remained in this office until the fall of 1893, when he went to Evansville, where he worked at his trade until late in the winter, when he returned home, where he remained until the following August, when he went to Newton to accept the position of foreman in the office of the Newton Press, which position he gave up to enter the service of his country. He became associated with the Illinois National Guard in June, 1895, as a private, was soon appointed corporal, and in May, 1896, was appointed to sergeant, which position he held until February, 1897, when he was elected first lieutenant. When the call was issued for volunteers, April 26, 1898, he went with his company and was mustered into the volunteer service as first lieutenant. When Captain Hersh resigned, to take effect March 18, 1899, Lieutenant Howell was, upon the recommendation of the colonel, appointed as his successor, which position he held until mustered out of the service, on May 2.

LYMAN HARRIS.

Lieut. Lyman Harris is a native of the little city of Newton, situated on the banks of Ambra river, where he was born. He enlisted as a private in Company B, Fourth Illinois National Guards, in March, 1893, and was elected second lieutenant of the company, May 27, 1895, and served in that rank in the Illinois National Guards during its history, taking part in the strikes service, encampments and other occasions when the regiment was called out. Was mustered into the United States volunteer service with the Third Battalion, holding the same rank until March 18, 1899, when he was promoted to first lieutenant and worthily bore that rank until with the regiment he was mustered out of the service.

HISTORY OF COMPANY B.

While the history of this company is one pecularly its own, and somewhat checkered, yet perhaps in the main not differing greatly from that of some of its associates in the regiment of which it has been a component part during the great part of its history.

Its organization as an Illinois National Guard was effected in Newton, Jasper county, Illinois, by the electing and commissioning of B. W. Harris as captain, David Trexler, first lieutenant, and E. B. Garrell, second lieutenant, and mustered into the Illinois National Guard service January 15, 1881, as Company B, of the Eighth Illinois, in which relation it continued until 1890, when the Eight regiment was changed to the Fourth, in which this company held its position during the remainder of its history in the National Guard service. By the following it will be seen that frequent changes took place in the commissioned officers of this company during this period of its career:

Capt. W. B. Harris commanded the company until September 1, 1888, when H. A. Faller was commissioned and took the place he vacated. The names of lieutenants holding commissions during the period above referred to, and date of their commission were not at hand when this volume went to press. E. W. Hersh was commissioned second lieutenant March 15, 1889, and as first lieutenant June 26, 1891, and as captain, taking the place of Capt. H. A. Faller, January 8, 1894. Lyman Harris was commissioned second lieutenant May 27, 1895, and W. A. Howell as first lieutenant March 12, 1897, who was commissioned captain, to take the place of Capt. E. W. Hersh, who resigned on account of ill health, March 18, 1899, and held the position until mustered out of the United States service May 2, 1899.

As a part of the National Guard this company has no shame in confronting its record. Whether at the annual encampment or when called upon to maintain public peace and order, and the good name of our soldierly, warrior state. In this line of duty it took its place in the suppression and control of the railroad strike or "tie up" of East St. Louis, in 1887, also of the great Chicago strike in 1894, growing out of what is known as the Pullman strike, which resulted in such great loss of property, and finally the proclamation of President Cleveland, putting the city under martial law.

The strain under which the people of the United States had been for months, because of increasing diplomatic tension between this government and Spain, had not been without its effects on the men of this company, and in consequence thereof every reasonable effort was made to have it as thoroughly fitted for an emergency as time would admit. Hence, when orders by wire from Governor Tanner reached Captain Hersh at 2 A. M. April 25, 1898, to report with his company at Springfield, Illinois, immediately, its full meaning was comprehended and preparations for compliance therewith were carried forward with alacrity. This, coupled with the fact that the men had bivoucked in the armory for several nights, enabled the captain to have all in readiness within sixteen hours. In the evening the armory was filled with friends, when Hon.

Hale Johnson, Judge Gibson and Reverend Johnson addressed the company with words of council, encouragement and assurance of the good will of those from whom they were going out. About 10 P. M. we boarded the north bound train and moved out amid the good byes and farewell greetings of friends on our journey to the "hub of our state," where after some four hours delay on the route, we landed at noon on the 26th, thirty-two hours after the order was received from the Governor, ovations having been the order at every city passed through on the way.

On arrival at Springfield we marched at once to the fair grounds, which was designated as Camp Tanner, where we were assigned quarters in one of the commodious cattle barns.

Here began in true fashion our soldier experience, growing out of what seemed to be unavoidable causes, want of sufficient clothing and bedding to meet the raw chilly weather induced by the rains during this period.

After weeks of anxious waiting, on the 17th of May we were ordered to the state house, where, under the skillful eye and trained mind of the examining board, under Surgeon-General Sternberg, of the State Militia, we were passed through the ordeal of physical examination to determine our fitness to meet the standard of a United States soldier. The maximum strength of the company in the National Guard being one hundred, and our company having been recruited to one hundred seventeen, gave us a neat surplus on which to work reductions. Three of these had been honorably discharged, still leaving one hundred fourteen men on the roll as state guards at this time.

But as the companies in the new United States service were restricted to eighty-four men, we still had a surplus of men to return to the civil occupations of life. On the 20th of May these eighty-four selected men took the oath as

United States soldiers, administered by Captain Roberts, of the regular cavalry, and were duly mustered into the United States service to be fully equipped and moved where they might render efficient aid in the conflict now being waged. Our equipment was not of the most modern, as we carried the Springfield rifle of the 1884 model, though by no means antiquated ordnance. The monotonous routine which had occupied us for the past four weeks did not continue much longer, for on the 25th of May, about 8 P. M., orders were received by the regiment to report at Tampa, Florida, immediately, which was welcome news to the boys, as was evidenced by their shouts that echoed through the entire camp. The following day our baggage was loaded and by 4 P. M. all were aboard and the long ride to the southern land was begun, leaving camp, visiting friends we loved and scenes we had learned to detest, to joyfully speed on our mission of mercy. All went "merry as a marriage bell," every city through which we passed ovating the boys in blue. In this connection we may mention a coincidence, though carrying with it no import, that is: The officers of this company, on leaving Springfield, were assigned to a sleeper named Springfield, and on arrival at Jacksonville camped in one of its suburbs named Springfield. The new recruits to bring the company up to its full quota of one hundred three enlisted men passed their physical examination at Effingham and were sworn into the United States service at same place by Capt. H. S. Parker, regimental adjutant, on June 18th to 23d, and at once started for Camp Cuba Libra, the last of them reaching their destination on the 26th of June.

In giving the history of this company during its stay at Jacksonville, we enter upon the most important period of its career. Whatever the impression created by first observations, as to the desirability of our quarters in Camp

Cuba Libre, our minds were fully disabused by the experience of later days. We entered the camp in excellent health and buoyant spirits, and mantained it until the rainy season had so far progressed as to change the whole aspect of the camp. It was here that the seeds were sown broadcast, that yielded their harvest of bitter fruits a little later on. The location of the third battalion was near depressions in the earth that filled with water from the heavy rains, making it the most undesirable as well as unhealthy portion of the entire camp, breeding malaria and fever under the hot tropical sun. While Company B had no general scourge of sickness in this camp, yet those who were affected became very sick, necessitating the best of care, which in order to render, hospitals were erected of temporary character and the proper nurses selected to give them the needed attention. To this most important and responsible duty George Anderson, and Eugene Files as assistant, were detailed, and took charge of the hospital, fitted up in this company, yet with the best of care that could be rendered, when the regiment was removed to the camp at Panama Park, in August, sickness had so increased in our ranks, that more than an ambulance load were unable to get there without the aid of this excellent vehicle. But for the want of proper facilities to make them comfortable in their new quarters, they necessarily had to submit to and share in the hardships that fell to the lot of the able bodied of the company. There were times when they had to lie in their tents in the full glare of the sun, while at others no precaution would prevent the rain from saturating their beds by beating through the tents or blowing in around the sides.

But no time was lost in getting up another company hospital, and into which our sick were at once moved, while the best of care was rendered that circumstances would admit. To the aid of the former appointment, George Anderson, re-christened by the boys "Major" Anderson, lent untiring assistance in the care of and ministrations to the sick,—at times carrying his cot and blankets about when needed at night, and stealing what sleep he could under the circumstances. But it remained for the latter days of August to develop the awful scourge that was creeping upon us in this climate and unhealthful camp, and which continued until the company seemed on the verge of being wrecked. So general was the demoralization, that from the middle of August until the company entered upon provost duty in the city of Jacksonville, it had only thirty-two men out of one hundred and two that were considered really fit for duty. And during these weeks of suffering the men able for duty were placed on guard one day and the next on "fatigue." It was during this time, also, that General Alger, secretary of war, paid a visit to Camp Cuba Libre, and, in the grand review that was held in his honor, this company, whose record was among the best, could only place twenty-six men in the line who were at all able to participate, and among these were the guards, and even the cook, who had been ordered to clean up and aid in swelling the numbers to their largest proportions. At other times, in division reviews, as few as thirteen men, including the guide, could take part, and he the right guide, at that. The same could be truthfully stated as to the daily dress parades in which the company took part.

During our sojourn in camp "Cuba Libre" the boys of the company conceived the idea of surprising their captain, and accordingly a fine sword was purchased, and on or about the 1st of September, Captain Hersh was duly made the recipient of the same, as a mark of respect from the men of his command.

It was while at this camp our company was detailed on special duty for nine days, that of patrol guard in the country, a duty in which they acquitted themselves so well as to win the unstinted commendation of their colonel as well also that of Brigadier-General Bancroft. But the rainy season came upon us and we were compelled to suffer many discomforts on account of it. Not the least among them that of the camps being covered several times with water reaching a depth of three feet between Company's B and K and the place where they assembled to partake of hash, over which they constructed a rustic bridge of poles. With the other companies of the regiment we were sent to Panama Park, where during our stay we had the experience of sickness, which so sorely afflicted us, at times so depleting our ranks as to unfit us for our part in the regular duties in the camp. It was during this time we lost comrade Charles V. Stark, the only death that occurred during our term of service.

During these sore straits through which we were called upon to pass, it was thought wise and best to remove as far as possible the convalescing from the discouraging scenes and conditions, and accordingly ten men from our ranks were granted sick furloughs, and sent to their homes. Reaching Newton, our home town, Ed Albright, Ed Arnold and Lowell Houchin were found still unable to get off the train, and, consequently, were carried by gentle hands to their homes for kindly care and tender nursing.

But, by experience or otherwise, level heads were led to believe that a change from these environments and conditions to that of the city would be beneficial to the bettering of conditions, which seemed to linger and cling with unrelenting grasp, and accordingly we, with our regiment, were ordered on provost duty, and transferred to the city under the command of Maj. Russel B. Harrison, provost marshal. The rapid change to good health, which soon set in, proved the wisdom of the change, for almost from the beginning a perceptible improvement took place, and continued until the company reached a standard of health which was never lost or even lowered. Hence with the return of our wanted health and vigor there was a corresponding return to the depleted ranks, until the incomers from furloughs brought our line up very near to its former strength, reaching ninety-five, while some had been granted discharges as further unfit for duty or more needed at home. But with a few absent on leave and one in the division hospital, we were only able to line up with eighty-six men fit for duty.

Meantime we were sent to Savannah, Georgia, to continue provost duty after the "well done" fashion of our work on this line in Jacksonville. It was here, on Thanksgiving day, we had the expressed opinion of the surgeon that we were in better health than any company in the regiment, while our ranks were not surpassed as to fullness.

Our location at Thunderbolt, in a sense, detached us from our regimental headquarters, and necessarily from certain advantages enjoyed by other companies. Under these conditions, with the experience of the past lingering in our minds, it was thought, not only prudent but wise, to be ready for any emergency that might arise similar to that of our Panama Park experience. Therefore "Major" Anderson, who was still company nurse, and had to a very great extent those matters in charge, seen to it that an emergency supply of medicine was at hand, and accordingly he was furnished with no stinted amount of such remedies as the wisdom of the surgeons suggested as proper, and especially since he had proven himself competent to handle them. After our location here, for a week or two one of the regimental surgeons made a daily visit to the camp, but as he discovered the qualifications of our nurse to handle simple remedies and the ability of the men to care for their health, he lessened his visits, trusting to our "Major" for the daily sick report, as well as other details in connection with the work in hand.

From this point we were ordered to report to Major Russel B. Harrison for provost duty in the city of Jacksonville, a change that proved very conducive to the health of the company.

In this duty Company B was assigned to district number five with company quarters at foot of Ocean street, while its headquarters were in the third story of the Mohawk building on Bay street.

This work came to a close on the 21st of October, when at 12:30 P. M. we started with our battalion for Savannah, Georgia, to follow the same line of duty in that city, when we located at Thunderbolt, a suburb, some four miles out, and connected by electric railway. At this place are the docks of the oyster growers and fisheries, and quite a resort.

Arriving after dark, we had little regard for regulations in pitching tents, leaving all the finer details of engineering for a time more suitable for seeing the point—*i. e.*, the point of the compass, and allignment of tent poles. But on the morn the finer details were looked after and the work of cleaning and beautifying was carried forward until our camp, located in a beautiful grove, overlooking Warsaw Sound, being thirty feet above it, became the pride of the one thousand villagers who occupy the homes at this point. The conduct of the company was such as to win their good will to the extent that they seemed to think they had a kind of claim on us, often referring to as "their soldiers." Nor were they slack in doing all that was reasonable to increase our comfort and happiness. To the point we look back and see one of the brightest oases in all our army experiences, and one that sank deep, *i. e.*, into our stomachs, making some lasting impressions on our minds, perhaps on account of the radical contrast between common army grub and the delicacies prepared by the deft hands of fair ladies. This very exceptional experience occurred on the 24th of November, Thanksgiving Day, when about twenty ladies of Savannah besieged our camp with well laden baskets of turkey and other rich viands, with which they loaded a long table in our company street and invited us to partake to our hearts content, while they untiringly served.

To say we did true soldierly justice on this occasion is putting it as mildly as truth will admit, for our very "teeth had been fairly made to water," as the delicate odor came from the company cook tent, which the ladies had captured for putting the finishing touches on some of the dainties, while our eyes fairly danced at the profusion that was crowning the table. No we will never forget that day unless it be when we gather our feet with those of loved ones under some well laden table in our own far away home land. True we bestowed our gratitude in lavish measure in return, and also about all the badges possessed by the company, on these fair ones who had the courage to undertake the capture of our camp. While Company B generally regards the days spent at Panama Park as their darkest, they are equally unanimous in pronouncing these of provost duty at Thunderbolt as those amongst the brightest and happiest of their army experience. But such conditions too long enjoyed might not prove conducive to good soldiery, therefore on the second day of December the authorities over us ordered the second battalion into camp southeast of the city, and Company B found itself again facing the routine duties of a military camp.

From here on the 3d of January, 1899, we embarked on the Mobile and sailed for Cuba with our regiment, and camped six miles northwest of Havana, near the sea coast, where, as a part of the army of occupation we did the work assigned us, as well as do our part in the capture of souvenirs, to bear home as trophies of our service. During our stay in Cuba, March 18, Capt. E. W. Hersh, on account of ill health, felt constrained to resign his position, which action was accepted by the war department, and he was released from the command of his company; the vacancy thus caused was filled by the appointing and commissioning of our young and popular first lieutenant, W. A. Howell, which gave place for the advance of another very worthy young man, Lyman Harris, who was regularly promoted to rank of first lieutenant and Sergeant Fred S. Barker, whose career proved his fitness, was commissioned and inducted into the office of second lieutenant. Tuesday, April 4, at 9:30 A. M., our battalion was ordered to embark for its return to the states, following the first which had just left camp, an order that required no official coercion on the part of Company B to have it executed, for soon we were on our "march to the sea," through clouds of limestone dust, at times obscuring the men six feet away, while the sun poured his rays upon us at the rate of ninety degrees in the shade. While the city of Havana, whose streets we must traverse some two miles, was more free from dust, yet their narrow limits and cobble-stone pavements were a doubtful improvement, at least as to temperature, still the farewells in broken English that came from Cubans as we passed, was construed as of most kindly feelings toward the departing American soldiers. Five o'clock finds us on the San Jose docks, watching the retreating tugs that bore the first battalion to its boat at anchor in the bay. Before sunset we were outside the harbor in conformity to harbor laws, comfortably located aboard the Yarmouth, which after receiving her cargo outside the bay at 8 o'clock began the journey to the states, reaching Mullet Key, twenty-five miles off Port Tampa, at sundown on the 5th and anchored for the night, which was a boon to the seasick soldier. On the morning of the 6th the Whitney came up in her creeping movement bringing the First Battalion Regimental Band and staff, having been outstripped some sixteen hours by our noble ship. About dark of the 6th inst., Company B was taken ashore on Egmont Key, the government quarantine station, near our stopping place of the evening before, and with Company D entered the tents in detention camp, which were in waiting for us.

On the morning of the 7th we were visited with a heavy rain and wind storm, which soon proved that while we were favored above others in not having to erect tents, we were "out of luck" in having tents through which the rain sifted under the pressure of the strong wind, wetting the floors until we could scarcely find a spot on which to lay our blankets. Under such circumstances, cooking out of doors was almost out of the question, hence meals were almost conspicuous for their absence. But our commissary-sergeant deserves great credit for the manner in which he met these difficulties, although he could not entirely counteract them. All and in all, our stay on this island was anything but desirable, and consequently we hailed with no little degree of pleasure the early dawn of Monday, the 10th, when we boarded the little bay steamer, with the other company's band and regimental officers, and hastened away for Port Tampa, where by 4 P. M., we were pulling out on the third section of the train for Savannah, Georgia, from which an order, received on the way, turned us to the camps lying near Augusta, Georgia, adding another disappointment to the many preceding, and surely if we had been a camel this would have come near breaking our strong backbone. But we endured it all, and landed in Camp McKenzie, west of Augusta, about 4 P. M. of the 11th of April, and were highly pleased with accommodations that awaited in this well-fitted camp.

A. W. Cone was detailed as one of the regimental clerks, in which capacity he served several months during the period we spent in Florida; and was again detailed on same duty for some weeks while in Camp Columbia, Cuba, and when not thus on detailed duty he acted in the capacity of company clerk. Private C. H. Beggs was detailed along with others from the regiment, to clear off and construct a rifle range for the practice of marksmanship. But during his first day's service he met with a painful accident, having his shoulder dislocated and collar bone broken by a falling tree. To fill the vacancy on the force caused by this mishap, C. S. Goff was put in his place, putting in faithful time from June 27 until July 25, 1898, only relinquishing his job when it became his duty to go on patrol guard, and that only two days before the range was completed. Only one detail from our regiment were privileged to use it. The men of this detail were taken a limited number from each company. One of the detail from this company was Jerry Allen, who won the laurels over all competitors by making the highest score up to that date, breaking all records in the Seventh Army Corps, thus carrying off the championship with a score of eighty-five points out of a possible hundred. Private Boggs was also placed on the permanent detail of Major Harrison during the entire time of our service on provost duty in Florida. During our sojourn in the island another of our privates was honored by being permanently detailed. This time it fell to the lot of Ira Hickson to go on Major Harrison's force of provost guards, in which capacity he served so faithfully and well as to receive from the major a recommendation for good character and gentlemanly conduct. Dave Adams, another private, was placed on duty with the signal corps, and while this term of service was brief, yet it was at a time when the duties were numerous and demanded heavy outlays of energy and effort, it being near the time of our departure for Cuba. On the 1st of January, 1899, Private Clinton Gibson was permanently detailed to guard duty at First Division headquarters, and served in that capacity until called back to the regiment on the 4th of March, in order to accompany his comrades to the point of muster out. It was his to win the distinction over his comrades of being the first man of the company to set his foot on Cuban soil. And as the men of this regiment were accustomed to good bread, it was well to have some one look after that interest who understood this branch of the culinary art, and accordingly Private Neal Weeks was detailed to the regimental bakery and given the honored position of chief baker. G. W. Boggs also had the pleasure of serving in this branch of the service while in Cuba. From this it will be seen that the make-up of Company B was of the stuff that can be relied upon in the hour of need, and only desired the privilege of giving evidence as a body of their courage and ability in the many arduous duties that fall to the soldier's lot on the field of carnage.

During the trying illness of Corporal Hinman from typhoid fever, while it raged as an epidemic in our camp at Panama Park, Private W. E. McClure, by consent of his captain, volunteered to nurse him, and at once repaired to the third division hospital, where his patient awaited his arrival. Another incident, illustrating his self-sacrificing spirit, occurred during our sty in Cuba, as reported by the Times of Cuba, a Havana daily: "Tuesday morning, while bathing near the railroad bridge east of Marianao, a member of the Fourth Virginia Regiment had a narrow escape from drowning, and was saved by one of his companions, William McClure, of Company B, of the Fourth Illinois. A good-sized party was in the water when one of them, whose name we were unable to learn, was seized with cramps and became entirely helpless. McClure, who is a fine swimmer, went to the rescue of the drowning man, and, after a hard struggle, he swam with the limp body a distance of more than twenty-five feet into shallow water. McClure was almost exhausted from the tremendous efforts made to save his comrade, and it is fortunate that the distance from shore was no greater, as in that case possibly both would have been lost. After reaching shore, strong hands carried the nearly drowned man to camp, where he speedily recovered from the cramps that almost cost him his life."

The health record of Company B during the occupancy of Cuba, was not second to any in the regiment; but having the smallest number on the sick report rather placed it at the head of the line in this respect. This perhaps could be accounted for, at least in part, from the aversion of our men to being on the sick roll and that of having a medical adviser of some competency in their ranks, as well as the belief in, and living up to it, that it was better to take medicine to avert disease than to cure it. Thus having the remedies and the man at hand to administer them, those reporting to the regimental hospital were very few. And it is but just to say here, that this man, Geo. Anderson, whose labors were so untiring and valuable in his company, was an humble private, who declined an unsolicited transfer from his camp to the First Division Hospital in the island, when promotion to rank for efficiency was awaiting him, preferring to remain with those to whom he had ministered and with whom he had passed through the dark days of affliction at Panama Park.

Only one death occurred in this company during the entire time it was in the service of the United States. This was Charles V. Starks, who died September 3, 1898, at the Third Division Hospital in Camp Cuba Libre.

Nothing out of the ordinary occurred during our stay in Camp McKenzie, which had any special reference to this company, except that on the 16th of April, seven privates and three corporals were detailed on provost duty in the city of Augusta, from which they were relieved on the 27th, giving them time to perpare for the muster out. On the 22d of the same month, the date on which the Third Georgia volunteers were mustered out, Captain Howell, with one sergeant, two corporals and twenty-five men, was detailed by Colonel Swift to act as provost guard in their camp, during the confusion attendant on getting out of the service.

Our last duty in the line of service was performed on the 28th of May, when we turned in the last of our ordnance, consisting of guns, belts and bayonets, to the United States arsenal located at this place.

COMPANY B ROSTER.

Those not otherwise mentioned were mustered in at Springfield, Ills., and mustered out at Augusta, Ga.

WILLIAM A. HOWELL, Captain, Newton, Ill.
LYMAN HARRIS, First Lieutenant, Newton, Ill.
FRED S. BARKER, Second Lieutenant, Newton, Ill.

COMPANY E.

SERGEANTS.

Powell, Robert L., 21, Newton, Ill., Clerk.
Crail, George W., 25, Newton, Ill., Pharmacist.
Webb, Sidney A., 25, Newton, Ill., Laborer.
McKinnan Wm., 28, Newton, Ill., Hostler.
Hester, Bert, 24, Newton, Ill., Laborer.
Robuck, Hi B., 22, Newton, Ill., Tinner.

CORPORALS.

Brooks, Bernie, 20, Newton, Ill., Laborer.
Dowell, Harry C., 19, Willow Hill, Ill., Laborer.
Hinman, Batson, 19, Newton, Ill., Clerk.
Hubbard, Charles, 24, Newton, Ill., Barber.
Parr, Jesse F., 24, Newton, Ill., Laborer.
Bruner, Otto, 21, Newton, Ill., Farmer.
Moshenrose, Paul, 18, Newton, Ill., Farmer.
Houchin, Lowell, 19, Newton, Ill., School-teacher.
Richardson, Ulysses E., 25, Lovington, Ill., Farmer.
Rentz, Joseph, 21, Newton, Ill., Laborer.
Cone, Artemus W., 25, Lovington, Ill., Book-keeper.

MUSICIANS.

Hoggard, Harry, 18, Lovington, Ill., Printer.
Arms, David, 24, Newton, Ill., Farmer.

WAGONER.

Upton, Albertus, 33, Newton, Ill., Wagon-maker.

ARTIFICER.

Theriac, Raymond, 20, Newton, Ill., Carpenter.

COOK.

Huss, Xavier, 20, Newton, Ill., Clerk.

PRIVATES.

Anderson, George A., 24, Willow Hill, Ill., Barber.
Albright, Edward, 23, Newton, Ill., Tinner.
Allen, Jerry L., 21, Oblong, Ill., Farmer.
Adams, David M., 21, Rosedale, Ill., Telegrapher.
Bright, Charles, 25, Greenville, Ill., Laborer.
Badger, Omer R., 21, Gila, Ill., Farmer.
Bowers, Elmer, 27, Lovington, Ill., Farmer.
Bever, Guy, 21, Newton, Ill., Laborer.
Boggs, Charles, 21, Newton, Ill., Farmer.
Beeman, Everet, 27, Hunt City, Ill., Carpenter.
Beeman, Harry, 18, Hunt City, Ill., Laborer.
Chapman, Otis F., 22, Yale, Ill., Farmer; mustered in June 18, 1898.
Chittenden, Bert, 18, Newton, Ill., Student; mustered in June 18, 1898.
Cooper, James, 22, Willow Hill, Ill., Laborer.
Coursey, Thomas M., 29, Willow Hill, Ill., Stavecutter.
De Frain, Jesse M., 20, Bogota, Ill., Farmer; mustered in June 18, 1898.
Downey, Henson B., 41, Colfax, Ill., Laborer; mustered in June 23, 1898.
Downey, Wesley W., 28, Colfax, Ill., Brickmason.
Ertell, Charles W., 26, Newton, Ill., Coal Miner.
Earnest, James K., 21, Falmouth, Ill., Farmer.
Ederer, John P., 23, St. Marie, Ill., Laborer.
Faller, Benard H., 23, Newton, Ill., Clerk.
Gleeson, John, 21, St. Marie, Ill., Farmer.
Gibson, Clinton, 22, Bass, Ill., Farmer.
Goff, Charles S., 21, Flat Rock, Ill., Farmer.
Hepner, Alba, 24, Pleasant Point, Ill., Farmer.
Huron, Nelson, 22, Newton, Ill., Farmer.

Hickox, Ira, 19, Yale, Ill., Farmer; mustered in June 18, 1898.
Hampsten, Albert T., 21, Yale, Ill., Farmer; mustered in June 18, 1898.
Johnson, Warren B., 32, Bogota, Ill., Farmer.
Jourdan, Elbert, 20, Newton, Ill., Farmer.
Lewis, Edward H., 42, Newton, Ill., Painter.
Mathews, James, 23, Newton, Ill., Farmer.
McColly, William, 21, Quincy, Ill., Lawyer.
Mills, Noah O., 19, Yale, Ill., Farmer; mustered in June 18, 1898.
McClure, William, 29, Villas, Ill., Farmer.
Needham, William, 18, Yale, Ill., Laborer; mustered in June 18, 1898.
Nelson, Frank J., 19, Newton, Ill., Farmer; mustered in June 23, 1898.
Ostendorf, Joseph, 19, Newton, Ill., Engineer.
Odell, Benjamin F., 22, Yale, Ill., Farmer; mustered in June 18, 1898.
Parr, Harry, 18, Newton, Ill., Laborer.
Ping, Roy, 21, Falmouth, Ill., Farmer.
Phillips, Wendall, 20, Newton, Ill., Farmer.
Parr, Charles, 21, Newton, Ill., Laborer.
Payne, Fred, 26, Newton, Ill., Laborer.
Raley, Walter, 19, Bradfordsville, Ill., Farmer.
Schneider, Julius, 19, St. Marie, Ill., Farmer.
Storer, Joseph W., 22, Newton, Ill., Clerk.
Smith, Walter, 23, Oblong, Ill., Printer; mustered in June 18, 1898.
Sheets, Elmer, 22, Oblong, Ill., Operator; mustered in June 18, 1898.
Smith, Otto, 21, Oblong, Ill., Printer; mustered in June 18, 1898.

Selby, Joseph B., 24, Newton, Ill., Clerk, mustered in June 23, 1898.
Threasher, Louis, 21, Hunt City, Ill., Farmer; mustered in June 18, 1898.
Tripp, George W., 21, Newton, Ill., Coal Miner.
Umsted, Heber, 18, Newton, Ill., Plasterer; mustered in June 18, 1898.
Vanderhoff, John Q., 18, Newton, Ill., Farmer.
Van Volkenburgh, Ruben B., 34, Hamilton, Mo., Printer.
Wagy, Charles, 25, West Liberty, Ill., Miller.
Weeks, Cornelius, 27, Comettsville, Ind., Baker.
Watwood, Charles, 31, Lovington, Ill., Barber.
Yelvengton, Calvin, 21, Newton, Ill., Laborer.

RESIGNED.

Hersh, Elijah W., 32, Newton, Ill., Lawyer; resignation accepted March 18, 1899.

DISCHARGED.

SERGEANTS.

Barker, Fred S., 21, Newton, Ill., Clerk; to accept commission in company March 17 1899.
Carrick, Thomas W., 30, Newton, Ill., Real Estate; discharged Aug. 24, 1898, for disability.

CORPORALS.

Johnson, Wm. F., 30, Newton Ill., Lawyer; discharged Feb. 10, 1899.

PRIVATES.

Hewett, Frank, 27, Lexington, Ill., Plasterer; discharged Sept. 12, 1898, for disability.
Hampsten, Charles, 22, Palmersburg, Ill., Farmer; discharged Oct. 17, 1898, for disability.

McKnight, John, 33, Ramsey, Ill., Musician; discharged Oct. 28, 1898, for disability.
Gregory, Lyman S., 39, Lovington, Ill., Physician; mustered in June 18, 1898, discharged Oct. 18, 1898.
Arnold, Eugene, 18, Newton, Ill., Student; discharged Dec. 19, 1898.
Weeks, Calvin T., 25, Deitrich, Ill., Real Estate; mustered in June 23, 1898, discharged Dec. 19, 1898.
Comstock, Charles M., 20, Yale, Ill., Clerk; discharged Dec. 7, 1898, mustered in June 18, 1898.
Epperson, Otis C., 21, Montrose, Ill., Blacksmith; discharged Dec. 9, 1898.
Tiles, Eugene H., 21, Bone Gap, Farmer; mustered in June 18, 1898, discharged Dec. 18, 1898.
Kent, John F., 23, Robinson, Ill., Farmer; discharged Dec. 19, 1898.
Riley, Ora I., 21, Gila, Ill., Barber; discharged Dec. 27, 1898.
Jones, Paul, 24, Zenith, Ill., Teamster; discharged Dec. 29, 1898.
Hammer, Wm. C., 24, Rose Hill, Ill., Lawyer; discharged Feb. 10, 1899.
Massey, Romeo, 26, Newton, Ill., Engineer; discharged Feb. 24, 1899.
Arnold, Edward, 20, Newton, Ill., School Teacher; discharged March 9, 1899.

TRANSFERRED FROM COMPANY B.

Syas, John F., 21, Paris, Ill., Student: transferred to Hospital Corps, June 10, 1898.
Burton, Charles O., 24, Falmouth, Ill., Nurse; transferred to Hospital Corps, June 10, 1898.
Little, Charles E., 24, Westborough, Ill., Wagonmaker; transferred to Hospital Corps, June 10, 1898.

Bishop, Ora A., Corporal, 31, Mattoon, Ill., Telegrapher; transferred to Signal Corps, Sept. 8, 1898.

Portlock, Jefferson, 19, Falmouth, Farmer; transferred to Hospital Corps, Nov. 28, 1898.

DIED.

Stark, Charles V., 21, Newton, Ill., Farmer; died at Third Division Hospital, Jacksonville, Fla.

THIRD BATTALION.

LOUIS B. WASHBURN.

Louis B. Washburn was born at Platteville, Wisconsin, January 24, 1872. He secured his literary education at the State Normal School of his native town. He moved to Vandalia, Illinois, where he applied himself to the study of law in the office of S. A. Prater, during the years of 1894 to 1898, while he was official court reporter in the Seventh and Fifth judicial circuits of Illinois. He was admitted to the Bar in November, 1896, which he makes his business in civil life. On July 26, 1890, he joined Company I, Fourth Illinois National Guards, as a private, and served in this capacity and as a non-commissioned officer until July 6, 1896, when he was commissioned as adjutant of the Second Battalion, with the rank of first lieutenant, under Major McWilliams.

On the election of E. E. Elliott to the position of major of the Third Battalion, he was commissioned adjutant of that battalion. He was mustered into the United States volunteer service with the Fourth Illinois Volunteer Infantry, and during his service in this capacity he acted as regimental ordnance officer, and for a long period served as regimental adjutant and as regimental commissary. After the muster out of the regiment he returned to the historic city of his adoption, and resumed the practice of law.

COMPANY M.

WILLIAM R. COURTNEY.

Capt. William R. Courtney, of Company M, was born in the city of Urbana, Illinois, November 7, 1861, spent the years from 1866 to 1873 on a farm in Howard township, Champaign county, Illinois, when he returned to Urbana, where he has resided since.

He enlisted in Company D, Eighth Infantry, Illinois National Guard, May 11, 1885. On July 15, 1886, he was appointed corporal, raised to sergeant March 26, 1888, and to first sergeant July 23d of the same year, serving in this capacity to March 11, 1890, when he was commissioned second lieutenant, holding this rank until March 21, 1891, when he was duly commissioned as captain of his company, which rank he held during all the transfers and changes through which his company passed until it became Company M, of the Fourth Illinois National Guard.

When the call to arms from the president brought the companies of the Fourth Illinois National Guard together at Springfield, he was the senior line officer in the regiment. He continued in command of his company during its service as United States volunteers, and was mustered out with it at Augusta, Georgia, May 2, 1899.

ARTHUR W. SMITH.

Lieut. Arthur W. Smith was born in Urbana, the site of the University of Illinois, September 22, 1875. He gave much of the time of his youth and early manhood to secur-

CAPT. W. R. COURTNEY.

1ST LIEUT. A. W. SMITH.   2D LIEUT. F. E. THOMPSON.

ing an education, and in June, 1895, enlisted in the National Guards as a member of Company M, which is the child of the twin cities, Champaign and Urbana. In January, 1896, he was made a corporal of his company and in August of the same year was promoted to a sergeant, filling this position until April, 1897, when another advance awaited him, and he was again promoted, this time to the rank of second lieutenant.

But the rapid steps with which he had reached this rank, were not to end here, and accordingly in May of the same year, only one month later, he was promoted to the rank of first lieutenant, and with his company was mustered into the United States service, in which he bore this rank with credit to date of mustering out of the regiment, May 2, 1899.

FRED E. THOMPSON.

Fred E. Thompson was born on the 25th of October, 1875, on a fruit farm near Urbana, Illinois, and until his sixteenth year, lived and worked upon the farm.

His father, James G. Thompson, was a veteran of the war of the Rebellion, having served three years in the Seventy-sixth Regiment Illinois Volunteers. He died in 1892, after which Fred and his mother moved to Urbana, where they have resided ever since.

In 1892 he was apprenticed to a carpenter to learn the trade, at which he has worked for several years during the summer months, and attended the High School during the winter.

In 1893 he enlisted in Company D, Fourth Illinois National Guard, which is now Company M, Fourth Illinois National Guard, and has been in the company since that time. He saw his first active service during the strikes of 1894, his company being sent to Danville, Illinois, where it remained fifteen days on duty.

In 1897 he entered the Champaign Business College, and on the 26th of April, 1897, or on the day his company was ordered to report at Springfield for duty, he graduated from that institution, and received his diploma.

His enlistment having expired during the winter, he re-enlisted just before the call for volunteers came and went to Springfield as a sergeant. On the 4th of May, 1898, he was elected second lieutenant of Company M, and was mustered into the United States service as such on the 20th of May, 1898. He served with his company through the Spanish-American war in Cuba, and was mustered out of the service in Augusta, Georgia, on the 2nd of May, 1899.

HISTORY OF COMPANY M.

One of the oldest, if not the ranking company in the organization of which it forms a part, is Company M, having been organized July 2, 1877, and attached to the Ninth Battalion, Illinois National Guards, being known by the name of Champaign Rifle Guards. Soon after its organization it was transferred to the Eighth regiment, then to the Fourth and later to the Fifth and finally in 1896 it was transfered back to the Fourth, where it has since been permitted peaceably to remain. Prior to its last transfer to the Fourth, it was known as Company D, but wears with equally as much grace the letter found a little farther down the line. The first commander of the company was Captain J. W. Langley, followed in the order here given, by the persons named: J. A. Monroe, J. R. Trevett, H. W. Mahan, A. T.

Engle and W. R. Courtney, who still holds that commission.

With these have been associated during these years, the following who held the rank of First Lieutenant: J. A. Monroe, John Van Arman, H. W. Mahan, J. W. Haines, M. E. Chase, C. C. Mittendorf, W. S. Rayburn, T. A. Holt, Ray Brown, W. A. Watson, W. A. Brown, M. J. Myers, J. P. Prather and A. W. Smith. Along with these were the following Second Lieutenants: E. T. Whitcomb, H. W. Mahan, J. A. Miller, J. W. Haines, M. E. Chase, A. C. Wilcox, C. C. Mittendorf, W. S. Rayburn, T. A. Holt, W. R. Courtney, Ray Brown, A. J. Hampton, W. A. Brown, M. J. Myers, J. R. Prather, E. B. Ellis and F. E. Thompson.

During the great railroad strikes of 1894 this company, which was then Company D, of the Fifth, spent fifteen days in state service at Danville.

During the winter of 1897, when the country was at a fever heat over the prospect of war with an eastern neighborn, and the call for volunteers was daily expected, the membership of this company increased rapidly, until the fifty or thereabout had swelled to one hundred and three brave-hearted men, while many, equally as loyal, had to be turned away.

On the 26th of April, that which we had longed and hoped for came in the form of an order from the governor to report at Springfield for duty on the following day. All was excitement while the armory was being dismantled, and everything belonging to the state as equipment was being packed ready for shipment, to be turned in to the state authorities at Springfield. Notice was given for all members to be on hand early on the morning of the 27th, and they began gathering the few articles allowed to a soldier, and prepare for the adieu to friends.

Scarce had the dawn began to streak the eastern sky when compliance with the notice was evidenced by the incoming and assembling of the men at the armory, and so eager were they for the start that long before the hour for the train's departure knapsacks, rifles and other accoutrements were in place on sturdy shoulders, ready for the start. Meantime relatives, friends, and it seemed about all the inhabitants of the twin cities had gathered, and were thronging the streets leading from the armory to the depot, until they seemed a seething mass of human beings, all desirous of bidding what might be the last good-bye to some of Company M.

Headed by the band of Uniform Rank, K. of P., and the G. A. R., we marched to the train which was in waiting for us and which we soon boarded, conscious that many sad hearts realized we were not booked for a holiday outing, but the serious business of war. Dread thoughts of what might be, involuntarily found a resting place in many minds, for it could scarcely be thought that all would return to share in the glad welcome that would be in long preparation. It was a day that has left its lasting impress on the minds of the boys of Company M.

Our train pulled out of the railroad yards amid the deafening roar of cannon, shrill whistles, silver-chiming bells and the shouts and cheers of the assembled throng, while we bid farewell to home and friends, for to us an indefinate time; some forever.

Reaching Springfield without accident, we marched to the state fair grounds where we were allotted one half of a cattle barn for our camp quarters. And as the sheds were new they truly made us an excellent barracks. While for a kitchen and dining hall we used the pig pens, which filled the bill admirably since they also were new.

Thus we were gently making the transition from well equipped homes to what commonly falls to the soldier's lot.

During the one month we spent in Camp Tanner it seemed to rain almost constantly, while the weather in general was of a cold disagreeable type, which was another degree in our initiation into the realities of army life. Our time in camp, not only between showers, was mostly occupied in drilling the new recruits, and taking almost daily an afternoon practice march of from five to ten miles, which from the blisters on our feet seemed like doing penance for having committed the sin of being awkward, ignorant civilians. But what seemed to be so great a hardship at first was doing its work of hardening, toughening our brawn for our coming duties. Along with this came the careful physical examination which was to determine who were fit for enlistment in the United States service. Only eight of one hundred and three failed to meet the requirements, thus necessitating their return home, which was a sore disappointment. While on the morning of May 20, about 10 o'clock, every man of the company who had filled the bill in the examination, was formed in line and marched over near the regimental headquarters where a platform had been erected, before which we were halted and with uncovered heads and our strong right hands lifted toward heaven, we stood waiting the moment that would complete our muster in.

Nor was it a tedious suspense, for exactly at 10:20 Capt. C. S. Roberts, of the Seventeenth United States Infantry, took his place on the platform and administered the oath that placed us in the United States service for two years, unless sooner discharged. Having at last attained the happy position of United States soldiers, the question soon arose, when shall we leave Camp Tanner? But this was settled five days later on the morning of May 25, when about 6 o'clock orders were received to put everything in readiness for a move to Tampa, Florida, by the next morning. This was the news we were awaiting, for it meant we were soon to see Santiago, and the camp rang with hearty cheers, followed by the hustle that attends the new soldier on packing up for a move. All were up at the sound of reveille the next morning and ready for breakfast, after which our quarters were thoroughly policed and at 10 o'clock we began our march to the train awaiting us on the siding of the C. & A., near the fair ground entrance, where the tedious wait of five hours was endured, when at 3 P. M. we ate our first travel ration and soon bid farewell to Camp Tanner and were off for the south land, making a brief halt in the capital city. At every station on our route great crowds of people had assembled with flowers and nice things to eat—the girls especially were there looking for a button or something else as a souvenir and to arrange for correspondence with a soldier. The boys of Company M were not napping, but were on the alert for souvenirs, also, and when we arrived at our destination there were enough hat pins and ladies' neckties in the company for all the girls in Florida. Sleep was almost a stranger to us the first night, although we had the best of Pullman sleepers. At St. Louis we were run onto the Illinois Central tracks and we were carried by that company until 6 P. M. the next day, when at Holly Springs, Mississippi, we were transferred to the Kansas City, Memphis & Birmingham. At 8 o'clock the next morning we arrived at Birmingham, Alabama. Here we were transferred to the Central of Georgia and took our first ride behind a wood-burning engine. At 3:10 that afternoon we arrived at the union depot at Albany, Georgia, a place long to be remembered by the boys. The citizens of that town, like a great many others, were anxious to do something to benefit the soldiers and they did it. All along the platform were barrels of lemonade, ladies were there by the dozens with cigars, cigarettes, chewing gum, tobacco and a great many other things. These were a great treat as we had not had a pay day yet. Company M was never known in a case of that kind to decline; so they were well supplied when they left Albany at 5 o'clock. We arrived at Columbus, Georgia, where orders were received to report at Jacksonville, Florida, instead of Tampa. This was not well received by the company for it was ominous of what we did not desire—continued camp life.

At 2 A. M. Sunday, May 29, we arrived at our new destination, and after a brief stop in the city our train was run out to what was called Camp "Cuba Libre," not improperly named, either. After breakfast that morning we left the train, and went into camp among the tall pines to realize a beautiful southern day, but O! how very warm compared with the cool breezes of our north land. It was often said that the first day in Florida was the hottest we experienced while in the service. But soon our tents were up, and many of the boys stretched themselves out in the shade for a rest, being tired from the long ride, while others sought a bath in the St. Johns river, while a few went to the city. The first night the entire company was placed on guard duty. Everything went well while in camp, there being very little sickness in the company. June 21 we received two hundred dollars from Hon. F. B. Carson, United States Internal Revenue Agent; this was a loan until we got a pay day, but the next day was pay day and all were made happy. June 22 twenty-five recruits arrived from home, raising the company to one hundred and six men; three were transferred to the hospital corps during the month of June. July 5 the company was present at the first review of the Seventh Army Corps, which was held in the city of Jacksonville. After marching down to the city and forming for the review it began to rain, and kept this up until the next day. On our return to camp at 6 o'clock supper was found ready, and had been for some time, needing only to be put on the tables, where the rain, which came through the roof of pine needles, soon saturated everything, cooling the coffee and giving to the food a taste of pine tar. Our clothing was soaked, and but few of the boys had a change at that time, compelling them to sleep in what they had on, while the tents, being old, leaked badly, making the night as uncomfortable as could be. At the lower end of the company street, where the ground was quite low, the water began to back up into the tents during the night and the boys had to move out. The next morning water was from eighteen to twenty-eight inches deep in the three last tents, while in a small ravine between the company street and the mess hall water was waist deep. During the day the boys of Companies M and H, being close neighbors, built a corduroy bridge over two hundred feet long across this ravine, working in water waist deep. In three days this water had all disappeared in the sand, and everything went on as before.

It fell to Company M to bear the honor of being the first company in the regiment to be chosen as provost guards, and on July 18 they were ordered to move to the city the following day. This news was received with cheers, as it would be a change of life. Early the next morning everything was packed that we would need while gone, and other articles were stored in one tent and a guard left over them. At 8 o'clock we marched from camp at a port arms amid the deafening cheers of hundreds. We went into camp just opposite Seventh Army Corps headquarters, where we remained ten days, July 21 being our first day as provost guards, and it was one of the days long to be remembered by the boys of Company M.

During our short stay we won the hearts of the citizens of Jax, and especially of the young ladies. But we were permitted to remain on provost duty only ten days, as it seemed they wished to divide this only good thing they had, around, giving all a small slice, and accordingly we were marched back to camp Cuba Libre, and entered again into the old camp life, daily drill, dress parade and fatigue duties too numerous to mention. August 10, we moved to what afterward proved to be the fever stricken Panama Park, for immediately upon our arrival there the boys began to get sick and were sent to the hospital until there were only a few men able for duty, even the officers were all sick and it looked as though Company M had seen better days elsewhere. At 8:50 on the evening of September 22, occurred the death of Private Percy N. Tittle. Although it was known early in the evening that he could not live, yet the news of his death came as a shock to the company, for he was a good soldier and loved by all the members of the company.

At 8 A. M. next morning, September 23, while arrangements were being made for the funeral of Comrade Tittle, the company was again shocked by the news of the death of Private Herman E. McFarland.

Hence arrangements were made for a double funeral, which was held on the following day, and the remains of Comrade Tittle were shipped to his home at Arcanum, Ohio, and those of Comrade McFarland to Mendon, Illinois. Soon after this, on October 4, occurred the death of Private George Turner, which was the third and last death in this company. His remains were sent north and buried at Mahomet, Illinois.

Shortly after these sad occurrences, Company M was moved to the city of Jacksonville to again enter upon provost guard duty, and were camped at Provost Station No. 4, where it remained a little more than a week, when it was moved to Station No. 5, in the central part of the city, where very good quarters were furnished in a building.

On October 16, 1898, Captain Courtney and Lieutenant Thompson, who had been sick, were granted leave of absence to return home and recuperate, while on the 24th of the same month Company M bid farewell to their friends and the city of Jacksonville, Florida, and moved to Savannah, Georgia, and went into camp at Provost Station No. 5, at Collinsville, a suburb of that city. It was there that the boys enjoyed the best time while in the service, for they soon became acquainted with both young and old of the vicinity and were invited out to suppers and entertainments nearly every evening. While here a cake walk was given by the members of the company one evening, under the electric light in a corner of the camp, and fully one hundred men, women and children were present, and all had a good time. Thanksgiving, 1898, was a day that will never be forgotten by the boys of Company M. It would take entirely too much space to begin to describe the dinner we sat down to that day. After dinner army wagons were brought into use and the young ladies who had been so kind to us were given a ride. December 6th the company moved into camp at Camp Onward, and again began drill and dress parade, which lasted until January 3, 1899, when Company M, with the rest of the regiment, embarked on the United States transport Mobile for the long desired island of Cuba.

Early on that morning the city friends of Company M were assembled at the river docks, awaiting our arrival, which was not until about 9:00 A. M., to bid us farewell, for at least a short time. About 11:00 o'clock the transport, with the aid of a tug, began to move toward the great Atlantic, while whistles blew, bells rang and as long as we were in sight, the people with tears in almost every eye waved a farwell. Just fifty-one hours later, with two bands playing the "Star Spangled Banner" and two thousand five hundred soldiers standing on deck with uncovered heads, the Mobile entered Havana harbor, passing Morro Castle, the armored cruiser Brooklyn, the battleship Texas

MOBILE ENTERING HAVANA HARBOR.

and the wreck of the Maine, having made a distance of eight hundred and fifty-five miles without having passed through a station or stopped for water, finishing a trip that we will not soon forget.

Our stay in Cuba was well spent and enjoyed by all, there being but little sickness or anything else to mar our comfort. The company made two practice marches to

Guines while in the island, the first with the Third Battalion, under command of Major Elliott, and the second with the First Brigade, under Brigadier-General Douglas, the distance being about thirty-five miles from Havana. We camped near Havana harbor a day on the return. From the first march the boys of this company had the name of being explorers, and nothing ever went by with a mystery that they did not solve. This time they went down under the fifteen feet of water in Havana harbor, where the Spanish had thrown car-loads of ammunition rather than have it fall into the hands of the Americans. Here the boys secured all the relics they desired, in the line of Spanish ammunition, in the shape of large shells and other munitions of war, which proved to be quite valuable on our return to the United States. On the second march we were camped two days at the foot of a mountain, where Company M boys were the first ones in the regiment to discover swarms of bees and secure their honey, which was a great treat to us at that time. They also were the first to discover a large cave near the top of the mountain, and after discovering it they must explore it. It proved to be about eight feet in diameter, extending some forty feet perpendicularly in the mountain, and increasing in its dimensions so far as it could be explored. They secured a large rope and tied one end around one of their venturesome companions, and lowered him into this grewsome pit. Having descended some twenty feet, his eye caught sight of a huge snake in a crevice of the wall, and it took but a moment to decide what to do. Lowering another rope with a noose in one end, which was fixed so the snake would have to crawl into it in coming from the wall, with some dry grass and a match, a smoke was started, which soon proved too much for his snakeship, and he readily became a captive to Yankee ingenuity and push. It proved to be a species of the boa constrictor, measuring eleven feet and seven inches in length. Several others of the same kind, though not so large, were captured and brought back with the regiment.

On April 11, thirty-two members of the company made application through proper military channels for a discharge from the service, and three hours afterward an order was received discharging them. At 11:30 o'clock that night, orders were received to return the company to the United States for muster out. This was the news the boys had been waiting for and it was well received, and no more slumber was indulged in that night by members of this company, and by 6 A. M., of the 12th, everything was packed, tents down and all ready for the wagon train, which arrived a few minutes later. Very soon all of our belongings were aboard, and Company M was again ready to bid adieu to another camp and its surroundings, and truly the most beautiful of all our camps was this "Camp Columbia."

A march of about one-quarter of a mile brought us to Buena Vista, where we boarded a special train for Havana, where on leaving the train we started on our last march in Cuba, viz.: From the depot to the wharf of Havana harbor, on arriving at which a rest of an hour was taken, after which we were taken by a small United States quartermaster's boat out near the wreck of the Maine, where we boarded the United States Mail Steamship Whitney about noon. All afternoon we lay in the harbor waiting for the baggage, etc., to be loaded and a few minutes before the sun went down the Whitney began to move in the direction of the sea, while all were on deck to witness, for us, the last sunset and other scenes about this historic city and harbor. We encountered a rough sea, and sea sickness was the common thing on board our ship.

As morning dawned we were in sight of Key West, but

throughout the remainder of the day no land was visible. About 11 P. M. the boat began going around in a circle, which movement she kept up until morning, when we found ourselves near a small island, and in a short space of time were treading its sandy surface, and learned we were on Egmont Key, United States detention camp, where we remained three days. No sickness developing we were allowed to go on our way, and boarding the Plant steamer Margaret at 9 A. M., we arrived at Port Tampa at noon, and all were glad to once more plant their feet on United States soil, where everything seemed so different; rations tasted better and everything was better in general, and all were well pleased. We remained here until 3:30 P. M., when we went on board a special train over the Plant System railroad, and journeyed over a country we had never seen, and after a good night's rest we awoke next morning to find ourselves still in Florida, but soon to pass over the line into Georgia, and a little later to find ourselves near the city limits of Savannah. Here the company met with one of its greatest disappointments, when the word went from car to ear that we would not get to stop in that city, but must enter camp at Augusta, farther up the river.

Soon the officers were taken down to the city in a special car that they might get something to satisfy their hunger. But there were hungry boys, also, and a great many of them started through the drizzling rain in the direction of the city in quest of something their appetites craved, and the consequence was that five of them were left in Savannah, but reached the company during the night while on the siding near Augusta, Georgia, where we had arrived at 6 P. M., April 18. As it was quite late, we remained on the train until the next morning, when we went into camp once more in the United States. The boys were made happy at noon by a message stating that the Hon. T. B. Carson, United States internal revenue agent of New York, would arrive during the day, and, as he had been like a father to the company during their former stay in the United States camps, and had always seen that they did not want for anything he could furnish. When he drove into camp that afternoon, all the boys were eager to get to shake hands with him first. But another happy surprise awaited us the day following, in the announcement that our battalion, the Third, would be mustered out with the regiment on the 2d of May, an event we could scarcely hope for, since the First and Second Battalions had been at work on their books preparing for this event for near two weeks prior to our arrival. These days soon sped by, not being burdened much with guard and other camp duties, and we enjoyed ourselves by seeing the officers and clerks sweltering over their final reports and muster-out rolls and in our trips to the city.

May 2d at last arrived and the muster out was done in a few minutes, every man receiving an honorable discharge. The baggage had been checked early in the morning and the company was mustered out at 10:30 A. M., being in the service just one year and one week to the hour and minute. After the muster out all left camp as citizens once more. The company left Augusta on a special train at 4:20 P. M. and arrived at Atlanta next morning, where we took breakfast, reaching Chattanooga for dinner and Nashville for supper. This was the last opportunity we had of taking a meal until we arrived at home on the 5th, at 2:20 P. M. At Mattoon we were met by a committee representing the citizens of Champaign and Urbana, who explained clearly the fact that a good dinner awaited us and that the people expected a parade. It did't take a lot of hungry soldiers long to decide the proper order of things would be dinner first and parade afterward. While time was beginning to lag at this switch end of the trip, yet it was not long after the plans were agreed upon until the shrill notes of the whistle notified us that the home station was at hand.

As we passed through the Illinois Central yards all the whistles in the city began to blow and all the bells began to ring a welcome home coming. The boys had gotten their hand baggage ready, and as many as the small space would admit of, had taken their places on the steps, making all the haste possible to again stand on home territory. When the train came to a halt, it was apparent that one thousand two hundred people had gathered to join in one glad welcome, while two bands were discoursing music, and the Sons of Veterans fired a salute with shotguns. Along with all this the secret orders and the Champaign Fire Department were there in full uniform, expressive of gratitude at the safe return of those who had gone forth to lay their lives on the altar of their country.

Through the surging crowd could be seen fathers, mothers, brothers and sisters crowding their way to press a kiss on one whose absence for a year had strengthened the tie of kindred love. Sweethearts and friends were there also, and such a glorious welcome will hardly be given Admiral Dewey on his return from glorious victories in a distant land.

After doing soldierly justice to a good dinner, a line of parade was formed on Main street, and a line of march was taken up including the principal streets of the city, preceded by the Champaign Fire Department, Grand Army of the Republic, Sons of Veterans and all the secret societies of the twin cities. After marching through the principal streets in Champaign, the march was started to Urbana. Arriving there in front of the court house, two short addresses of welcome were made by Col. J. S. Wolfe, of Champaign, and Judge F. M. Wright, of Urbana. After this the company was allowed to go home or wherever they wished. Receptions, balls and entertainments were given in honor of Company M every evening for over a week afterward. The citizens of the twin cities and the members of Company M will long remember April 27, 1898, and May 5, 1899.

COMPANY M ROSTER.

Where not otherwise designated, the members of this company were mustered into the United States service on the 20th day of May, 1898, at Springfield, Ill., and mustered out at Augusta, Ga., May 2, 1899.

WILLIAM R. COURTNEY, Captain, Urbana, Ill.
ARTHUR W. SMITH, First Lieutenant, Urbana, Ill.
FRED E. THOMPSON, Second Lieutenant, Urbana, Ill.

SERGEANTS.

Doty, George E., First Sergeant, Champaign, Ill.
Ellis, Edwin B., Quartermaster Sergeant, Champaign, Ill.;
    mustered in June 20, 1898; made Corporal July 4, 1898; made Quartermaster Sergeant Sept. 1, 1898.
Teeple, Wallace D., Maringo, Ill.
Frazee, John W., Champaign, Ill.
Neville, Charles W., Urbana, Ill.

CORPORALS.

Driskille, Frank K., Champaign, Ill.; reduced to ranks June
    21, 1898; appointed Corporal July 4, 1898.
Hendricks, Andrew J., Urbana, Ill.
Willskey, Lewis C., Champaign, Ill.
Edwards, Henry R., Urbana, Ill.; made Corporal July 4, 1898.

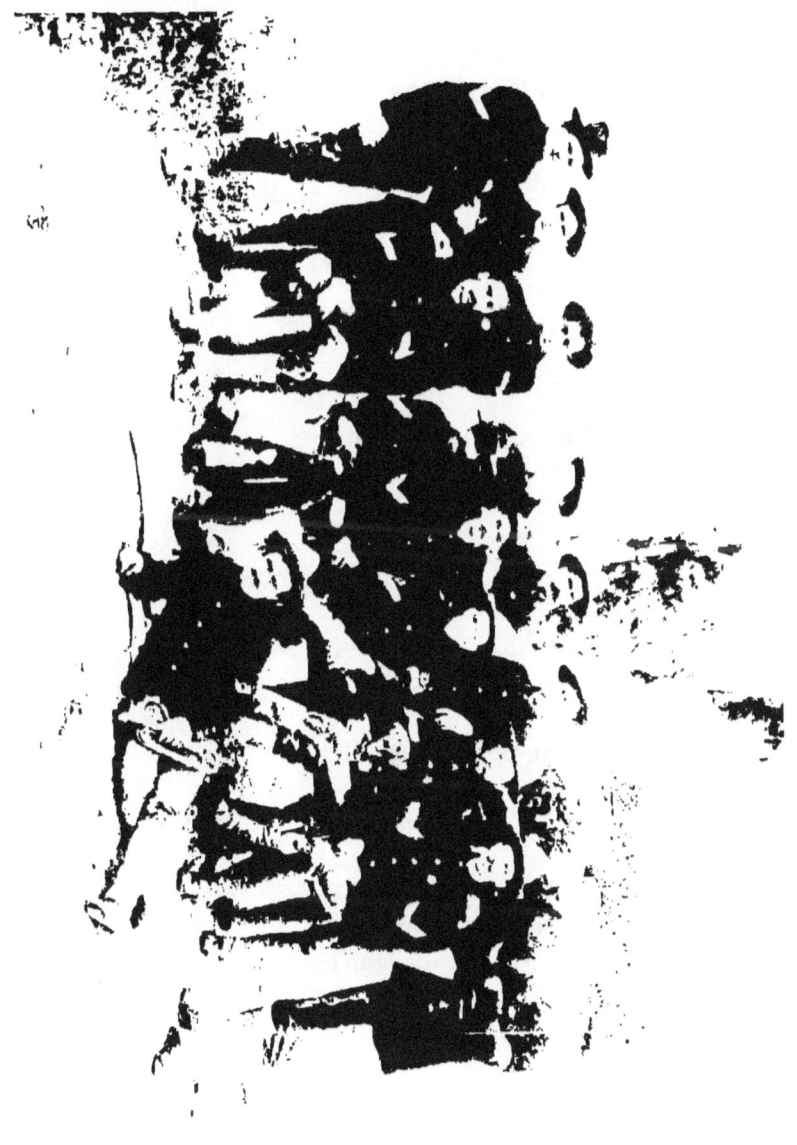

NON-COMMISSIONED OFFICERS, COMPANY M.

Patten, William G., Urbana, Ill.; appointed Quartermaster Sergeant June 1, 1898; reduced to Corporal Sept. 1, 1898.
Golden, Cecil L., Urbana, Ill.; made Corporal Dec. 1, 1898.

ARTIFICER.

Railsback, Bert; made Artificer, Dec. 1, 1898.

MUSICIANS.

Edwards, Ellwood, Urbana, Ill.
Fletcher, Clarence A., Pesotum, Ill.

PRIVATES.

Anderson, Oliver E., Homer, Ill.; mustered in June 20, 1898.
Buchanan, Samuel A., Urbana, Ill.
Bundy, Herman W., Tolono, Ill.; mustered in June 20, 1898.
Crabtree, Arthur O., Urbana, Ill.
Creech, William J., Urbana, Ill.
Cusick, Thomas O., Homer, Ill.; mustered in June 20, 1898.
Duncan, Ora M., Urbana, Ill.
Ensley, Sheldon D., Champaign, Ill.
Eldridge, Jerry N., Champaign, Ill.
Everman, James A., Urbana, Ill.
Flatt, Ira J. W., Champaign, Ill.; mustered in June 20, 1898.
Gates, Frank E., Seymour, Ill.; mustered in June 20, 1898.
Gilkey, Edward C., Portland, Me.
Gray, Leone S., Homer, Ill.; mustered in June 20, 1898.
Holden, Alexander E., Hope, Ind.

Harris, Roy, Danville, Ill.
Jewell, Frank, Tuscola, Ill.
Jewell, Fred N., Tuscola, Ill.; mustered in June 20, 1898.
Jamison, Ira T., Homer, Ill.; mustered in June 20, 1898.
Kirby, Francis M., Urbana, Ill.
Lacy, Hubert V., Homer, Ill.; mustered in June 20, 1898.
McCloud, Fred., Cook, Urbana, Ill.
McQuay, Fred, Champaign, Ill.; mustered in June 20, 1898.
Moon, Orris E., Champaign, Ill.
Moore, Charles L., Tolono, Ill.; mustered in June 20, 1898.
Mitchell, Joseph H., Urbana, Ill.
Morrow, Clarence G., Urbana, Ill.
Norton, Joseph G., Champaign, Ill.
Oneil, Barney, Champaign, Ill.
Park, Andrew H., South Chicago, Ill.
Priley, Fred, Urbana, Ill.
Sands, Richard E., Tolono, Ill.; mustered in June 20, 1898.
Schilling, Walter H., Urbana, Ill.
Stockwill, John W., Urbana, Ill.
Stockwill, Nathaniel P., Urbana, Ill.
Voight, Harry M., Champaign, Ill.; mustered in June 20, 1898.
Zanos, Edward, Urbana, Ill.

DISCHARGED.

Hawker, Frank A., Linden, Ind., First Sergeant; appointed Corporal July 4, 1898; appointed Sergeant Dec. 1, 1898; appointed First Sergeant Dec. 1, 1898; discharged April 10, 1899.
Courtney, Albert M., Urbana, Ill., Sergt.; discharged Nov. 3, 1898.

Hays, Fred H., Urbana, Ill., Corporal; discharged April 10, 1899.
Ekbom, Albert R., Champaign, Ill., Corporal; discharged Feb. 9, 1899.
Fox, Charles S., Saybrook, Ill., made Corporal July 4, 1898; discharged April 4, 1899.
Russell, Edward T., Champaign, Ill., made Corporal July 4, 1898; discharged April 10, 1899.
Stockwill, Willie V., Urbana, Ill., appointed Corporal July 4, 1898; discharged Dec. 24, 1898, on account of physicial disability.
Baker, Loein C., Champaign, Ill., made Corporal March 21, 1899; discharged April 10, 1899.
Mason, Charles E., Urbana, Ill., Artificer; discharged Oct. 18, 1898.
Brownfield, McClelland, Salem, Ill., Wagoner; discharged March 30, 1899.
Amerhein, Charles B., Rantool, Ill.; discharged April 10, 1899.
Blanchard, Arthur S., Urbana, Ill.; discharged Sept. 5, 1898, for disability.
Cady, Frederick R., Urbana, Ill.; discharged April 10, 1899.
Campbell, Matthew, Urbana, Ill.; discharged April 10, 1899.
Corbin, William A., Owensburg, Ind.; discharged Sept. 25, 1898, on disability.
Carson, Lewis P., Rantool, Ill.; discharged April 10, 1899.
Choat, Sidney G., Monmouth, Ill.; discharged April 4, 1899.
Dahlenburg, William, Urbana, Ill.; discharged April 10, 1899.
Davis, Harry J., Champaign, Ill.; discharged Jan. 14, 1899.

Dorr, Thomas C., Urbana, Ill.; discharged April 10, 1899.
Durand, Rolland D., Chicago, Ill.; discharged April 10, 1899.
Dollinger, Hubert H., Champaign, Ill.; mustered in June 20, 1898, discharged April 10, 1899.
Eldridge, Calmer, Champaign, Ill., mustered in June 20, 1898; discharged April 10, 1899.
Fisher, Charles P., Charleston, Ill.; mustered in June 20, 1898, discharged April 10, 1899.
Gordon, Charles C., Mayview, Ill.; mustered in June 20, 1898; discharged April 10, 1899.
Havens, Charles H., Champaign, Ill.; mustered in June 20, 1898; discharged April 10, 1899.
Hodge, Edward F., Urbana, Ill.; mustered in June 20, 1898; discharged April 10, 1899.
Johnson, Elmer H., Urbana, Ill.; mustered in June 20, 1898; discharged March 7, 1899.
Lake, Edward H., Bondville, Ill.; discharged April 10, 1899.
McAuley, Joseph H., Champaign, Ill.; discharged April 10, 1899.
Maguire, Morley, Hamilton, Mo.; discharged April 10, 1899.
Moore, Walter A., Champaign, Ill.; discharged April 10, 1899.
Moore, Clarence A., Champaign, Ill.; discharged April 10, 1899.
Moore, Thomas W., Roanoke, Va.; discharged April 4, 1899.
Myers, Willis I., Champaign, Ill.; discharged April 10, 1899.
Powell, Harry A., Champaign, Ill.; discharged Aug. 29, 1898, on disability.
Pattengale, John T., Champaign, Ill.; discharged April 10, 1899.

Snyder, William O., Urbana, Ill.; mustered in June 20, 1898; discharged April 10, 1889.
Small, William S., Farmland, Ind.; discharged April 10, 1898.
Satterwhite, William P., Urbana, Ill.; discharged Sept. 5, 1898, on disability.
Stonebruner, Clarence M., Champaign, Ill.; mustered in June 20, 1898; discharged Nov. 20, 1898, on disability.
Stevens, John J., Urbana, Ill.; mustered in June 20, 1898; discharged April 10, 1899.
Robins, Earle E., Champaign, Ill.; discharged March 29, 1899.
Wilson, Ira L., Lebanon, Ind.
Wollam, Ira, Owensburg, Ind.; discharged April 10, 1899.
Yount, John H., Mayview, Ill.; discharged September 5, 1898, on disability.

TRANSFERS.

McCoole, Claud S., Cleutons Heights, Kan.; transfered to Hospital Corps June 10, 1898.
Perry Geo. G., Urbana, Ill.; transfered to Hospital Corps June 10, 1898.
Musgrave, Andrew, transfered to Hospital Corps June 20, 1898.
Oglesby, James V.; transfered to Hospital Corps July 24, 1898.
Twitchell, John, Virden, Ill.; transfered to Regimental Band December 24, 1898.

DEATHS BY DISEASE.

Tittle, Percy H., Arcanum, Ohio; died at Third Division Hospital, Jacksonville, Fla., September 22, 1898, of typhoid fever.

McFarland, Herman E., Mendon, Ill.; died at Camp Cuba Libre, Jacksonville, Fla., September 23, 1898, of typhoid fever.

Turner, George E., Ogden, Ill.; died at Third Division Hospital, Jacksonville, Fla., October 4, 1898, of typhoid fever.

COMPANY H.

WILLIAM N. PIPER.

William N. Piper was born in Edgar county, September 21, 1871, and moved with his parents to Paris, in 1873. Here he attended the schools of the city, during his earlier years, after which he served an apprinticeship as a harness-maker, and later became a member of the firm of A. A. Piper & Sons, dealers in harness and saddlery.

In 1893, he enlisted in Company H, Illinois National Guards and in May, 1894, was appointed a corporal. Elected second lieutenant June 20, 1898, and was mustered into the United States Volunteer service May 20, 1898, and on November 5, 1898, was commissioned first lieutenant of his company, in which rank he continued until mustered out May 2, 1899. During his relation to the Illinois National Guards he was with his company in Chicago at the time of the great strikes.

HISTORY OF COMPANY H.

Company H, Fourth Illinois National Guard, was organized at Paris, Illinois, in the year 1881. Its first officers were Captain Vance, First Lieut. Douglass Mann and Second Lieut. William Macbeth. The organization was Company C, of the Eighth Regiment, and was transferred to the Fourth in 18—. The company has been commanded in succession by Captains Vance, Jaquath,

CAPT. W. H. SLANKER.

1st Lieut. W. N. Piper.   2d Lieut. H. E. Shutt.

Macbeth, Crowell, Lang, Davis and Slanker. Captain Slanker was in command of the company at the time it answered the call to arms, April 26, 1898. He was seconded by First Lieut. William Barr and Second Lieut. William N. Piper.

During the strike at East St. Louis stockyards in 1886, Company H accompanied the Eighth Regiment and served fourteen days. The next call came July 9, 1894, when their services were once more asked for in the interest of the state. Here they served eleven days at Camp Hopkins.

In October, 1892, and September, 1893, the Company spent several days at the World's Fair at Chicago. The next pleasure trip was to Charleston, Illinois, to attend the laying of the corner stone of the new State School. On July 22, 1897, the company left the state camp, Camp Lincoln, and attended the unveiling of the Logan monument in Chicago, returning July 24.

The order directing Captain Slanker to report at Springfield, Illinois, for duty, was received at 2:30 A. M., April 26, 1898. Immediately the city was awakened, and the news spread like fire. As soon as possible those members who did not live in Paris were notified of the presence of the order to report at once. At daybreak the boys began to arrive, and by noon almost the entire company, as well as a large number of recruits, were gathered at the armory. In the afternoon the Company fell in and marched to the southwest steps of the court house and listened to an address by Rev. Bell, of Paris, and were presented with two flags, one the Stars and Stripes by the the G. A. R., and the other a Cuban flag by the Baptist Young People's Union, of Paris. Afterward all returned to a hall on the west side of the square, and partook of a supper prepared by the Ladies' Aid Society and Relief Corps.

At 8:30 P. M. the company left over the Big Four for Springfield, where they arrived at 2:30 A. M. (Apr. 27), just twenty four hours from the time of receiving the order. They immediately marched to Camp Tanner and reported for duty. Although they were the second company to arrive in camp they were the first to report, for the other company did not report till the next day.

Company H, with Company E, was quarted in Barn H of the cattle section, where they remained until they left for Jacksonville.

At the time Company H received the order it consisted of three commissioned officers and eighty-four enlisted men. While waiting for a train more men were enrolled, increasing the number to one hundred and seventeen enlisted men. When they were examined for the volunteer service it was reduced to seventy-eight men and the shortage was made up by the transfer of the following men :

PRIVATES.

John F. Fowler, Company A.
Carl Heap, Company L.
Thomas Puyear, Company L.
Isaac Montgomery, Company L.
James M. Clark, Company E.
Stephen A. Shyrer, Company E.

This raising the number to the maximin of eighty-four enlisted men and three officers.

During the stay in Camp Tanner many of the friends and relatives of the company visited them, and always came with well filled baskets.

Company H was mustered into the volunteer service May 20, 1898, by Captain Baker, U. S. A. They left with the regiment May 26, bound for Tampa, Florida, but some place in Georgia an order was received directing the regiment to report at Jacksonville, Florida, where they arrived May 29. When the Fourth Illinois was placed on provost duty in Jacksonville, September 28, Company H occupied Station No. 1, at Forsythe & Jefferson streets and remained there till their removal to Savannah, Georgia, where they occupied Station No. 8, at Franklin Square, near the Yamacrow.

Company H was the last of the Fourth Illinois to leave Jacksonville, and had charge of the prisoners, fifteen in number.

On Thanksgiving day Company H's mess hall at Franklin Square was invaded by a number of the ladies of that district, who served the members of the company with a bountiful repast. This was under the leadership of Miss M. L. Landershine, of Savannah, and is an event which will never be forgotten by Company H.

The company was relieved from provost duty in Savannah by Company C, of the Second South Carolina on December 5, and then took up quarters with the regiment at the Dale avenue camp. On New Years' day, 1899, an order was received to the effect that the Fourth Illinois would leave for Cuba, January 3. The next day all were busy packing up and writing farewell letters to friends.

During the trip only a few from Company H escaped the experience of being sea-sick. Upon our debarkation at Havana the entire company was placed on guard at the wharves where the baggage was placed waiting transportation. About noon, January 8, Company H was relieved by Company D, and then proceeded to the camp which was distant about five miles. Some of the boys rode on the wagons while others more curiously inclined preferred to walk and take in the sights. Several had cameras and many interesting scenes were procured. All arrived in camp in due time for supper and were much pleased to find their tents all ready to receive them.

On January 22, 1899, the company accompanied the Third Battalion of which it was a part on a practice march to the City of Guines, which is forty-eight kilometers (thirty miles) from Havana and a little east of south in direction. The entire march covered a distance of nearly seventy-eight miles, the battalion arrived in Camp Columbia at 9 A. M., January 29. On January 24, while in camp at Guines, they were visited by General Lee. That night a ball was given in his honor by the residents of the city.

The day before the return to camp the battalion was camped near the shores of the harbor of Havana and not far from a powder magazine which had at one time been used by the Spanish army. A great deal of ammunition had been thrown into the harbor by the Spaniards, and "Major Elliot's Indians," having located the spot, proceeded at once to get some of the ammunition for souveniers. Quite a number of cartridges and other articles were "fished" out by the enthusiastic boys. During the night of February 13 the entire company was compelled, through necessity, to turn out in a heavy wind and rain storm to hold their tents down. The weather was cold enough to make overcoats very comfortable.

On Februaay 19 the company again started on another practice march, this time in company with the entire brigade, which then consisted of the Second South Carolina and Fourth and Ninth Illinois, under command of General Douglas. This march was taken over the same ground covered by the Third Battalion, of the Fourth Illinois, the month previous. On February 23 the brigade passed in review before General Gomez, the great Cuban commander. This was in the city of Guines, Cuba. On April 3 the order came directing the regiment to move at once to the

United States and prepare for muster out. The packing up was done that night, and the next day the First and Second Battalions left for the wharf. About noon an order came directing the Third Battalion to wait until the Friday following. When Friday came no boat came with it, so we waited until the 12th, when the return trip was begun. Leaving Havana about 6 P. M. we soon struck a very rough sea, and the little river boat, which carried us, had a hard time getting across, but upon striking the west coast of Florida the gulf became very tranquil, and the remainder of the trip was very pleasant.

Landing at the United States quarantine station at Egmont Key, on the morning of the 14th, we were held there 'till the next Monday (17th), when we proceeded to Port Tampa and took the cars for Augusta, Georgia. Arriving in Augusta on the evening of the 18th and staying aboard the train that night, we went into camp with the rest of the regiment and work was at once begun on the company books, getting ready to once more become citizens. This work finally completed, Company H was mustered out of the volunteer service of the United States, about noon, May 12, 1899.

COMPANY H ROSTER.

Where not otherwise designated the members of this company were mustered into the United States service on the 20th day of May, 1898, at Springfield, Illinois, and mustered out at Augusta, Georgia, May 2, 1899. Figures following name indicate age.

WILLIAM H. SLANKER, Captain, 38, Paris, Ill., Carpenter.
WILLIAM H. BARR, First Lieutenant, 27, Paris, Ill., Brickmason; discharged at Savannah, Ga., per resignation, Oct. 19, 1898.

COMPANY H.

WILLIAM N. PIPER, First Lieutenant, 26, Paris, Ill., Harnessmaker; mustered in as Second Lieutenant, commissioned as First Lieutenant Nov. 22, 1898, vice Wm. H. Barr. On special duty as signal officer from Dec. 6, 1898 to Jan. 9, 1899.

HARRY E. SHUTT, Second Lieutenant, 26, Paris, Ill., Cigarmaker; enlisted as Sergeant, detailed Sergeant-Major of the Second Battalion, May 20, 1899, commissioned Second Lieutenant, Nov. 22, 1898, vice Wm. N. Piper.

SERGEANTS.

Tracy, Howard T, 31, Paris, Ill., Painter; absent on recruiting service June 11 to 23, 1898.

Simons, Francis M., 29, Paris, Ill., Laborer.

Hill, Moss, 22, Chrisman, Ill., Clerk.

Patterson, Lockard, 30, Paris, Ill., Painter.

Rives, Harry C., 23, Paris, Ill., Clerk; enlisted as Sergeant, appointed Quartermaster-Sergeant Dec. 1, 1898.

Jacobs, John O., 20, Laborer; mustered in June 20, 1898, as private, appointed Corporal July 1, 1898, appointed Sergeant Dec. 1, 1898.

CORPORALS.

Buckler, William C., 22, Paris, Ill., Printer; enlisted as Corp., reduced to ranks June 28, 1898; on special duty in Engineering Corps July 18, 1898; appointed Corp. Dec. 1, 1898, reduced to ranks Feb. 22, 1899; discharged at Havana, Cuba, April 12, 1899.

Lientz, Ulysess B., 26, Chrisman, Teamster; discharged at Hospital, Ft. Myer, June 3, 1899.

Patterson, William, 24, Paris, Ill., Musician; detailed to band, returned to Co. Dec. 24, 1898; detailed to band Feb. 9. 1899.

Boyd, Enos A., 23, Paris, Ill., Cook; discharged at Paris, Ill., Feb. 3, 1899.

Lackey, Ross, 25, Paris, Ill., Laborer; enrolled as Corp., reduced to ranks June 1, 1898; appointed Corp., June 24, 1898; died at Third Division Hospital, Seventh Army Corps, Aug. 16, 1898.

Wasson, Orie E., 20, Chrisman, Ill., Student; discharged at Savannah, Ga., Dec. 14, 1898.

Sizemore, Denver, M. 26, Paris, Ill., Farmer; appointed Corp. Sept. 1, 1898.

Conover, Joseph C., 23, Chrisman, Ill., Farmer; appointed Corp. Dec. 22, 1898.

Durham, Herman E., 35, Casey, Ill., Farmer; appointed Corp. Dec. 7, 1898.

Scott, Purl A., 20, Chrisman, Ill., Student; on special duty with Engineering Corps July 18, 1898; appointed Corp. April 19, 1899.

Cardwell, Robert F., 18, Paris, Ill., Student; appointed Corp. July 1, 1898.

Scott, Edgar M., 28, Paris, Ill., Painter; appointed Corp. June 1, 1898.

Wetzel, Thomas M., 22, Paris, Ill., Laborer; appointed Corp. June 17, 1898.

Whalen, Thomas W., 27, Leroy, Ill., Photographer; appointed Corp. July 1, 1898.

Smith, William E., 26, Paris, Ill., Lineman; appointed Corp. July 1, 1898.

Cale, Charles E., 25, Paris, Ill., Laborer; appointed Corp. July 1, 1898; discharged at Havana, Cuba, April 10, 1899.

Owen, Stephen L., 22, Paris, Ill., Painter; appointed Corp. July 1, 1898; discharged at Savannah, Ga., Nov. 9, 1898.

MUSICIANS.

Howard, Edward T., 24, Paris, Ill., Painter; transferred to regimental band Dec. 24, 1898.

Fouts, Bert B., 22, Chrisman, Ill., Carpenter.

Russell, Clark A., 22, Chrisman, Ill., Clerk; appointed musician July 1, 1898; dischargrd Nov. 1, 1898.

Kelly, Waldo B., Casey, Ill., Printer; mustered in Dec. 1, 1898; transferred to Co. from regimental band Dec. 23, 1898.

ARTIFICER.

Barr, Charles C., 24, Paris, Ill., Brick-mason; discharged at Jacksonville, Fla., for disability Aug. 25, 1899.

Sell, William, 21, Paris, Ill., Carpenter; appointed artificer September 1, 1898.

WAGONER

Wilson, Stephen A., 33, Paris, Ill., Drayman.

COOK.

Bright, John F., 22, Paris, Ill., Hostler; appointed company cook January 19, 1899.

PRIVATES.

Anderson, John, 21, Kansas, Ill., Baker; on special duty in regimental bakery July 28, 1898, and Dec. 6, 1898.

Augustus, Willis O., 25, Paris, Ill., Student; detailed to Regimental Hospital Corps May 20, 1898, transfered to United States Army Hospital Corps June 27, 1898.

Black, Charles N., 30, Paris, Ill., Laborer; on detached duty as provost guard July 30, 1898—Aug. 6, 1898, discharged for disability at Jacksonville, Fla. Sept. 21, 1898.

Brown, Fred W., 21, Paris, Ill., Baker; on special duty at Regimental bakery at Camp Cuba Libre, detailed to Regimental bakery Dec. 6, 1898.

Beard, Aurthur J., 20, Paris, Ill., Clerk.

Black, Charles M., 36, Charleston, Ill., Druggist.

Conklin, Frank M., Paris, Ill., Fireman.

Cayton, Burt, 20, Paris, Ill., Laborer.

Conklin, Walter, 24, Paris, Ill., Laborer.

Camahan, David L., 38, Paris, Ill., Laborer; discharged September 21, 1898, for disability.

Caster, Louis, 31, Rolmore, Ill., Laborer.

Clark, James M., 27, Mattoon, Ill., Mechanic; detailed to regimental stables.

Ewing, Alva A., 35, Paris, Ill., Farmer.

Fowler, John W., 24, Tuscola, Ill., Blacksmith.

Gage, Leonard C., 22, Paris, Ill., Broom-maker.

Goodwin, George W., 21, Newman, Ill., Baker; special duty engineering corps July, 1898, died at Third Division Hospital, September 23, 1898.

Huffman, James F., 20, Paris, Ill., Clerk; transferred to United States Army Hospital Corps June 29, 1898.

Hardy, Aurther E., Paris, Ill., Laborer.

Bartlett, John, 25, Paris, Ill., Farmer; mustered in June 20, 1898.

Boes, Dan, 22, Paris, Ill., Laborer; mustered in June 20, 1898.

Gardner, Leroy, 35, Grand View, Ill., Carpenter; mustered in June 20, 1898.

Holding, Elton, 18, Grand View, Ill., Farmer; mustered in June 20, 1898.

Hardy, Harley C., 19, Paris, Ill., Laborer; mustered in June 20, 1898.

Keller, Martillis, 19, Shelbyville, Ill., Clerk, mustered in June 20, 1898.
Tone, George L., 19, Kansas, Ill., Tailor; mustered in June 20, 1898.
Layman, John L., 21, Paris, Ill., Hostler; mustered in June 20, 1898.
McClellan, Edward T., 33, Paris, Ill., Painter; mustered in June 20, 1898; appointed company cook Aug. 29, 1898; relieved Jan. 18, 1899.
Mitchell, Ogden, 20, Paris, Ill., Farmer; mustered in June 20, 1898.
Moody, William I. F., 19, Paris, Ill., Plumber; mustered in June 20, 1898.
Helm, Louis S., 28, Paris, Ill., Jeweler.
Huston, Samuel A., 19, Paris, Ill., Laborer.
Haish, William, 21, Paris, Ill., Broommaker.
Inge, Edwin A., 18, Chrisman, Ill., Clerk.
Inge, George B., 19, Chrisman, Ill., Painter; on special duty at provost headquarters at Jacksonville, Fla., and Savannah, Ga., until Jan. 1, 1899.
Jackson, Charles T., 22, Paris, Ill., Laborer.
Longfellow, Hiram, 21, Paris, Ill., Farmer.
Logan, James, 26, Warrensburg, O., Farmer; transferred to Hospital Corps, U. S. A., Sept. 19, 1898.
Mitchell, Stephen, 18, Paris, Ill., Farmer.
Montgomery, Isaac, 22, Ingraham, Ill., Farmer.
McMorris, Charles E., 18, Metcalf, Ill., Farmer.
Moore, Albert B., 21, Paris, Ill., Broommaker; mustered in June 20, 1898.
Miller, Harry A., 26, Paris, Ill., Printer; mustered in June 20, 1898.
Nail, Elmer, 23, Paris, Ill., Carpenter; mustered in June 20, 1898.
Quinn, Geo. E., 23, Paris, Ill., Farmer.

Robinson, Ira P., 25, Kansas, Ill., Farmer; mustered in June 20, 1898.

Sizemore, Oda, 22, Paris, Ill., Painter; mustered in June 20, 1898; discharged at Paris, Ill., Jan. 14, 1899.

Owens, John T., 19, Paris, Ill., Printer; mustered in June 20, 1898; honorably discharged at Joseph Simpson Hospital, Oct. 13, 1898.

Stark, Otis O., 20, Kansas, Ill., Laborer; mustered in June 20, 1898; discharged at Havana, Cuba, April 10, 1899.

Bagley, Chas. O., 21, Paris, Ill., Photographer; mustered in June 20, 1898; transferred to United States Army Hospital Corps, Sept. 19, 1898.

Low, Edward, 24, Paris, Ill., Carpenter; mustered in June 20, 1898; transferred to Hospital Corps, United States Army, Sept. 16, 1898.

Newton, Wm. R., 44, Paris, Ill., Carpenter.

Owens, John H., 23, Chrisman, Ill., Farmer.

Owen, Leslie A., 21, Paris, Ill., Clerk; honorably discharged at Havana, Cuba, April 12, 1899.

Putman, Homer C., 34, Livingston, Ill., Broommaker; transferred to United States Army Hospital Corps, Sept. 11, 1898.

Poulter, Harry E., 21, Kansas, Ill., Laborer; honorably discharged at Joseph Simpson Hospital, Feb. 10, 1899.

Puyear, Thomas A., 40, Mattoon, Ill., Engineer.

Shaw, Perry E., 18, Paris, Ill., Laborer; honorably discharged at Paris, March 13, 1899.

Scott, Daniel, 26, Chrisman, Ill., Clerk.

Scott, Samuel, 31, Chrisman, Ill., Farmer; discharged at Havana, Cuba, April 10, 1899.

Secres, Albert M., 18, Paris, Ill., Painter.

Sarvis, Wm. S., 35, Paris, Ill., Farmer.

Spires, Henry, 28, Paris, Ill., Butcher; special duty; provost guard Jacksonville, Fla., Aug. 5, 1898–Jan. 4, 1899.
Shryers, Stephen, 26, Arcola, Ill., Farmer.
Trine, David, 25, Paris, Ill, Laborer.
Thompson, Walter, 19, Paris, Ill., Machinist.
Tierney, Fred W., 18, Arcola, Ill., Farmer.
Walden, Levi W., 37, Paris, Ill., Miller.
Wyatt, James, 18, Chrisman, Ill., Farmer.
Wiley, Charles H., 21, Horace, Ill., Farmer.
Wallace, Claude, 18, Paris, Ill., Paper Hanger; discharged at Jacksonville, Fla., July 19, 1898, disability.
Heap, Karl L., 21, Olney, Ill., Farmer.
Moss, Harry, 20, Chrisman, Student; discharged at Jacksonville, Fla., Aug. 27, 1898, disability.
Green, Carlos T., 33, Tuscola, Ill., Contractor; mustered in June 25, 1898; died Aug. 8, 1898, in the Second Divison Hospital.
Wilson, Walter A., 21, Owensburg, Ill., Farmer; mustered in at Mattoon, Ill., June 20, 1898; deserted Sept. 20, 1898.

COMPANY A.

CHARLES M. DAVIS.

Charles M. Davis was born in Arcola, Illinois, July 27, 1870, graduating from the high school in 1887. Being of a studious trend of mind he wished to at once take up the study of law, but at the earnest desire of his mother, who thought it a part of wisdom for all young men to first adopt a trade before entering a profession, he discarded for the time the idea and learned the carpenter's trade, and gave his attention awhile to architecture.

In business he was always honorable and reliable, of industrious habits and of some means. He is an Episcopalian in religion and in 1897 joined the "Brotherhood of St. Andrew." Previous to this, he was for several years a member and secretary in the local "Order of Good Templars," in which he was a very active worker.

Among his ancestors for generations back were those who participated in every conflict in which the United States has been involved. There were also among them distinguished statesmen and jurists.

Capt. William Watts Davis, his father, was a Federal veteran of the Civil war, commanding principally Company K, Seventy-ninth Regiment Illlinois Volunteers, and in which service he lost his eyesight. His maternal great grandfather, Levi Sterling, was an officer in the American Revolution, and was wounded at Valley Forge.

The maiden name of Lieutenant Davis' mother was Ida M. Dolson, for many years a prominent worker in Ma-

sonic circles, a descendent of John Hart and James Wilson, signers of the Declaration of Independence. Her father was a first lieutenant in the Black Hawk campaign. His grandmother was the daughter of a Welsh nobleman by the name of Croson. She married Tunis Dolson, an American of wealth and prominence.

In 1888 Charles joined the Illinois State Militia, then known as Company A, Fourth Illinois National Guard. Some time later he entered the law office of States Attorney James K. Breeden, where he remained until that gentleman sent him to South Dakota on a business mission. After eight months he returned and was made first sergeant in his company, about the time of the strike of 1893, and was with them the two months, having headquarters at Chicago.

In 1896 he joined a party of excursionists to Anniston, Alabama, where he accepted a position as superintendent of the Novelty Wood Works. This place he resigned at the call for volunteers in the American-Spanish war. Hastening back home, and as his time in the militia had expired, re-enlisted, having then been a member nearly ten years, having been elected to the first lieutenancy in the spring of 1898. When, on the 26th of May, 1898, Company A, Fourth Regiment, Illinois Volunteer Infantry, boarded the train for Camp Tanner, Springfield, he went as first lieutenant of that company. During its year's servics, both in the United States and Cuba, he was in command about three months, and although a good drill master and strict disciplinarian, he was conscientious in his care for the privates' welfare in his personal attention to their mess and sickness. While duty came first, he spared no trouble to obtain for his men a favor or pleasure that would drive away the dull monotony of camp life. He enforced obedience and proficiency by careful instruction, supervision and courtesy, and remained with the company until mustered out at Savannah, Georgia.

RICE J. MOORE.

Rice J. Moore was born October 4, 1870, at Arcola, Illinois. Lived with his father on the farm until nineteen years of age, when he left home for an education, going to the Northern Indiana Normal School at Valparaiso, Indiana. After three years in this institution he returned home and resumed life on the farm. March 31, 1894, joined Company A, Fourth Infantry, Illinois National Guard; saw field service in Chicago during the Chicago strikes in July, 1894; appointed corporal July 10, 1895; appointed quartermaster sergeant March 15, 1897; commissioned second lieutenant May 22, 1897; entered United States service as second lieutenant, Fourth Infantry, Illinois Volunteers, 20th day of May, 1898; detached from Fourth Regiment July 25, 1898, and assigned to engineering corps of Seventh Army Corps. He resigned his commission November 9, 1898.

HISTORY OF COMPANY A.

STATE GUARD SERVICE.

The history of this organization began July 9, 1881, when, as Company A of the Ninth Battalion of State Militia, it was formed at Arcola, Illinois. William R. Armstrong was its first captain; D. A. Woodland and Al Snyder first and second lieutenants respectively.

Enlisted as privates at this time were S. A. D. Mc-

Williams and E. E. Elliot, both of whom have served with the regiment continuously from that date, the former having attained the rank of lieutenant-colonel and the latter that of major of the Third Battalion. Lieutenant Snyder, as he then was, is now regimental quartermaster, with rank of captain. In this same year (1881) the company was transferred to the Eighth Regiment, Illinois National Guard. In 1891 the Eighth was changed to the Fourth Illinois National Guard, but retained its organization.

Those who have served as captains of this company are Wm. R. Armstrong, D. A. Woodland, J. W. Goudy, S. R. Coan, E. E. Elliot and Jos. P. Barriklow. Of these, three reached the rank of major: Armstrong, Coan and Elliot.

Those filling the office of first lieutenant were D. A. Woodland, Al Snyder, S. R. Coan, Perry Bowers, S. A. D. McWilliams, J. P. Barricklow and Charles M. Davis.

The second lieutenants were Al Snyder, F. E. Wright, S. R. Coan, Perry Bowers, E. E. Elliot, J. P. Barricklow, W. C. Conners, Daniel Ghere, Judd Barricklow and Rice J. Moore. In addition to those previously mentioned, F. E. Wright also won the promotion of major.

The first encampment was one of five days, at Indianapolis, Ind., in 1882. A competitive drill, in which the company took part, was held there on July 4th.

The first real service that the company performed was during the strike of 1886 at East St. Louis. Orders were received April 10, and they remained on duty two weeks.

On October 12, 1892, the company attended the dedication of the World's Fair buildings at Chicago. The grand review of the state's troops was a magnificent spectacle, but the march of several hours over the hard pavements was a severe one.

Illinois Day, August 23, 1893, saw the state troops

once more assembled in Chicago. The company's quarters were at Windsor Park. A contractor engaged to supply all the troops with food during the two days of their stay. To this end he erected a very large tent, and the boys were fed on very tough beefsteak, and what little else was provided was equally as vile. This was too much to be endured. One morning the guy ropes were found cut, the tent collapsed, and the dishes demolished. The boys had been vindicated, and contract beef came suddenly to an end.

Again at Chicago, service was rendered eleven days beginning July 9, 1894. The company were in quarters at Thirty-ninth street and Wentworth avenue. Guard duty was performed on the Ft. Wayne Railway tracks. On July 16, great excitement was caused by the explosion of a caisson on the boulevard. The company were in line promptly, for the impression was that a riot had started. However, nothing further came of it.

Logan Day occurred on July 22, 1897. The Fourth being in State Encampment at Camp Lincoln, Springfield, left by rail to attend the ceremonies of the unveiling of the monument.

The company has, with its regiment, been in attendance at each of the State encampments, and has won for itself a full share of credit.

VOLUNTEER SERVICE IN THE SPANISH-AMERICAN WAR.

With the possibility of the State Guards being called into the service of the United States, came the order for recruiting. After the President's call for one hundred and twenty-five thousand volunteers, the company was almost immediately filled up to its full quota, and more.

On the evening of April 16, the ladies of Arcola presented Company A with a beautiful flag of silk. The exercises were held in Armory Hall. Mrs. Jno. R. Clisby, in choice thought, made the presentation, Capt. Jos. P. Barricklow responded on behalf of the company. Mr. George Cheney delivered a short but stirring oration upon the "Impending Struggle." The flag was not taken with the company until June 23, when upon the coming of recruits to Jacksonville, it was brought with them. On several occasions the company had the pleasure of seeing their banner carried as regimental colors.

Orders to report at Springfield were received at 2:00 A. M. April 26. It was an anxious, expectant day. Members of the company hurried from their homes, from farm and shop, from store and school, and from the neighboring towns, to the meeting place in Armory Hall. Roll call revealed a total of one hundred and seven. The veterans of '61, stepping forth with the spirit of those other stirring times, escorted the boys of '98 to the depot. At half past five in the evening, after the tearful leave-taking and the last sorrowful good-bye was spoken, the Vandalia train carried them away to the untried perils of war.

The train arrived in Springfield at 9:30. The boys slept the remainder of the night upon the cars with what little comfort they could.

In the first light of the morning the march of three miles to the State Fair Grounds was taken up. One or two companies of the Fourth and one of the Fifth regiment had preceded us into camp. Sergeant Blackwell and Private McBride, who, as part of a detail to accompany Captain Snyder, had left Arcola the previous morning, were the first soldiers to arrive in Camp Tanner.

The first breakfast was suggestive of camp life. It arrived late. It consisted of nothing but very tough beefsteak, which the cook issued to the men as fast as he could fry it. But half the boys, impatient at the long wait, cut forked sticks from the trees and toasted their portions before the fire.

Companies A and M shared quarters with each other in barn "Q," which, during the State Fair, had been used for cattle. The companies occupied the opposite sides of the building, both in the loft above and in the stalls below. A detail of men had carried each a bale of straw from one of the sheds about a quarter of a mile distant, and the quarters were fixed up with a fair degree of comfort.

At first the mess quarters were in the open, the cooking being done on improvised brick furnaces upon the hillside, but the weather being damp and chilly, and having had to eat in the rain on the fourth day, a removal was made to the sheep and swine building, which quarters were occupied the remainder of the stay in Camp Tanner.

Sleeping accommodations were not quite such as to satisfy the young men reared in comfortable homes. Most of the boys had left home without even an overcoat; the military overcoats were far too few. There was not more than half enough blankets, and even these had a provoking habit of taking a leave of absence in the night. One had almost to wear his blanket day and night to keep it from being "swiped." By the end of the first week Arcola responded to the need which the state had been slow to provide for, and some real home "comforts" came to make more endurable the chilly nights.

One of the first lessons to be learned was one of patience. It was commonly expected that in a few short days the men would be examined, the companies mustered in, and the regiment hurried away to some eastern or southern camp. But all the work of organization and equipment could not be done in a day; and while we waited impatiently, time hung heavily on the hands of the men. They drilled in company and drilled in squad, marched on dress parade and made practice marches into the city. These grew especially irksome when we thought it possible we might have to stay in Camp Tanner all summer.

War is a serious business. But men will not always be serious. When monotony threatens to overcome them they seek diversion. The volunteer, coming, as he does, from such varied walks of life, is especially fertile in means of enlivenment.

While the weather was gloomy without many an hour was whiled away in boxing and wrestling, in dancing and in athletic games. Some read books and all wrote letters. The old army game of poker furnished entertainment for some and beguiled the inexperienced youth into a new found pastime. Not last nor least in the list of amusements were certain "Initiation Exercises" in which the principal instruments were a paddle-shaped board and a pair of stout and willing arms. No one dared say he was not entitled to an initiation. The officers, too, sometimes came in for a good share of this enjoyment, i. e., the enjoyment of the boys. Sometimes the poultry-roosts of the vicinity suffered a depletion and the farmer, seeing so many bluecoats in camp, put two and two together and rightly guessed that it made four. But many found more sober enjoyments. The Young Men's Christian Association on the grounds, afforded interesting meetings, entertaining games, and a quiet place to read and write. Some twenty additional men came May 15 and 17, to recruit the company to a higher number.

The days preceding the physical examination was a period of much anxiety on the part of the boys. The time came on the morning of the 18th of May. Comparatively few of them failed to pass. Some time previous an order had been issued to cut the companies down to eighty-one men. Of the number above this of physically qualified men in Company A, six found a place upon the rolls of other companies — two in Company I, three in Company H and one in Company M. The remainder were sent home with those who had failed.

The date of muster in followed close upon the examination. At 11:10 A. M., May 20, Company A left the State Guard service to join the volunteer forces of the United States.

Six days later, according to orders received, the Fourth Illinois departed for the South, leaving Springfield, over the Chicago & Alton tracks. The Third Battalion did not leave until 4 o'clock.

All were eager to go. There had been days when the prospect for active service looked gloomy. Many thought they might be obliged to spend dreary weeks in the state camp and at last be sent back home. But now doubt fled. We were to go to Tampa, perhaps in a few days to embark on a voyage across the waters to join our brothers at Santiago. There was some little rumor that our destination might be Jacksonville. But that mattered little—any change was welcomed that promised to bring us nearer the front.

The travel accommodations were excellent and the tourist sleepers insured a good rest for each night.

This journey to the Southland was a new experience to most of the boys, and one which they thoroughly appreciated. The men of the regiment won attention both by their conduct and by their personal appearance. At Jackson, Tennessee, a white-haired veteran, looking up at Private Craft, is said to have remarked: "If that is the size of the men you have up there, it's no wonder you whipped us in '61."

It was a continuous ovation. The loyalty and hospitality of the South was very marked. Perhaps their feeling about the coming struggle was aptly put, in the words of a grey-bearded old warrior at Birmingham, Alabama. He said "I received three bullets at Gettysburg, but if you need me I am ready to go again." Every where we were greated with enthusiasm. We were treated with especial kindness at Sylacauga, Alabama, and again at Albany, Georgia, where they served lunch and lemonade to us.

The morning of the 29th found the long train upon the side track in the midst of the pine woods. We had arrived at Jacksonville, for orders had been changed. Here we were to go into encampment about a mile and a half north and east of the city proper. After breakfast the companies formed and were marched to the space assigned them. The Second Illinois, Fiftieth Iowa and First Wisconsin were already there and our regiment took its place to the north of them, i. e., on their left.

It was not till evening that arrangements were completed for the pitching of camp, and in the meantime we learned something of our new environments. It was a day of intense heat, and blankets were spread over the bushes, on poles, or in any manner to afford a shelter from the burning rays. The water from the hydrants that had been extended from the city, though of fairly good quality, was very warm. All about was a scattering timber of young pine. The clumps of saw palmetto, scattered about so profusely, formed a novel sight to unaccustomed eyes.

The grounds were level, and, covered with grass, seemed a goodly sight. Uninformed as to the nature of the country, men approached every bush with caution, not knowing what enemy in reptile form might lurk behind. A few days, however, sufficed to teach us that this land was no wilder than others.

Before night fell the tents, which had been brought

from the state, were erected. Each was large enough to accommodate ten or twelve men. Companies A and E, facing each other, formed the last company street on the south.

Now followed days of real camp life; of drills in the morning and dress parades in the evenings, and Saturday morning inspections. At first the men slept, simply spreading their blankets upon the ground; then, by way of luxury, some made their couch of the ever present pine bough, and some from the abundant gray moss that hung from the trees. After some time a few of the squads put in floors of lumber, purchased cheap at the neighboring mills. But most of the boys had long before spent their last nickel, and, without a cent to buy a bit of luxury, lived roughly in their tents, and subsisted on the coarse fare provided, often eating in the rain.

In the midst of this the volunteer remained cheerful. He was ever ready to sing, but it mattered not what. The average soldier sang with equal zest the songs of the Y. M. C. A. or those from the opera, and the evening twilight and the pine woods listened nightly to his music.

Two or three weeks had passed when the hearts of the boys were gladdened by the receipt of various boxes filled with useful toilet articles and dainty viands from home. Never before had edibles seemed so delicious.

The long looked-for pay day came June 23. It was the first, and right well did the boys appreciate it.

On this same day came twenty-five recruits under the charge of Private Everette Little, who had been sent back to Arcola for this purpose some time previous. With them they brought the company's flag, which henceforth was to remain with us.

An issue of blue shirts was made on June 24. The men had been very much in need of them. But we were now no longer the "Ragged Regiment." The transformation was quite striking.

The bath houses that were erected at the rear of the camp about July 1st, added quite a comfort, as well as being a necessity.

July 5, the company with its regiment took part in a grand review of the troops by General Lee. Unfortunately, soon after the line of march was formed, it began to drizzle, and before the companies got back to quarters they had undergone two hours of a drenching rainstorm. But all bore it cheerfully, and, strange to say, none seemed to suffer any serious effects from it. But it was yet to be learned what Florida rains were. On July 10, it rained so that the water stood over the low ground in the company street. Still raining all the next day, the water came up over some of the tent floors, and the men were obliged to wade over knee deep to get across to the mess quarters. There was now nothing left to do but to move out, and accordingly half the company transferred to the west side. A ditch had been dug along the south side of the camp, but it was not deep enough to drain the low ground. On the third morning Companies A and E went to work in the rain and mud and water building a causeway about a hundred feet long, of pine saplings and logs, thus bridging over the "pond." On this day, also, our company labored to build a mess house, so that we now had a rather respectable place in which to eat. Our first mess quarters had been a mere shack of poles, roofed over in a rough way with pine boughs. The soot from the pine-log fire painted and repainted this primitive canopy as often as the rains from above washed it out. In the way of an improvement later on, a board roof had been placed over the kitchen part.

On the evening of July 14, some excitement was caused, when, after dusk the order came down the line for the men to fall in with rifles and side arms. The first thought was that some serious trouble was on hand, needing our services. Even some that were ailing left their cots to join in something that promised a bit of excitement. After we were in line with the rest of the companies, some one remembered that Governor Tanner was coming to visit the Illinois regiments. This surmise proved correct, for we were marched to the depot; but as he did not come that evening our march was repeated next morning.

Twenty of our men, with a like detail from the other companies, went upon the rifle range, July 28. Captain Muench of Company L, was in charge. Some good scores were made. August 8th saw the removal of our regiment to Panama Park, two miles to the north of us, where it was placed with the Third Division.

Now came the season of our greatest trial. The unsanitary condition of our other camp, the coarse food, together with inexperienced cooking, the dull monotony, the steady heat of the sun, and the presence of the dread malaria and typhoid in the very air, all combined to make a condition under which the constitution of our men began to give way. Heretofore there had been but little sickness. Up to the 3d of August there had never been more than three upon the company's sick report at any one time. But now it seemed that one after another, and in two's and three's, they would have to be taken to the hospital.

Added to this was the doubt as to whether the regiment would remain in the service, and the discontent aroused over the absurd rumor that the men might be allowed to decide for themselves.

At times there was hardly a score of men fit for duty. Things were fast moving toward a demoralized state, when a change came for the better in an order for the regiment's removal to Jacksonville to do provost duty.

Before leaving Panama we were called upon for the first time to mourn the loss of a comrade. Allen F. Clare had come with the recruits in June. It seems that the fever had fastened its fangs upon him almost from the very first. He was sick in quarters almost continuously after August 2. A furlough was granted him September 9, but ere he reached home a mortal illness was upon him. After lingering three days, he died at his home in Lovington, Ill., September 15, 1898. Thus, in the cause of his country, in the flower of his youth, had he been cut down by the soldier's worst foe.

All the companies had gone but A and E when we broke camp September 30. In the evening of that day we pitched our tents next neighbors to Company C, with whom we were to take up the work at Provost Station No. 2 in the north central part of Jacksonville. All that night and the next day the wind blew a gale and the rain fell in gusty showers. We awoke, to find some of the tents down and several trees uprooted. Awakening almost any hour of the night, one could hear some one resetting his tent stakes. Amidst the storm our men went on duty next morning at General Lee's headquarters and at the city waterworks.

The death of Sydney Matters on the 6th of October, came as a terrible shock, alike to his comrades and to his friends at home. He had been under treatment of a resident physician for a periodic trouble. He had gone that morning requesting an operation. But at the moment of its beginning he was seized with convulsions and died. Poor Syd! whole-hearted, generous, best loved comrade! He had long expected his furlough but for some reason it was never granted. How much his disappointment had to do with the hastening of his death we cannot tell. Sadly we accompanied his remains to the depot whence they were shipped home to be buried in the Arcola cemetery.

Hardly more than a week passed by ere death came again into our midst. James Robertson died in the Third Division Hospital, October 14, carried away by a brief attack of typhoid fever. A telegram was sent to the address of his mother in Indiana, but no mother answered. When a reply did come back it was that there was no one to assume the expense and that he should be buried at Jacksonville. Arrangements, however, had already been made to do so. These circumstances made his funeral a peculiarly sad one. We followed his body to its sepulcher on the sandy slope. The bugles played taps over his open grave, and, firing the parting salute, we left him there with the tall pines above him to guard his resting place.

The events of these few days did nothing to dispel the gloom that was settling upon the men. Jacksonville, with which our first acquaintance had been one of pleasure, now seemed little short of a pest hole. Is it little wonder, then, that we received the order to report at Savannah with new and eager hopes? We were one of the first four companies to depart, leaving over the Plant System railway near midnight of October 20. We arrived at our destination about 7 o'clock next morning. It was prophetic of our later experience that we left Jacksonville in the rain and entered Savannah in sunshine.

Companies A and K were assigned to Station No. 3 and went into camp on the wide green in the center of Oglethorpe avenue and on opposite sides of Habersham street. Police headquarters were but half a block south of us, and in these grounds we were allowed to have our mess quarters.

At first the people of Savannah looked with doubt and misgiving upon the coming of the soldiers. But such was the uniformly good behavior of our men, and the firmness and vigor with which they dealt not only with the disorderly volunteers but with the unruly negro or white citizen as well, that they won respect and approval, admiration and friendship, in turn. Nor could any people have treated us better, more kindly or more hospitably than did these. We were received into their houses like sons and brothers, and many a little comfort and many a delicacy found its way to our tents. It was a usual occurrence for the sentinel, as he went on post in the early morning, to find a cup of hot coffee ready to be handed out to him by some kind-hearted lady.

It is not necessary to describe our duties as provost guards. It was, in reality, police work. Suffice it to say that the men did their duty fearlessly and well. Our district was known as Crawford ward, and men were not allowed to enter except under special and limited passes.

When November 24 came the good people of Savannah outdid all previous generosity in the spreading of a magnificent Thanksgiving dinner for the twelve thousand soldier boys encamped in and around the city. Our two companies were feasted near Chatham Artillery Hall, K at 1 o'clock and we at 3. Can we ever be grateful enough, or speak too much in praise of such hospitality? And to the Savannah ladies we must give full credit for their tireless efforts and skillful planning.

November 25 we gave up our old Springfield rifles in exchange for new United States magazine rifles. After more than two months of provost duty, our regiment was relieved and removed to the country camp. Such was the satisfaction we had given that the police department, fire department, mayor and citizens joined in a petition for our retention. But it availed nothing. Our company broke camp December 5, and was relieved by Company I, of the Ninth Illinois.

It seemed a bit odd to get back into company drills and regimental drills once more, but old habits soon reasserted themselves.

We were encamped partly in a meadow, partly in a peanut field, a very nice location withal.

The days were now getting rather cool. A damp wind often blew in from the ocean, making it very chilly and disagreeable. On the night of December 9, and on several others, ice formed a quarter of an inch thick, and one morning we awoke to find a sleet upon the ground and trees. This was unusual for Savannah. It was not exactly comfortable for open air meals.

The army stoves, which were provided us December 10, afforded much comfort. For the benefit of those who have never seen a government stove, one is briefly described here: A funnel of sheet-iron about twenty inches high inverted over a shallow pit in the ground, four inches wide at the top and eighteen at the bottom; an inverted $\wedge$ shaped notch at the bottom for the admission of air; a door on the side fastened with ordinary hinges; three or four joints of four-inch stove pipe. The tents were arranged in clusters of threes, all facing the little square, in the center of which was the stove.

Our regiment joined in the grand review before President McKinley December 17. The companies were well filled up, averaging eight sets of fours. Not since the early days at Jacksonville had we gone out with such full companies.

As the year drew to a close we began to feel assured that we should be taken across to Cuba. Amongst other special preparations, good, strong boxes were made, each large enough to hold the extra goods of six men. These proved very substantial in the rough handling of shipping.

Reveille sounded early on the morning of January 3, for orders had been received to embark on the Mobile that day. It was almost like parting with our own home friends to leave the Savannah people. We had had a happy stay with them.

Our great ship, with both the Fourth and Ninth Illinois on board, moved off at 11:30, dropping down the river with the tide. From window and door of every factory and home, a multitude waved us farewell. The voyage upon the sea was without particular incident, though it was a new experience to the greater number of us. At 11:25 A. M., January 5, we first caught sight of the high coast line of Cuba; after fifty hours of ocean journey we slowly drew in under the grim old walls of Castle Morro, into the great Havana harbor, past the wreck of the Maine, to our landing place. Here we were obliged to lay two days before the ship could finish unloading. On the afternoon of the 7th we made the march to our camp, located nearly seven kilometers (about four miles) northwest from the city.

So strangely different from the familiar scenes of homeland, the succession of new and unexpected sights was almost overwhelming. Streets were narrow, crooked, and filthy; doors and windows of homes barred. There were great ox-carts and little horse-cars. Everywhere strange scenes met our eye and a strange tongue greeted our ears. A curious throng looked on as we passed by. There were ragged, unkempt children and naked infants. At almost every home men, women, or children, waved the Cuban flag in one hand and with the other the Stars and Stripes. Every appearance of our beloved banner was greeted with a burst of cheers.

As we passed out of the city into the country still

other novel sights met our gaze. Stone walls and cactus hedges served as fences. A fortified hill appeared on our right, and one with a block house upon it some distance to the left. We crossed a fine little stream of clear water, with a waterfall a few yards below. Our winding, hilly road led us through several suburban villages. We reached the site of our camp in the evening, and pitched our tents on the red hill slope overlooking the sea, two miles away. A row of royal palms extended along the south side, and a lane of banana led off from the north.

Our large new tents, 14 x 14, were erected before night fall, and six men occupied each. That night the rain fell heavily. We had not had time to dig trenches around our tents and some of the squads awoke to find themselves in several inches of water that had filled the hollows. The next morning we wondered if we would ever enjoy this Cuban experience, for the pasty, red soil seemed worse than the black mud of Illinois.

On the third day of our encampment we were issued good, substantial folding cots. These provided much toward our health as well as comfort.

Now followed days of the usual routine of camp duties, the boys using their spare time in getting acquainted with the country around us.

Not a little stir was created when we learned that the Third Battalion was ordered on an eight-day march to Guines, thirty miles southeast of Havana. We left Camp Columbia near 8 o'clock on the morning of January 22, Major Elliott in command. The band accompanied us for a mile or more. The men were in cheerful and expectant spirits. Our road led us northeast through El Cerro, Tulipan, and Jesus del Monte, suburbs of Havana. Turning to the east through this latter place, and then to the southeast, which general direction we followed all the way, we soon left the city to our backs.

The roadway was well built of crushed rock. Every culvert and bridge was substantially made of stone, or brick and iron. A short post of gray rock marked each kilometer and its number from the city.

On our left, as we left Jesus del Monte, the great harbor remained in view for some distance, while on our right, a mile away appeared a series of fortified hills.

At noon we reached San Francisco de Paula. A mile farther we left the winding hill road and emerged upon the more level upland. About 1 we reached the village of Cotorro, near which we pitched our camp. We had marched twelve miles and a half and were somewhat tired, yet much pleased with the interesting things we had seen.

The village had had four block-houses to protect it. These structures, for the most part of stone, and two-thirds of them in ruins, became a familiar sight ere the end of our journey was reached.

This was our first night under field tents. We made an early start next morning and traveled with much more ease than on the previous day. Four miles out from Cotorro we crossed a fine little stream of pure water that afforded us a good watering place. Three miles farther we passed the peaks of Somorostro, tall, rocky masses that rose on each side of our road to the height of about four hundred feet.

We passed through San Jose at 10:30, and twenty minutes later reached a second camping place. We had again marched about twelve miles.

The third day we passed through the hills of Candela, from whose summit we caught an indistinct vision of the Caribbean. Three miles further lay our destination. At

10:30 we had established our camp in the northwestern part of Guines.

We found this to be a place of about eight thousand inhabitants. There were nine or ten block-houses surrounding the town, but nearly all were in ruins.

We remained in encampment here three days, including that of our arrival. General Lee came down from Havana the first day, and, escorted by some two hundred Cuban cavalrymen, visited our camp.

A battalion of the Second Louisiana, which had been sent out under orders similar to our own, arrived on the day following.

The people received us kindly, and altogether our short stay amongst them was both pleasant and profitable.

We broke camp once more at 6:15 the morning of the 27th. We made a particularly good march this day, for at 12:50 we reached the watering place previously mentioned, a distance of eighteen and one-half miles.

The next forenoon we encamped at Luyano, in sight of the harbor, and the third morning we marched into the home camp, led by the band that had come a mile or so to meet us. Colonel Swift complimented both commander and men on their good appearance after their long march.

The days of February 12th and 13th were very stormy ones, the wind blowing a gale from the north and the rain falling in gusty showers. Many found it chilly enough to wear an overcoat.

February 19 found us for the second time upon the march to Guines. This time it was the entire brigade—the Second South Carolina, Ninth and Fourth Illinois regiments. We followed the same route as before and therefore it was not entirely a new experience to a part of us.

On the evening of the second day we pitched our camp on the southern slope of Lomas de Candela (Candela

Hills). The ground was very stony, fit hiding places for more than one centipede that was found ere we made our couch for the night. The following day we did not break camp till at noon. The forenoon was spent in the manner usual to the American soldiers when he has a bit of leisure time, viz.: in exploration and investigation. It is a part of his nature to do so.

A grove of bananas and cocoanut palms that stood a quarter of a mile to our west claimed first attention. We had never seen quite so much of the first in one patch. Some of the boys amused themselves with their pistols in shooting the cocoanuts from the clusters. Some one early discovered a great cave up near the hill top. Most of us had the good fortune to see this wonder of nature. The entrance was rather difficult to find, the ground being so overgrown with shrubbery. There was no beautiful stalactite formation, only damp and dirty walls. There were great rooms, and narrow winding passageways. One dome-shaped apartment was about thirty feet across; an aperture in the center opened out into the sunlight above. We left the cavern by another opening which we afterwards found to be several hundred yards west from that where we had entered.

At 2:00 in the afternoon we moved on to Guines, the Third Battalion leading the way. Our camp was established near a swift flowing stream of pure water, about a mile northeast of the city. Here we remained until Friday morning the 24th. Many of our friends, whose acquaintance we had formed when on our previous visit came out from the town to see us. The 22d being Washington's birthday, we formed a parade through the principal streets. General Gomez witnessed the review of the troops.

The evening of the first day's return march brought us

again to the Somorostros. The other regiments were not with us.

We had not stretched our tents a half hour till shouts from the hill-top proclaimed that several adventurers had already scaled the steep, rocky ascent. Soon all sorts of reports were coming in as to the strange, wild creatures to be seen up there. Matthews found a meek-eyed house cat that had had both ears and tail abbreviated, and with a stout cord tied it to his tent pole. The news got out, and boys were to be seen coming from all parts of the camp to see the "mountain lion."

It need not be told here how, during our stay, the boys gathered bucketfuls of honey from a great natural hive in the rock, nor how they found and entered a snake den, capturing some of the reptiles; for these will very probably appear in the story of the other companies.

We rambled over nearly every foot of the sharp, craggy summits. We found wild oranges, limes and guava upon the hillsides, and many varieties of small wood. From the topmost tree we could see the waters of the northern coast about fifteen miles away.

On the evening of the 26th, orders came to break camp once more. So unexpected to the boys was this, that quite a number were beyond the peaks, and out of range of the bugles. But most of them got back in time to join their companies in line, if they did miss their supper.

It was about 5 o'clock when we left. Marching about three miles we entered the village of Carninoso. Here we turned to the south. A fairly good road led out for two or three miles, but after that it became nothing better than an ox-cart track, narrow, often deep rutted and stony, and sometimes sunken ten or fifteen feet below the surrounding country. Night coming upon us added nothing to the convenience of our traveling. At a quarter of eight we reached

Managna, a town of considerable size, twenty kilometers south of Havana. Here we entered another good road, similar to the other by which we had left Havana. An hour and a half more of marching brought us to a camping place for the remainder of the night. We had come about thirteen miles. Without further incident we reached our home camp at 12 o'clock next day, tired enough, and glad to get a rest. Colonel Swift praised his men for their cheerfulness, and was pleased and satisfied with their conduct. The remaining days in Camp Columbia were uneventful. All felt that the time was drawing near when we should recross the waters to the home land.

But we were enjoying ourselves. Never had there been a better condition of health. The weather was of the very finest. It was not often it rained; in fact, there was none in the last seven weeks of our stay.

Daily we were acquiring valuable information. Many a pleasant hour, away from camp duties, we spent by the seaside, roaming over the fields, in the villages, or in the great city itself. We learned much of the country, its soil and its products; of the people, their language, their customs and their social conditions.

Our battalion went aboard the side-wheel steamer Whitney, April 12. The other two had gone a week before. Just as the sun went down we passed out the harbor, bidding goodby to Cuban scenes and Cuban experiences, that were ours no longer, except in memory.

On the morning of the second day we were unloaded at Egmont Key, where we remained in quarantine three days. We were at the entrance to Tampa Bay, Florida. The barbed wire enclosure, in which we were tented, was much like a prison to the boys, for we could not leave it except on duty. Each day we were examined by the United States Surgeons, but not a man was sick. Our blankets had been fumigated when we first came off the boat, and our other goods later.

The pilot boat Margaret carried us away from Camp Detention on the morning of April 17th. We reached Port Tampa at noon. After several hours wait, while our baggage was being transferred to the train, we took the Plant System line for the north. We reached Savannah at about 11 o'clock next morning. Owing to a conflict of orders we were obliged to lay here in sight of the steeples of the city till near 11 o'clock. We reached Augusta at nightfall, remaining on board the cars till morning. We marched out to Camp McKenzie next morning, finding the tents some other regiment had left, already up and waiting for us.

The days passed by quietly. We had drills occasionally and dress parades in the evening and light guard duty.

In the meantime we had opportunities to learn even more of Georgia hospitality.

We were examined for muster-out on the 21st, turned in our guns and accoutrements on the 28th, and at noon of May 2nd, received the final papers that discharged us from the service of the government and made us private citizens once again.

Need we add that the home-coming was a joyous event? A reception was tendered the members of Company A at the Armory Hall May 6. Through the untiring efforts of the many friends, led by the Army and Navy League, a magnificent banquet was spread, at which soldiers, both old and young, were feasted. Surely we owe a great debt of gratitude to those who, throughout the twelve months of our service, provided us many a comfort and cheered us with their sympathy!

The following poem from the pen of Mart H. Bassett was presented to each member as a souvenir of this reception:

Back to our homes, back to our hearts,
    Our boys are welcomed tonight—
From tented fields to civil marts
    They come with records bright;
The volunteers of Company A
    Are hailed with proud delight;
We grasp your hands and proudly say:
    You're welcome home tonight.

Not yours to stand where bullets flew,
    'Mid mad alarms of strife,
But pestilence and fever grew
    Where brave you offered life,
That Cuba might uplift her eye
    To Freedom's holy light.
You willing were to do and die,
    You're welcome home tonight.

We've missed you in the year that's past,
    The days have sped but slow;
And now, we have you home at last,
    We'd have you all to know
Arcola viewed, with leaping joy,
    Our soldiers' record bright;
And fondly tell each patriot boy
    You're welcome home to-night.

COMPANY A ROSTER.

When not otherwise specified, mustered in May 20, 1898, and mustered out May 2, 1899. Figures following address indicate age.

JOSEPH P. BARRICKLAW, Captain, Arcola, Ill.
CHARLES M. DAVIS, First Lieutenant, Arcola, Ill.
HOVEY S. MCBRIDE, Second Lieutenant, Arcola, Ill.

COMPANY A.

SERGEANTS.

Waldo, Hazen J., Mattoon, Ill., Hotel.
Bouck, Wm. E., Arcola, Ill., Farmer.
Gere, Ross E., Arcola, Ill., 22, Farmer.
Barricklaw, Samuel E., Arcola, Ill., Farmer.
Clement, Charles W., Oakland, Ill., Farmer; made Corporal June 24, 1898; promoted to Sergeant Nov. 19, 1898.
Munsen, Fred F., Arcola, Ill., Clerk; made Corporal June 24, 1898; promoted to Sergeant Mch. 19, 1899.

CORPORALS.

Thomas, Alfred M., Arcola, Ill., 22, Tailor; made Corporal Aug. 30, 1898.
Sitz, August G., Arcola, Ill., Farmer; made Corporal Aug. 15, 1898.
Walz, Charles A., Carnie, Ill.; made Corporal June 24, 1898.
Clayman, Earl, Arcola, Ill., Clerk; made Corporal June 24, 1898.
Smith, Henry W., Arcola, Ill., 24, Teacher; made Corporal June 24, 1898.
Watson, John H., Chesterville, Ill., 24, Farmer; made Corporal Oct. 20, 1898.
Timm, William, Tuscola, Ill.; made Corporal Oct. 20, 1898.
Cross, William A., Tuscola, Ill.; mustered in June 25, 1898; made Corporal Oct. 20, 1898.
Holler, Robert L., Lovington, Ill.; mustered in June 20, 1898; made Corporal Feb 1, 1899.
Butler, Austin, Hindsboro, Ill.; made Corporal Feb. 1, 1899.

Nelson, Otis M., Ottumwa, Iowa, Miner; mustered in June 20, 1898; made Corporal Feb. 1, 1899.
Fletcher, Montelle, Tuscola, Ill.; made Corporal Mch. 19, 1899.

ARTIFICER.

Scott, John, Arcola, Ill., 27, Farmer; made Artificer Feb. 1, 1899.

WAGONER.

Hall, Lee, Arcola, Ill., 30, Farmer.

COOK.

Bates, William S., Hindsboro, Ill., 26, Farmer; made Company Cook Mch. 24, 1899.

MUSICIANS.

Skinner, Elgie R., Arcola, Ill., 20, Student.
Spellman, James, Arcola, Ill., 14, Painter.

PRIVATES.

Armstrong, Samuel G., Tuscola, Ill., 32, Farmer.
Bales, Stewart N., 18, Tuscola, Ill., Stonecutter.
Barnett, Mosie, 23, Arcola, Ill., Laborer.
Boone, Winfield S., 18, Arcola, Ill., Student.
Branson, John, 32, Chesterville, Ill., Farmer.
Brown, Albert, Lovington, Ill.; mustered in June 20, 1898.
Bird, Harvey D., 22, Tuscola, Ill., Carpenter.
Chester, Earnest K., 24, Oakland, Ill., Laborer.
Conley, Guy, Sailors Springs, Ill.; mustered in June 20, 1898.
Coon, Ollie P., 24, Hindsboro, Ill., Painter.
Cox, John C., Oakland, Ill.; mustered in June 20, 1898.
Craft, Walter I., 25, Arcola, Ill., Laborer.
Ehlenbach, Hans C., Arcola, Ill.

Fulton, John C., Philadelphia, Pa.; mustered in June 20, 1898.
Gasman, Thomas, Jr., Tuscola, Ill.; mustered in June 20, 1898.
Gray, Fred M., Lovington, Ill.; mustered in June 20, 1898.
Grigsby, Lon, Sullivan, Ill.; mustered in June 20, 1898.
Hartford, William R., 23, Arcola, Ill., Farmer.
Hendricks, Harry M., 23, Oakland, Ill., Laborer.
Howard, John W., Arcola, Ill.; mustered in June 20, 1898.
Kennedy, John, Findlay, Ohio; mustered in June 20, 1898.
Kurtz, Edwin A., 19, Oakland, Ill., Laborer.
Land, Edward J., Tuscola, Ill.; mustered in June 20, 1898.
Lentz, John N., 21, Mt. Vernon, Ill., Farmer.
Logan, Stephen, Arcola, Ill.
Ludolph, John H., Arcola, Ill.; mustered in June 20, 1898.
McCallister, Thomas, Raridan, Ill.
McCowen, George, Sullivan, Ill.; mustered in June 20, 1898.
Maris, George A., 32, Tuscola, Ill., Engineer.
Matthews, Riley B., 36, Arcola, Ill., Brakeman.
Miller, George W., Atwood, Ill.
Northway, John, 26, Toledo, Ill., Farmer.
Pfeifer, Lawrence L., 24, Arcola, Ill., Farmer.
Pigg, Leonard, Kemp, Ill.
Potter, Palo L., Lovington, Ill.; mustered in June 20, 1898.
Price, Thomas, 30, Arcola, Ill., Farmer.
Rhodes, James D., Plymouth, Ind.
Sandy, Charles F., 19, Sullivan, Ill., Student.
Short, Harvey A., 26, Hindsboro, Ill., Farmer.
Short, Zeddie I., Hindsboro, Ill.
Sich, Henry, 27, Garrett, Ill., Farmer.
Sipes, Fred, 21, Arcola, Ill., Plasterer.
Smith, Samuel R., 25, Arcola, Ill., Farmer.
Southard, John M., 34, Arthur, Ill., Laborer.

Strain, John A., Lovington, Ill.; mustered in June 20, 1898.
Swisher, Earnest O., Sullivan, Ill.; mustered in June 20, 1898.
Thein, John W. E., 35, Arcola, Ill., Farmer.
Thompson, Alecuph R., 21, Colony, Kans., Farmer.
Thompson, Eugene, Hawesville, Ky.; mustered in June 20, 1898.
Watts, William W., 25, Hindsboro, Ill., Farmer.
Wingate, Ernest G., Lovington, Ill.; mustered in June 20, 1898.
Wirshing, Edward A., 26, Tuscola, Ill., Wood Engraver.
Wolf, Albert J., 23, Hindsboro, Ill., Farmer.
Wood, Nicholas B., Lovington, Ill.; mustered in June 20, 1898.
Woodrow, George N., 20, Tamaroa, Ill., Farmer.
Wright, Chauncey S., Lovington, Ill.; mustered in June 20, 1898.

RESIGNATIONS.

Moore, Rice J., Second Lieutenant, 28, Arcola, Ill., Farmer; resigned November 9, 1898.

DISCHARGED FOR DISABILITY.

Matthias, Charles W., August 26, 1898.
Graham, Ernest, 24, Arcola, Ill., Farmer; discharged July 27, 1898.
Tick, Julius, 21, Lafayette, Ind., Laborer; discharged September 12, 1898.
Allen, Mark, 30, Oakland, Ill., Laborer; discharged September 17, 1898.
Bonkofski, Alex., 34, Arcola, Ill., Painter; discharged September 17, 1898.
McCarty, Thomas F., 28, Grand Rapids, Mich., Clerk; discharged December 29, 1898.

DISCHARGED BY ORDER.

Funston, Rolley E., Lovington, Ill.; mustered in June 20, 1898; discharged November 2, 1898.
Million, Andy, Lovington, Ill.; mustered in June 20, 1898; discharged December 3, 1898.
Cross, Harry E., Tuscola, Ill.; discharged December 15, 1898.
Moorehead, Jason B., 31, Tuscola, Ill., Carpenter; discharged January 10, 1899.
Parker, Chauncey J., Casey, Ill.; discharged Jan. 11, 1899.
Little, Everette A., 21, Bookkeeper; appointed Corporal June 24, 1898; discharged Jan. 17, 1899.
Carroll, Thomas, 21, Arcola, Ill., Farmer; discharged Jan. 23, 1899.
Davis, Albert D., Arcolo, Ill., 19, Student; discharged Feb. 9, 1899.
Jones, Christopher L., Clairmont, Ill., 22, Farmer; discharged Feb. 16, 1899.
Wilson, William D., Tuscola, Ill., 42, Carpenter; mustered in as Corporal, discharged June 3, 1898.
Devine, Charles F., Rantoon, Ill., 22, Cigarmaker; dishonorably discharged July 24, 1898.
Bland, Allen L., Oakland, Ill., 31, Plasterer; discharged without honor or travel pay, April 10, 1899.
Harris, Claud S., Sullivan, Ill.; mustered in June 20, 1898, discharged Feb. 24, 1899.
Roges, Clay M., Baggstown, Ind., 27, Farmer; discharged Feb. 18, 1899.

TRANSFERS.

Wilkins, John P., Arcola, Ill., Farmer; transferred June 12, 1898, to the U. S. Hospital Corps.

Gasmann, Hans, Tuscola, Ill., Baker; transferred June 12, 1898, to U. S. Hospital Corps.

Frey, Leo J., Springfield, Ill.; transferred to Regimental Band Dec. 24, 1898.

Woodman, Joy, Virden, Ill.; transferred to Regimental Band Dec. 24, 1898.

DEATHS.

Clore, Allen F., Lovington, Ill.; mustered in June 20, 1898, died Sept. 15, 1898, at Lovington, Ill.

Matters, Sid H., Arcola, Ill., Clerk; died Oct. 6, 1898 at Jacksonville, Fla.

Robertson, James W., Waterman, Ind.; died Oct. 14, 1898 at Jacksonville, Fla.

DESERTED.

Bird, Harvey D., Tuscola, Ill., 22, Carpenter; deserted July 15, 1898, returned to duty without sentence.

COMPANY E.

ALVIN C. VORIS.

Lieutenant Alvin C. Voris was born at Neoga, Illinois, January 5, 1876, where he still resides and where in the public schools he secured his early or preparatory education. In the fall of 1892, he entered the University of Illinois at Champaign, Illinois, where he spent two years, during which time, in connection with his regular University studies, he also received something of a military education.

In the fall of 1894, he entered the North Western Law School, and in the following fall, that of the Chicago College of Law, from which he graduated with the class of 1896. Entered upon the practice of law in Beaumont, Texas, during the following year, and while there was a member of the fifth regiment of Texas Guards. The late war, or Spanish-American war, breaking out while he was spending some time at his father's home in Neoga, he joined Company E, Fourth Illinois National Guards, and was mustered into the United States Volunteer service as a private, on the 20th day of May, 1898. On July 1, of the same year he was appointed corporal of Company E, and was commissioned second lieutenant of same December 8, 1898, filling this position until the Company was mustered out of the United States service. From January 20th to April 13, 1899, he filled the position of judge advocate of a general court martial.

Capt. B. E. Rudy.

HISTORY OF COMPANY E.

Company E, of Mattoon, Illinois, was organized in that city on the 12th day of March, 1891, and became a part of the Fourth Illinois National Guard. Its first commander was Emory Andrews, with Charles E. Dole, first lieutenant, and Dr. C. E. Mack, second lieutenant.

During the year 1892 Captain Andrews resigned his command, and Lieutenant Dole was commissioned to take the place thus vacated. This occasioned a vacancy in the first lieutenancy, which was filled by the commissioning of Charles Rudy. Lieutenant Swan tendered his resignation some months later, and Frank Sencebaugh was regularly put in his place. Later on Captain Dole laid aside his rank by resignation, and Lieutenant Rudy was duly qualified to assume the duties thus laid aside. Frank E. Norvell was thereupon elected to take the first lieutenancy, and in due time commissioned as such. Next in the order of changes came the resignation of Second Lieutenant Sencebaugh, which vacancy was filled by the election and commissioning of Samuel E. Owen to that rank. In 1896 Lieutenant Owen made good the record of the company by tendering his resignation, which opened the way for the election of Richard L. Wright, whose commission bears the date of July 14, 1896, only to hold the office until November, 1897, when he in turn duly tendered his resignation, and later took his place in the ranks of the retired. This checkered history began to take on a new phase of changes, when, by order from higher authority, it was recruited up to the strength of one hundred and twenty enlisted men.

Following hard upon the heels of this came the anxiously anticipated order of April 26, 1898, at 9 A. M., calling the company to join the regiment at Springfield, Illinois; and accordingly on the 27th, at 5:10 A. M., the company took leave of their friends and embarked for the state capital, where they arrived at 11:30 A. M., of the same day, and joined the other companies of the regiment in the barns on the fair grounds.

On the 10th of May, while in Camp Tanner at Springfield, the company elected Second Lieutenant Krick to the position from which Lieutenant Wright resigned, thus raising him one step in the line of promotion. A few days later the company was marched into the presence of the United States examining board of physicians in the State House and went through a careful physical examination, and out of the number, about 110, who reported for this test of fitness for further duties, only eight failed to receive the approval of the examiners. But as the company was not allowed to retain as its full strength more than 84 enlisted men and their officers, the number of qualified men had to be reduced by subtracting 28 from their number.

With these eighty-four as its composite, the company was mustered into the United States service on the 20th of May, 1898, and six days later boarded a train for the sunny South, thus ending our first brief period of camp life and drill. On the 29th we landed at Jacksonville, Florida, and were marched to our quarters in Camp Cuba Libre, in the suburb Springfield, where we found anything but an inviting spot to an Illinoisan, so thoroughly unaccustomed to such stretches of burning sand as were presented to our view in this place.

Here we, like obedient sons of our great father, Uncle Sam, entered upon a career of grubbing, ditching, filling of swamps, building of fountains, etc., etc., while the business of drilling and marching was unremittingly kept up.

During our stay in this camp the companies of the regiment were ordered to be recruited up to the quota of one hundred and six men and three officers, but by some mis-cue the specific order in reference to this company, as perhaps some others also, only called for one hundred and three enlisted men and three officers.

With this enlargement of the company, we later accompanied the regiment, to another part of Camp Cuba Libre, which we called Camp Panama, having done a good job of clearing for some land speculators at the former place, and which it seemed was to be continued in this new camp.

But whatever the plans of our "superiors" were in this respect, the rapid rise and spread of typhoid fever and other diseases held us in check from anything quite so extensive as in the former camp.

This company had its full share of this scourge, having at times thirty-five on the sick roll, not including many who were "ailing" sufficiently to scarcely be able to attend to the duties devolving upon them. Yet the prevalence of disease made it necessary to "hold down" the sick roll to a minimum, at least for appearance.

After a time of this new experience in army life it was thought best to remove the regiment from these land improvement camps, and accordingly we were transferred to the city of Jacksonville, where we entered upon the novel duties of provost guard, being located at Major Harrison's headquarters.

After a brief period of service here, in which the boys rapidly recuperated their strength, we were removed to Savannah, Georgia, where we continued on provost duty, being located at the suburb of the city called Colinsville, and were assigned the unpleasant task of guarding the street cars. And while this furnished us with plenty of car riding and pleasant diversions, it brought also enough of the opposite to beat back any monotony that might attempt to creep in, for it was not uncommon that we had to haul in the "drunks," of course from other regiments encamped without the city, and confine them in the "bull pen," where we treated them to a shower bath from the hose, a thing in many cases very essential to the health of the victim, but uncomfortable to the stray grayback that might chance to have missed his lair in the seams of clothing before the ordeal was fully on.

While at Savannah, Georgia, Lieut. Frank E. Norvell resigned, September, 1898, opening the way for the promotion of Second Lieutenant Krick to his place, and the commissioning of corporal, Alvin C. Voris, to the rank of Second Lieutenant, being commissioned to that rank December, 1898.

Our last days at Savannah, which ended January 3, were spent in Camp Onward, and on the practice march and daily drill, duties that had not troubled us while on provost duty, and which had left us somewhat rusty as to military tactics.

Sunday, January 1, 1899, will long be remembered as the day so long looked for, the day of good tidings, tidings that brought a shout of gladness which echoed out upon the still chill air of the evening. It was the news that we had almost despaired of hearing,—orders to move to Cuba. Accordingly on the 3d of this initial month, with the rest of our regiment and the Ninth Illinois Volunteers, we started on our first ocean voyage, which permitted some of us to realize what it is to have one's stomach try to find larger space by getting outside of him, nevertheless we succeeded in retaining possession of all except its contents. Our experiences being about that of our comrades in the regiment we pass over the little events leading up to our sitting up house or tent keeping in Camp Columbia near the railroad station Buena Vista.

From this beautiful camp, after thirteen days' rest and

camp duties, the third battalion, of which Company E was a factor, started on an eight-days' practice march to the interior of the island, passing over one of the beautiful military roads which was built in the days of Spain's glory, and on which doubtless no American soldier had ever before set foot. Reaching the inland city of Guines, which is the terminus of this excellent road, we went into camp and during the days of our tarrying visited the places of interest and otherwise, learning the customs and habits of this to us strange people and purchasing many articles associated with the Spanish-Cuban war, to bear home as trophies or souvenirs of this our first outing in this delightful island. After more than two days rest we retraced our steps, reach Camp Columbia on Sunday the 29th, about the same hour of our departure, 9 A. M.

On the 26th of February our company was detached from the regiment and placed on provost duty in the towns of Marianao and Quemados, at provost headquarters, where we spent forty-six days, returning to Camp Columbia on the 12th of April to find the camp broken up and all in readiness to leave for our own beloved land. Joining the rest of our battalion, we marched to the Buena Vista railroad station and took the train for Havana, where, after a march across its entire length, through the hot sun and narrow paved streets, we called a halt at San Jose docks, from which we were conveyed by United States tugs and lighters to the "scrubby" little side-wheeler Whitney, of the Plant system, and about 6 P. M. steamed out of the beautiful and famous Havana harbor for the home land. Reaching Egmont Key, some twenty-five miles out Tampa Bay from that city, we entered upon a three days quarantine, being confined in a small barbed wire enclosure of perhaps less than one acre. We put it tamely when we say we were heartily glad to see the dawn of the day in which we were to pass out from these narrow quarters and embark on the little steamer Margaret for Port Tampa. Here we were soon on board a well-equipped train of the Plant system and moving with a true American gait for our new and final camp, McKenzie, at Augusta, Ga., where we met a cheery welcome from the First and Second battalions, and with them quietly awaited the dawn of the second day of May, when Uncle Sam would give us our clearance papers, and with a few greenback thank-you's, kindly permit us to return to our homes and peaceful occupations.

This company, although it had its full share of sickness during its career as United States Volunteers, yet it was the only one in the Fourth Illinois that did not lose a man by death.

ROSTER OF COMPANY E.

RUDY, CHARLES E., 37, Captain, Mattoon, Ill., Merchant.
NORVELL, F. E., 36, First Lieutenant, Mattoon, Ill., Paperhanger.
KRICK, WM. A., 24, Second Lieutenant, Mattoon, Ill., Clerk.

SERGEANTS.

Wright, R. L., 25, Mattoon, Ill., Clerk.
Garrett, Brown J., 27, Mattoon, Ill., Clerk.
Woods, Martin D., 27, Mattoon, Ill., Brick-mason.
Beem, Arthur M., 23, Mattoon, Ill., Fireman.
Jones, Oliver O., 16, Mattoon, Ill., Student.
Smithley, Wm. A., 32, Mattoon, Ill., Brakeman.

CORPORALS.

Cox, H. M., 24, Mattoon, Ill., Salesman.
Springer, Wm. H., 21, Mattoon, Ill., Laborer.

NON-COMMISSIONED OFFICERS COMPANY E.

Henneke, Edwin C., 23, Mattoon, Ill., Farmer.
Tracy, Joseph, 26, Mattoon, Ill., Farmer.
Ewing, Charles C., 21, Neoga, Ill., Clerk.
Glascock, Jasper, 43, Mattoon, Ill., Laborer; discharged October 19, 1898.
Voris, Alvin C., 22, Neoga, Ill., Lawyer; promoted to corporal July 1, 1898, Second Lieutenant December 22, 1898.
McFadden, John A., 40, Mattoon, Ill., Clerk; made corporal July 1, 1898.
Matthews, Fred W., 18, Carlinville, Ill., Student; promoted corporal July 1, 1898, discharged December 3, 1898.
Irving, Wm., 22, Humbolt, Ill., Farmer; promoted corporal July 1, 1898.
Sullivan, Wm. W., 22, Mattoon, Ill., Farmer; made corporal July 1, 1898.
Roberts, Carlton E., 25, St Louis, Mo., Electrician; made corporal July 1, 1898.

MUSICIAN.

Baldwin, Harry O., 23, Mattoon, Ill., Clerk; mustered in as bugler.

ARTIFICER.

Keller, Edward M., 29, Neoga, Ill., Carpenter; appointed artificer July 1, 1898.

WAGONER.

Workman, John F., 29, Windsor, Ill., Butcher; mustered in as wagoner.

PRIVATES.

Albeck, Fred F., 18, Mattoon, Ill., Printer.
Aye, Charles, 21, Mattoon, Ill., Farmer; appointed corporal December 23, 1898.

Alliman, Clarence, 21, Mattoon, Ill., Harness-maker.
Athey, John, 24, Mattoon, Ill., Laborer; mustered in June 17, 1898.
Auld, Frank P., 22, Shelbyville, Ill., Teacher; mustered in June 17, 1898.
Bassett, Albert A., 18, Neoga, Ill., Laborer; transfered to band November 20, 1898.
Burnett, George W., 22, Mattoon, Ill., Fireman.
Baldwin, W. L., 32, Mattoon, Ill., Clerk.
Kenney, Wm. D., 21, Mattoon, Ill., Fireman; mustered in June 17, 1898.
Lozier, Walter W., 28, Humbolt, Ill., Farmer.
Lacy, Edwin M., 24, Neoga, Ill., Lineman; transfered to Signal Corps.
Lash, George G., 27, Windsor, Ill., Laborer.
Lichtenwalter, Joseph, 22, Shelbyville, Ill., Laborer.
Michales, John W., 42, Mattoon, Ill., Carpenter; mustered in June 17, 1898.
Maxedon, Charles E., 25, Sullivan, Ill., Coal-miner.
Melick, Edwin, 30, Humboldt, Ill., Farmer.
Melick, Amos W., 26, Humboldt, Ill., Farmer.
Moris, Frank H., 20, Lafayette, Ind., Blacksmith; promoted corporal December 23, 1898.
Montgomery, Truman, 20, Windsor, Ill., Laborer.
Moxley, Aldin H., 21, Neoga, Ill., Laborer.
Maxey, Theodore, 30, Attwood, Ill., Farmer.
Mansur, George, 29, Cincinnati, Ohio, Clerk.
Mercer, Walter T., Shelbyville, Ill., Farmer.
Needham, Leslie A., 21, Neoga, Ill., Farmer; mustered in June 17, 1898.
Newman, James H., 21, Mattoon, Ill., Laundryman, mustered in June 17, 1898.
Norwood, Harry L., 22, Boston, Mass., Baker; mustered in June 28, 1898, deserted September 20, 1898.

Osborn, Leonard A., 25, Neoga, Ill., Student.
Parker, Wm. M., 24, Charleston, Ill., Merchant; mustered in June 17, 1898.
Patheal, Wm. H., 18, Mattoon, Ill., Copper-smith; mustered in June 17, 1898.
Ross, James T., 24, Mattoon, Ill., Coachman.
Robinson, George W., 24, Mattoon, Ill., Plasterer.
Robinson, Robert, 19, Mattoon, Ill., Teamster; mustered in June 17, 1898.
Richmond, Charles F., 29, Mattoon, Ill., Clerk; mustered in June 28, 1898.
Steers, Albert, 38, Mattoon, Ill., Printer; mustered in June 17, 1898.
Stairwalt, F. B., 21, Shelbyville, Ill., Student; mustered in June 17, 1898.
Shutts, Charles H., 21, Mattoon, Ill., Railroad call boy; mustered in June 17, 1898.
Spohn, Harry C., 21, Mattoon, Ill., Book-keeper; mustered in June 17, 1898.
Smith, Oliver, 20, Jonesville, Ind., Laborer; appointed corporal December 23, 1898.
Shinn, Oliver M., 20, Mattoon, Ill., Clerk.
Beck, Curtis, 21, Neoga, Ill., Farmer.
Briggs, William B., 38, Mattoon, Ill., Blacksmith.
Boren, Guy H., 22, Milton, Ill., Undertaker.
Bowen, Clyde L., 21, Windsor, Ill., Laborer.
Bartles, Thomas J., 26, Mattoon, Ill., Laborer.
Bayne, Frank, 20, Neoga, Ill., Laborer.
Bolan, William S., 27, Gays, Ill., Carpenter; mustered in June 17, 1898.
Buchanan, William D., 28, Neoga, Ill., Fireman; mustered in June 17, 1898.
Bond, William E., 42, Mattoon, Ill., Cooper; mustered in June 17, 1898.

Coons, Leon E., 19, Mattoon, Ill., Switchman.
Cooper, Clarence E., 30, Mattoon, Ill., Engineer; mustered in June 17, 1898.
Cramer, Harry W., 20, Shelbyville, Ill., Carpenter; mustered in June 17, 1898.
Cullum, Hubert J., 21, Neoga, Ill., Tinner; discharged Dec. 19, 1898, disability.
Cox, Charles, 31, Kinmundy, Ill., Brakeman.
Cunningham, William F., 24, Mattoon, Ill., Farmer.
Davidson, William W., 21, Neoga, Ill., Laborer.
DeGarmo, Francis M., 27, Mattoon, Ill., Hostler.
Everhart, Frank D., 21, Carlinville, Ill., Laborer.
Eberhart, Frederick, 22, Neoga, Ill., Laborer.
Elliott, John E., 26, Mattoon, Ill., Jeweler; mustered in June 17, 1898.
Findley, Virgil W., 23, Mattoon, Ill., Mailcarrier; discharged March 18, 1899, disability.
Fancher, George A., 21, Neoga, Ill., Laborer; discharged March 18, 1899, disability.
Fosnock, Joseph W., 36, Mattoon, Ill., Laborer; discharged.
Fulfer, Jacob A., 30, Mattoon, Ill., Laborer.
Gibson, Albert, 26, Oleny, Ill., Laborer.
Good, Charles W., 22, Neoga, Ill., Teacher; discharged March 6, 1899.
Greenawalt, Allen L., 21, Neoga, Ill., Laborer.
Harris, Everet B., 21, Shelbyville, Ill., Laborer.
Hall, Hiram V., 20, Mattoon, Ill., Laborer.
Husband, Thomas E., 19, Neoga, Ill., Laborer; mustered in June 17, 1898.
Howk, George F., 21, Neoga, Ill., Printer.
Jones, Joseph B., 35, Mattoon, Ill., Cabinetmaker; mustered in June 17, 1898.

Keller, Wade, 21, Mattoon, Ill., Machinist; mustered in June 17, 1898.
Keller, Walter C., Neoga, Ill., Laborer, mustered in June 17, 1898.
Strawn, Joseph, 24, Mattoon, Ill., Farmer.
Sackville, Louis T., 21, Mattoon, Ill., Farmer.
Seaman, Thomas M., 31, Toledo, Ill., Farmer.
Summerlin, Iran, 39, Mattoon, Ill., Printer.
Sparks, George S., 33, Hillsboro, Ohio, Laborer.
Tarpley, Joseph P., 24, Oleny, Ill., Laborer.
Tucker, William I., 32, Detroit, Mich., Clerk; discharged Dec. 25, 1898, disability.
Volaw, Alvin C., 21, Neoga, Ill., Farmer.
Welsh, Martin, 24, Mattoon, Ill., Clerk.
Elyu, Regan, 20, Shelbyville, Ill., Laborer; transferred to Hospital Corps.
Cullum, A. L., 25, Neoga, Ill., Pharmacist; transferred to Hospital Corps.
Dibble, Allen P., Mattoon, Ill.

In all cases not otherwise mentioned, mustered in May 20, 1898, and mustered out on May 2, 1899, at Augusta, Georgia.

THE REGIMENT.

While the history of this regiment, like that of most of of its companions, dates back in its organization several years earlier than its enrollment as a part of the United States forces, which were called out on account of the insulting and encroaching attitude of our sister nation, Spain; yet we do not propose to enter into that part of its career, only as it incidently relates to that of its history as a United States Volunteer regiment.

We also deem it wise, as far as clearness will admit, to avoid any repetition of that which pertains wholly, or in part, to any particular company, yet not forgetting the very potent fact that these lesser organizations are a part of and so closely related to the regiment, as to make their every act a part of its history, however remote the connection may seem.

The composite of this regiment is of the young blood and sturdy manhood of central Illinois, coming from the fields of her thrifty farmers, the shops, stores and offices of her provident towns, with no small sprinkling from the professional ranks.

The initial, therefore, of the present organization as a regiment, was the assembling of the several companies of the national guards at Springfield, Illinois, in answer to an order from Gov. John R. Tanner, issued on the 25th of April, 1898, which assembling was accomplished within the brief space of forty-eight hours. Headquarters were established in one of the barns of the fair grounds, with Col. John B. Washburn in command, while the companies were located in other barns in close proximity thereto. Scarcely had the camp been established, when it became very apparent that there was friction somewhere near the center of power, and in a few days, Colonel Washburn tendered his resignation (a variety of reason therefor gaining publicity), which was promptly accepted by the governor, and on the 19th day of May, 1898, Casimir Andel, of Belleville, was commissioned by the governor to take the place thus vacated. But a few days elapsed before Colonel Andel reported and at once assumed the duties made incumbent upon him in his new relation to the regiment.

Time hung heavily on our hands during the weeks that intervened before the time for our examination arrived. But it came, freighted with many disappointments and surprises; for the big, muscular fellow that always had things largely his own way about the village, could not understand why he was not permitted to go farther than the first physician, who turned him back to readjust his wardrobe, leaving him in blissful ignorance as to a serious lack of lung power. Not less puzzled was the fellow whose chest would expand like a poucher pigeon, when he stood before the last examiner, who kindly passed him on to join the civilian host of his native land, to learn later the serious defects in the great engine of his physical being, which, so far as he knew, had never made a mistroke. But the surprise came to on-looking comrades when the fellow with all the brawn necessary to endure the hardships of the farm, or tramp the weary miles with a full hunter's equipment strapped about him, claimed he was sorely afflicted with about all the ills flesh is heir to, and moved away from the examiner with a slight hitch in his gait and a solemn look on his face.

But this part of the programme was not without its touching scenes—when those with buoyant hope and strong desire to attend their comrades still farther in the experiences of the soldier were seen to turn away and weep because they were rejected.

All these preliminaries being disposed of, then came the work of uniforming the men—a thing very much needed in many cases, as the men had come to camp poorly clad, anticipating an early issue from Uncle Sam's store house, which was not fully realized, doubtless owing to the great demand made upon the quartermaster's department in fitting out the vast number of men that were needed immediately at the front, with but a very brief time in which to do it.

Added to this shortage was that of blankets, a need keenly felt at this season of the year, even though quartered in the commodious, well-arranged barns on the fair grounds. For even here we had no little experience in the hardships that fall to the soldier's lot, growing out of rainy weather and chilly atmosphere that seemed to find the very marrow of our bones, giving the old-fashioned ague shake to our chins, while our nerves fairly crept, as if seeking a secure retreat from this searching element of the north pole. But with all this, our condition and that of some others was far superior to what some companies experienced who were located on low ground, which was soon flooded by the heavy rains that visited our state during the month of May, while instead of barns, their shelter was the common tent.

But these discomforts of our regiment were not permitted to continue long, for no sooner was the fact known to our friends in their comfortable homes, from which we had so recently gone out, than thoughtful loving hearts began to plan, while strong hands, flush purses and well filled bedbing closets were brought into requisition, and soon large boxes of the needed articles came rolling into our quarters.

We may note in a passing way, that one of the causes incident to these discomforts, was the fact that some companies, anticipating a large falling off under government examination, had before leaving for camp, recruited their companies above the proper quota, increasing the number anticipated when preparations for their comfort were being made by the quartermaster's department.

Along with these conditions, so undesirable, came another trial that tests the metal of which a fellow is made, especially in the region of his appetite, viz: the dire want of those palatable delicacies that crowned the table in a goodly number of our homes; the very thought of which awoke the glands in proximity to our masticating machinery to a provoking activity, which in earlier years was, in common parlance known as " making the teeth water." Nor would it stop with this encroachment upon us in our waking hours, but intruded itself into the " half-fed " soldier's peaceful slumber on the "soft side" of the loft floor, or his downy bed of clay in the stall of some thoroughbred of the bovine family. But betimes the home friends would break this spell of woes by "dropping in upon us," with well laden baskets of the very article that would answer our dreams, and gratify our appetites.

If space would admit, we would like very much to give more than a mere passing mention of other severe trials, as that of the heart pangs caused by recalling the smiles and glances of the fair one whose affection had not perhaps quite reached the point of cohesion, and might be won by the other fellow whose patriotism was still a dormant quantity. But fortunately for the regiment, the number of this class was small.

Thus all and in all there was an evening up of these ills and joys, until later on the overdrawn stores of Uncle Sam's quartermaster's department were sufficiently replenished to enable us to exchange the little that remained of our wardrobes, for the others that made us presentable, either side foremost.

So likewise, in due time, the ordnance stores were opened, and the new recruits were equipped with Springfield rifles and other accoutrements necessary to give him the appearance of a soldier and fit him for practical drills and impressive dress parades, both of which were relentlessly kept up until the day we struck our tents in Camp Tanner and boarded the train for new scenes and a less monotonous career.

While we would not attempt to create the impression that the weeks spent in this camp were not devoted to such duties as were thought to be necessary to the fitness of the troops for more arduous and trying service, which seemed to be at no great distance in the future,—duties to which the men submitted themselves with becoming patience and zeal, being stimulated by the thrilling reports of the before unheard-of victories over the enemy by our marine forces—still, considering the inexperience and unhardened condition of the men, these first weeks of camp life were perhaps as keenly felt as any in the entire history of the regiment.

Once upon a time, as the story goes, while one of the sentinels of this regiment was faithfully performing his duty on one of the guard posts during the somber shades of night, his attention was arrested by approaching footfalls, and called out: "Halt! who comes there?" Just then the approaching object accidentally stumbled, and proceeded to express his disapproval of such awkwardness, or something else, before answering the guard, and in no unsubdued tone he exclaimed (pronouncing the sacred name of our Saviour), whereupon the guard sang out: "Call out the Chaplain." Of course, such a personage would find ready access through our lines, especially where one of such pious thoughts walked the post.

On the 25th of May, about 8 o'clock P. M., orders were received directing the colonel to report with his command at Tampa, Fla., immediately, and on the following day we had our first experience in packing our outfits and getting ready for a move—a task of no extraordinary character, as we had little more than the clothes we wore and our blankets.

Moving out to the railroad on the morning of the 26th of May we entered a train of well fitted cars, which was divided into three sections, where we waited with more or less patience for the moving of wheels, until the hours of the afternoon grew very narrow, when we pulled out of the capital city and hastened toward the land of sunshine, meeting with ovations all along the route, but especially after we reached the southern states, where the far-famed hospitality of these people was realized in a way not soon to be forgotten by the boys who appreciated their palatable dainties.

While enroute to the point of our destination, on the 28th of May, Colonel Andel received telegraphic orders from the war department, to report to the commanding officers of the United States forces at Jacksonville, Florida, which he proceeded to do by turning our train from its proposed route toward the last named place, where we arrived about 2 o'clock A. M. Sunday, the 29th. This brought us into the Seventh Army Corps, where we were assigned to the Second Division commanded by Brigadier Gen. A. K. Arnold, and the Second Brigade under command of Col. D. V. Jackson, Fiftieth Iowa Volunteer Infantry.

On June 13, 1898, Brig.-Gen. W. A. Bancroft reported to the commander of the Seventh Army Corps, and was assigned command on the Second Brigade, relieving Colonel Jackson.

On the 5th of August the regiment was transferred from the Second Division, Second Brigade, to the Third Division under Brig.-Gen. Lucius F. Hubbard and the Second Brigade under Brig.-Gen. James H. Barkley.

On the 29th and 30th of September and the 1st of October, the regiment was detailed by companies to do provost duty in Jacksonville, Florida, and ordered to report to Provost Marshal Major Russel B. Harrison. The regiment continued on provost duty during its stay in this locality, and during which time, on the re-organization of the Corps, it was transferred to the First Division under command of Maj.-Gen. J. Warren Keifer, and to the Second Brigade under command of Brig.-Gen. H. T. Douglas. While all this was going on in camp "Cuba Libre," the Fourth was having experiences not any more pleasant in its new quarters into which they had just moved. But their condition was very much improved by the kindly hospitality of the citizens of Jacksonville, and vacant buildings which we did not hesitate to occupy even without an invitation. Still it must not be inferred, that with all these advantages our lot was one to be desired or highly enjoyed.

We here diverge to give place to events touching the division. Along with all the other ills met with in Camp Cuba Libre was the storm of October 2. The day preceding was one somewhat ominous of storm, yet not enough so to have awakened any thought of an unusual occurrence, but the wildest midnight dream was to be realized in a few hours, for scarce had they pillowed their heads on pillowless cots, when the storm that had been hatching from the serpent's egg in the sea, burst in upon them in its fury, while the rain fell in sheets rather than drops, beating through our time-worn or otherwise non-rainproof tents.

Not only did the howling of the wind and cracking of the canvas bid successful defiance to the god of slumber and sweet dreams, but we awoke more fully to the fact that danger was upon us, and soon there was a stir in camp, and the sound of hammers evidenced that tent pegs were receiving attention, while voices, keyed well up in "G," told of the fruitlessness of all such efforts in this region of sand. Toward the dawn of day the storm began to assuage, and the early day, found about all out trying to learn who, if any, had met with more trouble and loss than they, for in the contest some of them had lost more than their hats through the collapse of their tents. But while consoling ourselves that the worst was over and that so little damage had been done, as though it had been hiding in some quiet nook noting the varied comments on its very recent visit and inability, until whet into a rage, it rushed upon us afresh, and with such increased fury as to put to shame the blow and rain torrents of the past night. Not only did it moan, but shrieked and howled among the pines, prostrating the weaker ones and compelling others to bow and kiss the earth with their topmost boughs, while only those sturdy from age were able to maintain anything near an upright posture.

The experiences of the night were but a foretaste of what each rapidly recurring blast now told us was at hand. Tents succumbed and went down in rapid succession, and the belongings of their occupants were scattered and drenched by the heavy fall of rain, necessitating prompt and vigorous effort to keep them in camp. The Third Division Hospital was feeling the weight of it, and the few who had rushed to its protection, proving insufficient for the task, General Barclay came to the rescue, not only putting forth his personal effort, but also urging others to come to the help of those who were battling with disease.

Poles were carried and laid on the lower edge of the sidewalls and men stood upon them as weights. Athletes climbed to the top and sat astride the ridge poles, others tugged at the ropes that had drawn their pegs, while within the nurses and others held blankets and other articles over the sick to shelter them from the rain that beat like mist through the canvas roofs above them. It was by such heroic efforts, in which none felt too high to lend a

STORM SCENE AT 3D DIVISION HOSPITAL.

strong helping hand, that the entire line of hospital tents were not demolished and the sick left to the mercy of an almost unmerciful storm.

On the 20th of October, the regiment was removed to the city of Savannah, Georgia, in advance of the Seventh Army Corps, where it continued to do provost service until the 4th and 5th of December, when it was ordered to quarters in Camp Onward, at the southeast part of the city of Savannah.

After outlining these changes, we return to take up other phases of the history of the regiment, pertaining to its stay in the vicinity of Jacksonville and Savannah. Having, as before stated, reached Jacksonville, Florida, in early morning of May 29, we remained on board the train until daylight, taking our breakfast before disembarking.

Having marched some two and a half or three miles, we found ourselves in a suburban district of the city, called Springfield, where our quarters in the great camp "Cuba Libre" were located, and which we named Camp Springfield, as it so well fitted the name of the capital city of our state.

Our camp site evidently was selected during the dry season of the year, since there is a wet season here as we learned from experience later.

The site was a level sandy stretch of country with nothing inviting about it, at least to an Illinoisan, so accustomed to the clay soil and its luxuriant growth of his own state.

Still this camp was not entirely void of vegetation, being overgrown to a great extent with dwarfed pine and palmetto (for the heat and rain here would dwarf anything but sand burrs and graybacks), which furnished very little shade and much discomfort. Thus our initiation was anything but that which tends to awaken admiration, since our arrival was welcomed by a blistering hot sun, that heated the sand almost to the burning point during the middle of the day, while that which was expected to furnish us shelter therefrom was scarcely more than a mockery as a shade; for these little sand pines are simply crowned with a small tuft or crest of needle like leaves. On the other hand the palmetto plants had to be cut away or dug up in order to secure a spot large enough on which to lie down with comfort.

Having come into camp in the forenoon, the heat continued to intensify, driving us to every imaginable device for protection. One of the simplest and most effective used in some parts of camp, being constructed by planting four of our guns with bayonets attached, points downward, forming a square, and then stretched a blanket over them attaching each corner to a gun, and propping the center with another gun. This formed an excellent protection from the sun's rays over a small space, but not from the wind, made unusually hot by its passage over the burning sand. But as the day wore on tentage was brought to camp, and with eagerness we moved to the pitching of the same.

Once settled, the grubbing, ditching, bridge building and other like duties attending the clearing and beautifying of a new country were entered into in a systematic and general way to the utilizing of about every enlisted man in the regiment, giving to our regiment the name of "The Florida Land Improvement Company."

While here mails reached the camp something after the olden time style of private conveyance. Nor was there danger of having to leave any of it in keeping of the city office for want of sufficient capacity to bring it to camp, however prolific our friends might be with the quill, fertile brain and loving hearts, as a picture of one of the "cannon ball" mail wagons will illustrate.

It was here and at such service, often wading slush and water several inches deep in order to accomplish it, we prepared the soil and planted many and deep the seeds that yielded to us so bountifully the harvest of disease and death which we gathered in the camp at Panama Park, to which we were removed; but not until it would have been apparent to either "half of a natural born fool cut in two in the middle" that nothing could ever redeem that sand swamp.

Although mud was a thing never seen here, however much rain visited the country, to have entertained the idea that we would ever be disturbed by this element would have been thought an indication of approaching insanity. But these delusions, as they proved, were completely swept away by the rainy season, which stole gently upon us about

FAST MAIL.

July, and for several weeks the rains were a daily occurrence, and the gentle shower became a torrent that filled every low place in the camp, until some of the companies had to build bridges to get from one part of the camp to another, while they were often necessitated to wade from place to place, in protecting their tents and belongings, in water from six inches to two feet deep. Among those who met with these difficulties to the greatest extent were Company B and those of the Third Battalion—the last three or four squads nearest the mess tents having to wade in and elevate their tent floors on piles or stakes and "walk the water" on going to their meals, while the frogs sang their lullaby under the tent floors to sooth the minds of the sleepers above.

Added to all this was the fact that our tents, which

CORDUROY BRIDGE.

were made of material little better than common shirting, were almost no protection from the torrents of water that fell upon them, so that our ponchos had to be used as the top cover of our beds.

Such were the conditions existing in our camp on entering the sunny south, and from which we were transferred to Panama Park, still in the limits of Camp Cuba Libre, but some three miles from our Springfield camp. It was here the effects of the former camp conditions and life showed themselves in the sickness that so rapidly reduced the men of the regiment able for duty, to less than one-fourth its regular strength, while hospitals and hospital forces were taxed to their utmost capacity.

SCENE IN PANAMA PARK.

As a pen picture cannot present these things in anything near their reality, we forego a further delineation, leaving it to a vivid imagination to paint it, with no fear of its being overdone.

During the early part of June an order from the war department directed that all volunteer regiments be recruited up to the regular quota of one hundred and three

COMPANY STREET IN CAMP CUBA LIBRE.

enlisted men, which gave to each company of our regiment, with one or two exceptions, an addition of nineteen. Accordingly, officers were duly appointed and sent into the localities from which the companies came, and in due time the requisite number was secured, examined, mustered in, and sent forward to join the regiment, where they were assigned to their respective companies, thus increasing the regiment to over twelve hundred men. This called for an additional drilling, of which we all thought there had been enough before. Aside from drill, dress parade, guard mount, guard duty and review, we had another duty, designated "fatigue duty," and comprehended about everything else required of a soldier. Nor was it necessarily such duty only as is imposed in the line of punishment, but

BREAKING CAMP AT CAMP CUBA LIBRE.

for which any soldier may be detailed. Our illustration shows part of a line of such detail carrying lumber for the erection of "mess shacks" and tent floors, during the stay at Camp Cuba Libre.

This camp has been called also the "drill grounds" of the Seventh Army Corps, and certainly the Fourth has no reason to complain because of a lack of this kind of seasoning in its military pie, any more than that of fatigue duty.

Battle tactics were something into which variety entered almost without end, from the simplest movements that at first tangled the feet of a "tenderfoot," as well as his head, to the more complicated battle manœuvers, which

FATIGUE DUTY.

our boys had no opportunity of proving as to their value in the hour for which they were designed.

Marches were another phase of exercise in this camp, designed to toughen the muscle, and to give one "wind" for the toilsome march following up fleeing Spaniards.

The reader can here look upon a company ready for such a "hip."

There were some things not necessarily connected with what constituted a high proficiency in ordinary drill or battle tactics, yet extremely pleasurable to all who took part in it, except the other fellow who was sent on short but rapid marches toward the moon.

This blanket drill was a very common thing in some localities in camp, even going to the extent of drafting a negro woman into the least desirable part of it.

The accompanying cut is from a snap-shot taken in an adjoining regiment, and in which an old darky figures prominently in the ascending act. Still with all the real pleasure connected with it, our boys never indulged in it,

SKIRMISH DRILL, CAMP CUBA LIBRE.

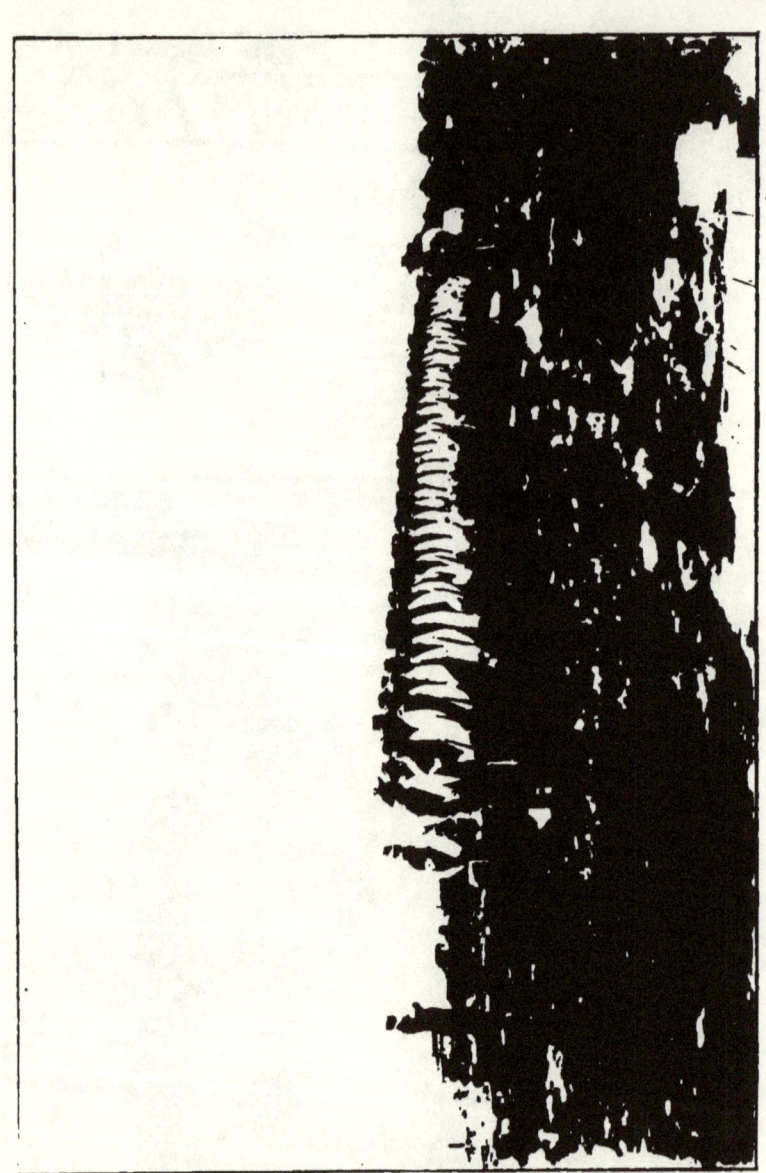

READY FOR THE MARCH.

except as a remedial exercise, *i. e.*, when the important party in the transaction was "liver grown" or something of that sort.

Along with the very undesirable conditions growing out of the ill health of the regiment at this time, came that of unharmonious feelings and conditions among certain officials, which at times seemed to threaten the existence of the organization. But not desiring to impose a personal opinion as to the causes leading to the merits in the case, neither as to the proceedings or finding of the court—much less to attempt the settling of blame where it justly belongs, or cast reflections on any one directly or indirectly concerned, we shall content ourselves with simply giving the facts as we have been able to gather them from records accessible at this time.

On the 25th day of August, 1898, officers' call was

sounded summoning them to headquarters where they were interrogated by the Colonel as to the correctness of certain reports that had become current through the daily press of the country. Being informed by Major Elliott as to the correctness of the same, the colonel thereupon read an order placing Lieut.-Col. S. A. D. McWilliams, Maj. L. E. Bennett, Maj. E. J. Lang and Maj. E. E. Elliott in arrest. But owing to the fact that Lieutenant-Colonel McWilliams was on duty as inspector of the Third Division Seventh Army Corps, under command of Brig.-Gen. Lucius F. Hubbard, he was not technically at any time in arrest. Major Bennett being field officer of the day for the Third Division Seventh Army Corps, and Major Lang being at the same time field officer for the Second Brigade of the Third Division Seventh Army Corps, were exempt from the order of arrest until relieved from their respective duties on the following day, August 26th. The foregoing arrests being made on special order from Colonel Andel's headquarters, and those in arrest were kept in close confinement in their respective tents until September 2nd, when Major Elliott was released and charges preferred against Major Bennett, Major Lang and Lieutenant-Colonel McWilliams. The general charge preferred against those accused was, "conduct unbecoming an officer and gentleman in violation of the sixty-first article of war;" while the specifications were substantially as follows: "That these officers joined in sending a telegram to Gov. John R. Tanner, of Illinois, in which the statement was made that a very large percentage of the members of the regiment were in favor of going to Cuba, and asking the Governor to use his influence to that end."

In addition to the above, Major Bennett was also charged " With conduct to the prejudice of good order and military discipline, in violation of the Sixty-second Article of War;" the specification being, substantially, that Major Bennett had called upon General Lee and General Barclay without permission being first had from Col. Casimer Andel.

Also this additional general charge was made against Lieutenant-Colonel McWilliams, viz.: "Conduct unbecoming an officer and gentleman, in violation of the Sixty-first Article of War." Specifications under this charge were substantially as follows:

FIRST SPECIFICATION.

Disobedience to orders, in that Lieutenant-Colonel McWilliams did leave camp one night when he had been left in command of the regiment by Colonel Andel.

SECOND SPECIFICATION.

That Lieutenant-Colonel McWilliams did not report for duty to Colonel Andel when he (McWilliams) was relieved from duty as provost marshal of the Second Division of the Seventh Army Corps.

On September 12 counter charges were preferred against Col. Casimer Andel by Lieutenant-Colonel McWilliams, as follows:

FIRST CHARGE.

The first general charge was, "Incompetency to command and ignorance of military matters, usages and forms, to the prejudice of good order and military discipline, in violation of the Sixty-second Article of War."

The specifications under the charge were substantially as follows:

1, Col. Casimer Andel, while in command of his regiment at Springfield, Illinois, did cause his regiment to form in columns of two's, and commanded substantially as follows: "On right and left, go each way, march!"

SECOND SPECIFICATION.

"That Colonel Andel did on various occasions, being prepared to pass in review and being in line of masses, did give the command change direction by the right flank."

THIRD SPECIFICATION.

"That on many occassions he did halt the regiment and ask his subordinate officers the necessary commands to manoeuver the regiment into such positions intended."

FOURTH SPECIFICATION.

"That Colonel Andel, on or about May 20, 1898, said of Company K, of the regiment, that he would rather it would not be mustered into the United States service; that he could furnish a company from Belleville in twelve days to take its place. That it was not necessary for officers to be acquainted with drill regulations to command troops."

FIFTH SPECIFICATION.

"That Colonel Andel said to Captain Courtney, of Company M, substantially that if Lieutenant-Colonel McWilliams, Majors Bennett, Lang and Elliott wanted to go to Cuba they would go without their arms."

SIXTH SPECIFICATION.

"That Colonel Andel permitted private, afterward Sergeant Ropiequet, to sign his official signature, to-wit: 'Casimer Andel, commanding Fourth Illinois Volunteer Infantry,' to official papers to superior officers."

SEVENTH SPECIFICATION.

"That Colonel Andel established a regimental bakery and detailed enlisted men with more or less experience as bakers, and promised such enlisted men that he would cause one hundred loaves of bread to be issued to each company for each one hundred pounds of flour from the company's ration, the surplus flour to go to the said bakers as extra pay. This said extra flour was stopped in a few days by the colonel, who ordered that such extra flour should be baked into pies, rolls, buns and other healthful breadstuffs which should be sold to any person wanting the same, provided the purchaser paid for the same with canteen checks only; turning the surplus, if any, after paying the expense of the baking, into a common fund, which was to be distributed to the company fund. This was not followed out, and the bakers sold and delivered bread to any person wanting the same, for legal tender money, from any bread on hand, whether the companies had drawn their full amount or not, all with the full consent of the colonel."

SECOND CHARGE.

"Conduct unbecoming an officer and gentleman, in violation of the sixty-first article of war."

FIRST SPECIFICATION.

"That Colonel Andel did, on many occasions in August and September, sign certificates to requisitions for fuel, forage, straw and illuminating supplies, in words as follows: 'I certify that the above requisition is correct and just; that the articles required have not been previously drawn for any part of the time above charged; and that the private animals for which forage is required, are actually owned and kept by the officers of my command in the performance of official military duties, being on duty with troops in the field or military post or station.' Which certicate is false, in that it made requisition for one private horse owned by Chaplain H. W. Todd, when said H. W. Todd did not own a horse in the United States service."

A general court martial was convened pursuant to the following order at 9 A. M., September 15, 1898, to try these case above cited, and such other matters as should come before them.

HEADQUARTERS SEVENTH ARMY CORPS,
CAMP "CUBA LIBRE,"
JACKSONVILLE, FLORIDA, SEPT. 13, 1898.

Special Order No. 99. — EXTRACT —

Par 5. A general court martial is hereby appointed to meet at this camp at 10 o'clock A. M., on Thursday, September 15, 1898, or as soon thereafter as practicable, for the trial of Majors Edward J. Lang and L. E. Bennett, Fourth Illinois Volunteer Infantry, and such other persons as may be properly brought before it.

DETAIL FOR THE COURT.

Brig.-Gen. Henry C. Hasbruck, United States Volunteers.
Brig-Gen. Lloyd Wheaton, United States Volunteers.
Brig.-Gen. H. T. Douglas, United States Volunteers.
Col. W. H. Mabry, First Texas Volunteer Infantry.
Col. James S. Pettit, Fourth United States Volunteers.
Lieut.-Col. Calvin D. Cowles, First North Carolina.
Lieut.-Col. Curtis Guild, Jr., Inspector-General United States Volunteers.

Capt. Henry A. Wise, Fourth United States Volunteer Infantry, Judge Advocate.

A greater number of officers than these named cannot be assembled without manifest injury to the service.

By command of

MAJOR-GENERAL LEE.

R. E. L. MICHIE, Assistant Adjutant-General.

This was the only court convened by corps order from corps headquarters, all other cases having been tried by courts convened by order from division headquarters.

Capt. Joseph P. Barricklow and Capt. E. Wood Hersh, Fourth Illinois Volunteers, were introduced as counsel for the accused.

Maj. L. E. Bennett was brought to trial September 15, 1898.

Maj. E. J. Lang was brought to trial September 19.

Lieut.-Col. S. A. D. McWilliams was brought to trial September 21.

The findings of the court in the several cases were as follows:

Major Bennett, to charge under the sixty-first article of war—Not guilty. To charge under the sixty-second article of war—Guilty, and sentenced to be reprimanded.

Major Lang, to all charges—Not guilty.

Lieutenant-Colonel McWilliams, to all charges—Not guilty.

On the 23d of September Col. Casimer Andel was brought to trial on the charges and specifications that were lodged against him.

Attorney Gustavus A. Koerner, of Belleville, Illinois, was introduced as counsel for the accused.

The findings of the court in the case were as follows:

Under Charge 1, not guilty; but under Specification

2, guilty, to which he pleaded guilty. Under 3d Specification, guilty, but attaching no criminality. Under 4th Specification, not guilty. Under 5th Specification, guilty, but attaching no criminality. Under 6th Specification, not guilty. Under 7th Specification, not guilty.

Under Charge 2nd, not guilty; but guilty of conduct to the prejudice of good order and military discipline, in violation of the sixty-second article of war. Under 1st Specification, guilty, excepting the word "false," substituting therefor the words "carelessly made;" and of the excepted words "not guilty," and of the substituted word "guilty."

SENTENCE IMPOSED.

Maj.-Gen. J. Warren Keifer, in command of the First Division of the Seventh Army Corps, being in command during the temporary absence of Maj.-Gen. Fitzhugh Lee, in reviewing the findings of the court martial, stated: "The proceedings, findings and sentence of the court are approved, and the sentence will be executed. Col. Casimer Andel is therefore suspended from the rank and command as an officer in the Volunteer Army of the United States for the period of six months, from this date, and he will forfeit to the United States one-half of his pay as an officer for the same period of time. Col. Casimer Andel is released from arrest."

Major Bennett having been found guilty and sentenced to be reprimanded, the reviewing authority said: "In administering this reprimand, the Major-General commanding reminds Major Bennett, that the sentence of the court is light, considering the gravity of the offense; and the sentence can be justified only on the ground that his conduct was mitigated by unusual circumstances. Major Bennett is, however, further reminded, that an officer honors his high character by good conduct at all times, regardless of conditions and circumstances surrounding. Major Bennett is released from arrest and will return to duty."

APPEAL OF COLONEL ANDEL.

Colonel Andel through his attorney carried his case before the President of the United States, who caused a special order from the War Department to issue rescinding the findings of the court martial and restoring Colonel Andel to duty.

The Colonel held his commission until November 17, 1898, when he resigned, returning to his duties in connection with the First National Bank of Belleville, Illinois.

Eben Swift, captain of the Fifth United States Cavalry, then lieutenant-colonel of the Ninth Illinois Volunteer Infantry, was commissioned to fill the vacancy, and at once entered upon the duties of this higher position, taking command of the regiment at Savannah, Georgia, from which place he led it into the island of Cuba as part of the army of occupation.

Provost duty in the city of Savannah having been turned over to others and the Fourth having had a month of camp life, they hailed with joy and no little demonstration the order that reached camp and was delivered to the staff and line officers by Colonel Swift in his quarters at 8:30 P. M. on the initial day of the year 1899, directing that this regiment prepare to load baggage on the following day and to break camp and embark on the transport "Mobile," Tuesday morning.

The long cherished desire to enter the land of conflict having thus so nearly reached its realization, gave new life to the men, and on the morrow there seemed little if any need of orders, except for details, as every soldier seemed ready to do his whole duty in the work of packing and loading the effects of the different companies, as if to hasten the time for departure.

But it remained for Tuesday to develop the true eloquence of the "camp yell," which came at the "first call" of the bugle sounding out on the crisp winter air of Georgia, long before the dawn of day.

It was a call to every man able for duty, and under the circumstances, few were otherwise, to pack his knapsack and other personal belongings, and be ready for a hasty breakfast of "army rations," praparatory to the march to the river docks.

About 7 A. M. the companies lined up in heavy marching order and turned their backs upon their tent homes, which were to be left behind, to bid them a final farewell as their feet began to mark time to the music of the band in a march which led through the streets of this beautiful Southern city, in which they had won a high reputation as provost guards, as well as the respect and esteem of the better classes, who were in no wise stint in their praise, as well as expressions of regret at their departure.

It was the privilege of the writer to meet a goodly number of the business men of the city without disclosing his relation to the regiment, and in all cases they spoke in highest praise of the regiment for the service it rendered in unison with their police force in maintaining order in their city. So persistent were their pleas for the retention of the Fourth as guards of the city, that a lengthy petition was presented to Maj. R. B. Harrison, praying him to countermand the order relieving them therefrom.

But with all this, the time had come for the Fourth to take its departure from the city: a brief stay in Camp Onward having been thought best prior to their departure for Cuba.

But the time having arrived for their final leave of the camp and the city, they did it in a most commendable way, marching through the streets in an orderly, soldierly manner, reaching the wharf about 9 A. M., and were soon

GOING ON BOARD THE MOBILE.

wending their way up the narrow gang plank and entering the hull of the great transportation ship "Mobile," on which the Ninth Illinois Volunteer Infantry had embarked the day previous and awaited our arrival.

While this mighty mansion of the ocean was once a cattle ship plying between England and the United States, her reconstruction has so completely transformed her interior and to some extent her exterior, as to cause the loss of identity, so we have been told. Her dimensions can be best comprehended when we consider that upon this trip she carried two entire regiments with tentage, baggage and officers' horses and the necessary forage therefor, besides a cargo of iron for ballast; she is virtually a five-story structure, with bunks sufficient to accommodate all she took on board: while it may be said that her deck room was not adequate to give the men that elbow room during the day they so much desired. But this congested condition of the decks was soon relieved when we got out to open sea, by the light-headed boys seeking their berths below.

MOBILE OFF FOR CUBA.

It was 11:30 when this great ship loosed her moorings and slowly swung off from the dock, in answer to the line from a tug that gradually tightened as its whirling wheel set the river in commotion: while an overfull comrade ran along the dock shouting at the top of his voice, and waving his arms frantcially, hoping to induce the captain to halt, and push his little boat ashore for the accommodation of one who had allowed his appetite to get the mastery of his mind. But to his dismay he discovered that although large bodies move slowly, they do not stop easily or quickly. Our passage down the river was one continuous ovation, as the people lined the docks, the banks of the river and filled the balconies, doors and windows of shops and factories, waving handkerchiefs, hats and "Old Glory," while they shouted their good-byes.

About twenty miles brought us into the blue sea where for the first time opened to the view of most of the boys from the prairie state, the grandeur of the old ocean's expanse. Here our river pilot and the little tug took their leave, and the massive machinery of the great engine, hid away in the inner chambers of our floating house began to move and soon the peculiar tremble, so well known to every sea fare:, was felt from bow to stern, as the stately ship plowed the deep under the pressure of her own giant engines.

The trip was one of no significant occurrence, except a dense fog that settled on us a few miles out, and which led to repeated soundings of the great fog-horn whistle, the loud, hoarse, mournful tone of which almost sent a chill through the frame of a sturdy soldier, while the prevalence of that unpleasant accompaniment called "sea sickness" made a goodly number feel like taking their departure to some more desirable place, as it twisted them into laughable contortions of body, making heavy claims on their breakfast if not the supper of the previous evening, while their more favored comrades consoled them with the fact that it was not fatal, but rather a normal health-producing process.

On the third day of our voyage, about 11 A. M., we

sighted the land of our destination, and soon her beautiful hills and valleys, covered with rich verdure, became quite visible, and the distinct outline of the stately royal palm came gradually into view, producing a picture to the eye, of one just from the frozen north, that would not be easily forgotten. But the burden of desire seemed to be a view of old Morro on his high uplifted rock bed, at the entrance to Havana harbor.

But this desire was not realized until afternoon. As we moved in a westerly direction toward the bay, we sighted the light-house which towers many feet above the battlements on the walls of this grim old fort.

Cabannas also stood out in all her defiant glory, and as we neared them the mouths of their large guns gaped at us, but rather in amazement than with unfriendly mien. Near 2 o'clock we stood off the mouth of the bay, where the quaint old buildings of the city, smaller forts beyond the entrance, and the ancient-styled boats with their jabbering crews, all joined in the formation of a scene of antique grandeur, beyond the ability of my pen to picture, and which only increased as its larger dimensions came in view while we slowly steamed up the bay, until it formed a bewildering panorama as the eye ran the entire circle of the shore, clad with structures of every seeming ancient type, from the thatched cabin of the poor to the stately mansion and warehouse.

Thus we entered the rockbound, fortress-crowned gateway, to the capital of this famous island; just one year later, and about the same hour of the day, when that majestic ship of our navy, the Maine, moved quietly and peacefully through the same channel, never to move out again with her noble crew.

Very impressive was this coincidence on the minds of many of our own and the companion regiment on our boat,

WRECK OF THE MAINE.

the Ninth Illinois. But to the novice not only do these scenes of the city attract the eye, but also the line of hills that gradually rise from the plain which entirely surrounds the city and bay (except a few valleys) on whose crests the frowning fort, blockhouse, or barbed wire trocha is seen at short distances from each other, telling to the thoughtful mind the fact that this, the capital of the once cherished isle of Spain, was prepared to defend herself against an equal foe for no short length of time. The bay itself, practically land-locked, is a stronghold of nature's own forming, while upon its bosom are seen ships flying the flags of many nations, as well as some of our own bulldogs of war and merchantmen, while near us, almost buried in the murky, filthy waters of this bay, lie the remains of the ill-fated Maine, upon which, as we gaze, the thought of the terrible wholesale murder committed in her destruction about one year ago, and the unsuppressed thought of revenge is heard to fall from many lips. Assisted by a United States tug, the Mobile was soon pressing her side hard against one of the spacious docks that project tooth-like from the San Jose wharf sheds, and the work of unloading was begun by a motley gang of white, black and intermediate colored men, all of whom spoke in a strange tongue to the American ear.

From the manner in which they entered upon and continued their work, the critical onlooker would begin the task of reconciling the facts before his eyes with the statements he had so often met with as to the inborn laziness of this people. The unloading continued during the next day, while the army wagon train was transporting our tents and equipage to the camp, to which the regiment took up its march during the second afternoon, reaching their destination a while before sundown. The detail sent ahead not having been able to erect all the tents, the tired men

SAN JOSE ESPIGON (WHARF).

detailed themselves and aided in the work until by considerable crowding, like sardines in a can, sufficient shelter for all was secured.

Nor was the work done sooner than was really necessary, for as the shades of evening approached they were prematurely deepened by a dense cloud that rose up as if out of the sea and poured its liquid contents upon us in torrents, while a stiff ocean breeze pressed the sides of our tents, testing the strength of the guys and the depth of the pegs, while the water ran into many tents, stopping only where it came in contact with some early sleeper's blanket. As the storm allayed, the ax and hammer could be heard in different directions throughout the camp, redriving tent pegs preparatory to the next gust that seemed imminent.

The next day, being Sunday, and a few days following, our camp was a veritable bee-hive of busy men, resetting tents, cleaning, and otherwise putting the camp in a com-

WAGON TRAIN ON WAY TO CAMP.

fortable, tidy condition. Camp Columbia, the home of the Seventh Army Corps, in whose bounds we are quartered, is located six and one-half kilometers northwest from Havana on the military pike leading from that city to Pinar del Rio and on the Havana & Marianao railroad, with General Lee's headquarters at Buena Vista station. Our location was in the northeast part of the camp west of the military road, and a short distance south from General Lee's headquarters, overlooking the camps of most of the other regiments of the corps, and the blue sea just beyond to the west, with the First Division hospital, the beautiful hills and valleys to the east, beyond which lies the city and bay of Havana, clearly seen from the brow of the hill. A more beautiful location could hardly have been found; while its topography and immediate surroundings were equally as favorable and attractive. Beginning with the fine cement-covered stone wall eight feet high and eighteen inches thick, on the east side along the pike, our camp was quite level for some twenty rods west, and where our regimental headquarters, hospital, band quarters, exchange, guard house (tent), gospel tent, and guard mount grounds were located, thence sloping gradually westward to the railroad near one-quarter of a mile distant. On the east part of this space, reaching to headquarters street, the line of officers and companies were located, with company streets running west to the beautiful, commodious drill and parade ground. At our north and south, near the pike, were situated two fine homes which, in the palmy days of Cuba, were surrounded with every conceivable convenience, as well as beautiful adornment of lawns. Massive iron gates and fence, connecting with the stone wall, guarded the front along the pike, of the home to the south, while stone walls and a most beautiful gateway opened into a street leading to the north home, on either side of which stood a

GUARD MOUNT, CAMP COLUMBIA.

NORTH GATE, CAMP COLUMBIA.

row of stately Royal palms, lifting their crested heads high toward heaven, furnishing another of those most beautiful pictures of Cuba.

Not only was the camp beautiful for situation, but its sanitary condition was not excelled by any regiment in Camp Columbia. And this was not the result of any natural causes, but the product of a persistent, energetic watchfulness on the part of those in charge, coupled with a systematic and to some extent laborious application of muscle and disinfectants. A brief account of the manner and means to the accomplishing of these results may not be out of place just here. First, we may say the design of the government, however slow in carrying it out, was to the health, comfort and convenience of the soldiers.

To this end commodious wall tents, nine by nine feet for the officers and sixteen by sixteen for the men, each provided with a fly, all of good material, were provided, and as rapidly as the transportation of lumber would admit, these were provided with floors, placed well up from the ground to prevent mould and decay beneath them, and the floors were required to be treated to frequent applications of water, with which, after some delay, our camp had

STREET SCENE AT DRILL HOUR, CUBA.

an abundant supply of the purest and best. Beneath these floors, and on the clay floors of other tents, a lavish supply of air-slacked lime was scattered several times a month, as well also, though not so frequenly, over the streets of the camp. When the weather would warrant it, the tent walls must be rolled up twice or three times every week, and daily the folding cots with which the men were provided, all and bedding, must be carried to the street, where all was exposed to the clear sun light and pure air. Ordinarily, six men occupy one of these large tents. Three times a week the detailed broom brigade, armed with rattan brooms, sweep the entire camp from headquarters to the foot of the company streets, while the Cuban gang, with their machettes, go over the entire camp as occasion requires and cut any weed, flower or spear of grass, allowing no vegetation to grow for decay, while every day after breakfast the regiment is marched through the entire length and breadth of the camp quarters, picking up scraps of paper, orange peel and other useless things, which later, the sanitary police, consisting of a commissioned officer, two non-commissioned officers, and ten men, would take them from the heaps in which they were placed and put them in an army wagon or the camp cart for conveyance to a safe distance from camp or to where they were burned or buried. But this is not all. Deep sinks are dug at convenient places in which all refuse from kitchens and tents is deposited, and from five to seven times a day this refuse is covered with a thin coat of earth and a sprinkling of lime, only to be followed by another detail, who wash all the seats and floors of the closets with diluted carbolic acid, giving the already limed sinks a good supply of the same.

And oftentimes, as if to make doubly sure of a sure thing, the force that occupy the guard house, some times larger and some times smaller than others, owing to various causes, are marched through the camp with suitable tools for the work in hand, and the little details are looked after in a scrutinizing way. Along with all this the white-wash gang, usually Cubans, make their trip through camp two or three times a month and white-wash about everything in sight except tents, as our pictures show, not even sparing the clothes and bedding hung out to the sunlight. With all this care it was a surprise that we were expected to pass the ordeal of quarantine and fumigation in order to fit us for admission to a state, where disinfection seemed equally as important, looking to the protection of our regiment. Lest the foregoing should lead the mind of the reader to form a wrong impression as to the proper service a soldier should render while in camp, it is therefore but just we mention the fact that the colonel of this regiment did not impose upon his men extra duties merely for the sake of artistic ornamentation or beautifying the grounds to no practical value to the command; hence, no monuments, or decorations, other than a clean camp, was left to mark the spot on which the Fourth Illinois Volunteers bivouacked during their history as an army of occupation in Cuba.

The health of the men in this regiment was remarkably good—not excelled by any period of their waiting in the United States.

Death visited our ranks but once, on the fifteenth of January, and that by drowning while bathing in the river. Only one incident or accident of note occurred while in this camp, that of the fall of the immense water tank, erected for flushing the sewer pipe leading from the camp to the sea. This was a substantial superstructure erected at the south end of the line of headquarter tents and near the band and hospital quarters. The frame work on which the immense wooden tub or tank twenty by twenty-four feet was placed, evidently was strong and well made, but its posts, twelve in number, were placed on pillars of small dimension, made of the soft native lime-stone, which is not capable of sustaining any great pressure, and also becomes very brittle or rotten when saturated with water. Hence when completed ready for roof, on the twenty-second day of January the water was turned into it to prove its fitness for the task it was expected to perform, the joints and seams permitted the escape of a considerable quantity of water, saturating the earth beneath it and soaking the stone pillars until they crushed beneath the preasure, and the structure careened, and with terrific crash the whole was precipitated to the earth a complete wreck of bent rods, bands and broken timbers, while the unpent water like a flood deluged all that part of the camp, wrecking

WRECK OF THE TANK.

several tents in the band quarters and seriously twisting some in headquarters row, damaging considerable property and bruising up the cook of the band mess. Still life in such a camp could not well be other than pleasant.

Scarcely had we gotten our quarters in condition to

live as comfortably as camp life will admit, on entering this camp, until it was thought necessary, or something else, to change the order and begin the re-enacting of the old program of the states, with which we had become so familiar as to lose our relish for it, that is the "grand review."

We were introduced to it on Cuban soil in the form of a big review before Major General Douglas on the afternoon of the 16th of January, a short distance southeast of the village of Quemados, which lies at the south side of Camp Columbia. This was, by the unanimous consent of our regiment, voted to be the "rockiest" affair of the kind we had ever participated in, for the face of the field on which it took place was literally covered with stone of various sizes and shapes. Of course it was a creditable (?) performance.

But this condition was broken into again on the afternoon of the 31st, when, in compliance with an order from General Lee, the whole corps was assembled on the spacious parade ground at the southwest part of the camp, and reviewed by their distinguished corps commander.

Again, on the 17th of February, another order brought the entire brigade together at the same place, at which it was reviewed by General Brooke, Governor General of Havana.

The hour for morning drill on the above day, as well as the day following, was put in on practice in pitching and striking shelter tents, preparing for what was in the near future. The value of this practice was demonstrated by the very brief space of time in which the work could be accomplished, not exceeding two minutes. Thus, in case of emergency, preparation for storm could be made in time for protection. The time for which this drill was more especially given, came on the morning of the

19th. An order having come down from the Second Brigade of the First Division, directing the regiments of this brigade to start on a practice march on that date, Sunday. Therefore the camp was astir at an early hour, and notwithstanding the mud, which was more like wax, caused by the heavy rains of the preceding night, yet with large quantities clinging to their feet the work of getting ready was speedily done, and the Second South Carolina, the Ninth and Fourth Illinois of this brigade, were in readiness for the march to Guines; and at about 9 in the morning this regiment filed out at the north gate of the camp in light marching order, taking the lead of the other two regiments during the first day's march. The day proved to be one of Cuba's balmy winter days, if anything a little hot. Still the march was a pleasant one, without any mishaps, except, that two or three who were scarcely able to enter upon the march, were compelled to give up to an ambulance ride which continued through the outgoing trip.

About noon a halt was called some ten kilometers beyond Havana and the midday lunch was partaken of in a true soldierly way and with an appetite that lingered after the plates were clear. After an hour or more rest, one of the most delightful things that ever comes to a weary soldier, we resumed the tramp, calling a halt at 4 o'clock east of Cotorro, on this, one of the splendid military roads built by Spain. Here we pitched our pup tents, and prepared for our night's rest. True to the characteristic of this regiment, there was scarely a foot of ground for two or three miles from our camp that some of the boys had not gone over, in search of something, whatever it might be, to serve as a reminder of the camp or a souvenir of the occasion.

A good night's rest and a typical ration breakfast, we were again ready to "hip," which we began about 7

MILITARY ROAD NEAR SAN JOSE, CUBA.

o'clock, reaching San Jose, twenty-seven kilometers out from Havana, by 11:30, where another halt was made for the midday lunch and rest. Having marched some twelve miles after lunch we found ourselves beginning a gradual ascent, which became more steep at times, winding its course around the ends of low hills and along ravines until we were at the summit of a large hill or small mountain overlooking a well watered extensive and fertile prairie, whose beauty and luxuriant growth of vegetation, reminds one of the fertile prairies of our own land. Out on this broad stretch before us and some five and one-half kilometers east we could distinctly see the city of Guines the objective point of our march; and beyond it the stack of a large sugar refinery rose above the plain, the capacity of which, as we learned later, having camped near it, was three thousand pounds per day and was in operation at this time.

At our feet the roadway entered a cut leading in a circular descending course through the promontory like brow of the mountain, for a distance of about one-fourth of a mile.

At its deepest point the perpendicular walls of soft lime stone rise to a height of perhaps fifty feet with a roadway twenty or thirty feet in width. In this again we see one of the monuments of Spain's glory, as well as an evidence that money, time and labor counted for little when an undertaking was on foot looking to her martial advantage and temporary glory and power. Passing out of this grand piece of engineering, so skillfully executed, we found the road rapidly declining and making another graceful curve to the left producing the letter S, thus lengthening the distance in order to decrease the otherwise steepness of the grade. Soon after emerging from the cut we turned aside into a field near the foot of the mountain or hill, where we pitched our tents, during a gentle shower, on a sloping field, literally covered with small stones, which we were under the necessity of gathering from beneath our little canvas roofs, prior to making our downy beds with moistened blankets, a fact that did not discommode us to any great extent, since the weather was mild and pleasant as in our beautiful balmy May days in central Illinois.

This was the end of another afternoon's march of about sixteen kilometers. While tents were being pitched the cooks were rushing the open kitchen fires and hurrying up supper on double time. Still our collapsed stomachs had to forego the pleasure of the delightful feast. For while hunger made our hard-tack and boneless ham, taken from the side of a hog, a delight to the palate, yet at times, it aroused a rebellious condition near the centre of one's phys-

MOUNTAIN CUT.

OUR CAMP AT FOOT OF MOUNTAIN CUT.

ical organism. Well, having "pulled through" another out of time meal, and the still hours of night having passed far up the dial, we were admonished that our little beds were the place for "good boys;" hence we decided to pass by the delightful pleasure of a ramble over the mountain sides. But the rising sun found birds of our camp that search for the early worm, moving about in the bushes on the hill side, but using the precaution necessary to hearing the breakfast call. This meal over and a stampede on a small scale took place from the camp, for the coatless blues were soon exploring every foot of the east side of the hill. While it was not a Klondike for curios and souvenirs, some of the men brought back lime formations as trophies gathered in the caves they had discovered, and whose dark chambers they had to some extent explored. As we remained in camp here most of Tuesday, ample opportunity was offered for a pretty thorough exploration of the surrounding country, a pleasure not to be forgone by the men of this command, whose bumps of curiosity and inquisitiveness are quite well developed.

At 2 o'clock in the afternoon camp was broken and our regiment moved out taking the lead in the march of the day, passing through Guines, another of the quaint cities of this island and the second in size in the province of La Habana; we again pitched our tents about one kilometer northeast of the city, partly in a rough corn field and partly on a beautiful grassy plot in the forks of a clear, deep, fast-flowing stream that rises from one spring at the mountain's base, some eight miles distant; and which is used for irragating this vast stretch of fertile plains, as well as for water power. Hence, unlike most streams, it forks at the wrong end, sending its waters out through a multitude of smaller streams that diminish in size, instead of taking on from incoming rivulets to their increase as they proceed to a confluence with some other stream or lose themselves in the great ocean. This pure, limpid stream was too much for a soldier who had been sweltering in the hot sun of that day, and grown dust begrimed on his march. Accordingly, before all tents were pitched, the heavy splash told that the weary soldier had reached one point of his glory, and would feel the better for it. In fact, even the Colonel and the Chaplain became so undignified as to try its cleansing qualities. Just across the east branch, on the north side, the Second South Carolina pitched its tents, while just across the highway east of us, the Ninth Illinois took up its quarters, thus putting us in close proximity to each other in fact, too near the fountains of cognac and other exciting decoctions that arouse the combative elements of a soldier nature. Now while "foraging," a mild name given to a practice in army life, which in a civilian is seriously repudiated, was in no sense necessary during the occupation of Cuba, and hence could not be justifiable from any standpoint, yet it is a fact that it was resorted to at times, and that not always because there was a vicious desire back of it, but from the spirit known as "fun" among the boys in blue: and which some of them had practiced sufficiently to have reached the point, where they had a kind of semi belief that it was within the bounds of a "pretty fair grade of army morals." Hence during our encampment at Guines, a little episode along this line occurred that led to the striking of a badge, that was not uncommonly seen on the coat or blue shirt of one of Uncle Sam's honor preservers, and which bore an inscription after this order: "Who stole the hog? Second South Carolina. Who killed the hog? Ninth Illinois. Who ate the hog? Fourth Illinois." The affair out of which this grew, at least so far as the best information the writer was able to secure, was this: In the city of Guines, as in every town in Cuba, about all the lesser and general merchants, carry along with their other line of goods, certain kinds of soft goods that can't well be kept without enclosing them in a vessel of some kind; and for which some of the soldiers had a strong proclivity for making themselves a suitable receptacle for preservation of these valuable (?) soft goods. So it seems a certain South Carolinian had been trying to take in a quantity of these goods, more or less, and as usual they had penetrated the fibre of his body, and created a kind of irritation which so affected his brain as to produce halluciations of the mind, leading him to believe things right and proper which at other times he would have seen in another light, or perhaps when there was no light.

So it happened on this occasion, in "broad-day light,"

as this soldier was returning from the place of business where he had been kindly assisting the poor Cuban in bottling or transferring of his soft goods from one receptacle to another, and under one of these peculiar hallucinations of mind, he saw a rope tied to a stake in the yard of one of the rustic Cuban homes and thereupon a strong desire took hold of him to possess it: which was "half the points" under the circumstances to its possession, and thereupon he deliberately untied the cord which added another fourth to the "points," and moved off toward the camp with one end of it in his hand. The occupants of the hut hastily followed him, doing loud talking, and fearful gesturing, which the fellow could not understand, being purely an American, he walked on, simply carrying the end of the cord. It was while on this peaceful pleasant march, our artist caught him with a snap-shot as he made a brief halt for contemplation.

But the unfortunate thing connected with the whole affair, and which seems to have exercised the minds of these Cubans so greatly was, that there was a hog, which they very much prized, at the other end of the rope. Well, to be brief, this was the hog which 'tis said the Fourth Illinois ate, which the Ninth got, which the Second South Carolina stole, which was on the end of the string, which was tied to the stake, which was in the Cuban's yard. Of course the Fourth Illinois did not know where the Ninth got the hog, nor they, how the Second South Carolinian became possessor of it, while he did not know he had it, for no soldier ever steals. The nearest he ever gets to that awful crime is to "swipe." On the following day, Wednesday, being the 22nd of the month, and that on which the "father of our country" was born, it was thought to be a fitting thing, though in a foreign land, that we emphasize its significance in some suitable way, as seen from an American standpoint.

SWIPING A PORKER.

Therefore Major-General Douglas issued an order calling out the whole brigade at 2 o'clock in the afternoon, and after marching to the city and through its principal streets, we passed in review before the commanding general and staff, who were located in the large park in front of the cathedral: which is the central object of reverence and admiration in this city of the plains. Under this structure it is said are located a number of dungeon cells, in one of which was confined a Spanish soldier awaiting his punishment. The following day by an unforseen providence, was destined to be another gala day in this city, and this brigade was to perform the conspicuous part, by passing in review before the celebrated Gen. Maximo Gomez, who was slated for a visit to this his home city, and where his mother still resided. Accordingly about 2 o'clock in the afternoon of the 23d, we fell in line with the other regiments of the brigade, and made about the same prominent streets as on the former day, passing the city hall, which is located on one of the narrow streets, thus necessitating the staff to form in double file to avoid crowding the people that over filled the narrow side walks, flanking the porch of the city building under which the noted personage, venerable with age, was stationed, in the midst of a dense throng of the elite and prominent personages of the city. All were decorated in their best attire, not neglecting a plentiful application of the everywhere present face powder, that brings out prominently the dark eyes and hair of this Spanish race, producing a very charming effect. As to what the noted veteran of two wars thought of the American blue coats we are unable to say, as his opinion was never given to the public. Yet the boys were none the less significant because of his august presence. Having shipped two of the disabled men by rail, back to camp Columbia, we spent the night of Thursday in our quarters, with orders to break camp the following morning.

Friday dawned upon us as had each day of the week, in all the beauty and warmth the sun is capable of diffusing in this tropical isle during the winter, only to reveal the activity of an American camp when orders require prompt action and careful preparation. All of which was true of Camp Swift, as we are pleased to call it, in honor of our leader. Breakfast over, and the hour for departure having arrived, 9 o'clock, a. m., we again moved out upon the highway an hour in the rear of the Ninth Illinois, the Second South Carolina having gone out the preceding evening, and soon our backs were upon the camp and the city; and thus we bid adieu to them, their scenes and their associations.

Ere we were aware of it, our first hour's march was

up, and we halted for the usual rest, when Colonel Swift dismounted to take part in the "tramp, tramp, tramp" of the boys when the next start was made. And not to be outdone, the staff followed his example, and soon we were ascending the "S" shaped curve of the mountain road leading to the deep cut; on the soft limestone walls of which the boys of the South Carolina and the two Illinois regiments, in no small number, had carved their names and some hieroglyphics, to be read and deciphered by the coming generations of the Cuban people, and to remind the traveler from America that friends had preceded him over this famous military road. Descending the gradual decline of the road through the foothills on the west side, we enter a rolling prairie country, in which the royal palm and other tropical vegetation are found in abundance, and

RUINS OF A CUBAN BARN.

the fine stone fences, massive gateways, and ruins of former stately mansions, are proof of the splendor, glory, and wealth of this country prior to the time when the despoiling hand of war was laid upon it.

Having referred to the remains of once beautiful but now ruined buildings, we insert here, in a parenthetic way, the ruins of a barn which stood on the south side of our quarters in Camp Columbia, and which we were told was the nearest point to Havana ever gained by the insurgent army. So many stories as to its ruin were circulated, that we do not venture to give any.

About noon of this first day of our return trip, having covered fourteen kilometers of the way, we filed into the fields in the midst of the tall grass and partook of the provisions which had been prepared before breaking camp in the morning, and of which we partook with such a relish that to speak of it as a lunch would be to cast a reflection on "Bill," the colored cook, for our condition made it a first class meal. Our usual rest over, we proceeded on our way, passing the town of San Jose, which is built after the order of towns in Cuba generally, that is, on either side of the main road in a single line of houses, continuing often for some distance. About two and one-half kilometers west the column turned to the right through a large gateway into a lane some sixty feet wide, with a fence on either side constructed out of small stone and mortar, and which led up to a one-story, well equipped farm house, at the foot of the north mountain, which aids in forming this beautiful pass through which the military road leads. Here rising out of the level plain almost perpendicularly to the height of perhaps three hundred feet, and extending back north and south from the pass for miles, widening out into low hills, are the twin mountains, that one's imagination might picture as having in the distant past, been broken asunder by

CAMP AT MOUNTAIN PASS, SHOWING LANE AND CAMP FROM THE NORTH MOUNTAIN.

some mighty power and pushed back, forming a beautiful gateway of about one-fourth of a mile in width. At this point, we were told by the dwellers in the community, was fought the battle of San Jose in the late Spanish-Cuban war. The Cubans, secreting themselves in the brush and clefts of the rocks on the mountain side, poured their deadly fire into the enemy as they were passing on the road in a wholly exposed position, with a high stone wall on the opposite side of the road from where the Cubans were in ambush. Whether the history of nations will record the glories of this victory or not, we do not pretend to say, yet our informants seemed to look upon it not only as a great battle, but a great victory for the arms of their countrymen. Of the temporary camps on this march, nothing equaled this for beauty of scenery or outstripped it as to conveniences. Our congenial Spanish-Cuban host, who, with quite a force of men, was just in the midst of repairing the ruins left in the track of contending armies, not only cheerfully gave permission to use water from his well, but put his own servants and mule at our disposal, to draw therefrom, until our camp was fully established, after which a detail of our own men, Sampson-like, pushed the sweep that operated the drum on which the rope coiled, in bringing the crystal fluid from its rock reservoir, some eighty feet below. At no time on the march had the boys been more eager to get the "pup tents" pitched and their luggage from their shoulders than at this time. And that after a long, rapid march; for they had pressed with such rapidity all day as to crowd the front rank of the band up alongside the horses of the staff. And when halted because of the close proximity into which we were coming with the Ninth Illinois in our lead, they earnestly called out for permission from the colonel to press on and pass them. During the whole day they kept up the regular one-hundred and twenty pace to the minute, if not exceeding it. But with all this, their eagerness to see and learn all that could be seen and comprehended about the camp was early manifested. For soon voices were heard echoing back upon the camp from the steep mountain side on the north, where one's gazing eyes could discern the forms of men, that appeared to be those of children, moving in a zig-zag direction, in and out among the crags and brushy growth that covered the mountain side, and to which they clung for support and means of ascent.

Thus they could be seen at intervals often of many feet one above the other, from t e base to the brush covered summit, where after a short rest, the adventurers began their descent over the same perilous route, reaching

WAGON TRAIN AND NORTH MOUNTAIN IN DISTANCE.

camp with no greater injury than impaired clothing, scratched hands and soiled faces. Soon after the evening meal, darkness having settled its sombre shades about us, voices were again heard in the same direction, as well also on the opposite side of the pass, where our eyes could detect a light flashing at intervals on either mountain and moving higher and higher up, which evidenced that the Fourth had in it men who could not be sati-fied with their achievements by daylight, but would excel them by similar feats accomplished by the help of an army search light, a paraffine or tallow candle. In due time the program was reversed and the descending light bearers reached the plain, entering the north and south parts of camp, without any mishaps greater than those sustained in the daylight adventure. Throughout the camp nothing more was thought of it, until next morning after breakfast, the men of certain messes where heard extolling the sweetness of mountain honey; when further inquiry revealed the fact that the daylight ascent of the north mountain, led to the discovery of a rich deposit of wild honey near the summit, and the night adventure was to secure the find, in which they were successful to a large measure, as the buckets full of delicious nectar in camp clearly evidenced. But the climbers of the south mountain would not be thus outdone by comrades of no higher rank or braver hearts. Accordingly after a hurried breakfast, groups of men, some equipped with long ropes and other articles that might be of use to mountain adventurers, were seen wending their way toward the rocky slopes of their choice, and in a few hours they began to return to camp with trophies of a very different character, from those of their comrades on the previous night. One of these was the person of his wise-looking monkey-faced owlship, others were reptiles looking somewhat like the little graceful chameleon that play about and capture the flies in our tents at camp Columbia, only much larger, rougher and more undescribable in their appearance: which they called Gila monsters. These were soon followed by another squad bringing a reptile of greater dimensions, being a beautiful sleek snake of about five feet in length, supposed to be of the Anaconda family, if not one of the direct descendants. Later three others of these graceful beauties were brought in, one measuring eleven and one half feet, their captors caressing and handling them as if but an innocent kitten, much to the seeming enjoyment of the captive. When Brigadier General Douglas, whose camp was only a short distance ahead, heard of these adventures, he remarked something like this: If those Fourth

Illinois men could be camped near hell, they'd soon have the devil out playing with him.

But the boys of the Fourth would have played with him only so long as they had him where things went their way, and beyond that there would have been a racket. These in-gatherings are looked upon as the regimental menagerie, and until muster out, almost daily exhibitions of their snakeships were being made, in the presence of distin-

SNAKES AND OTHER TROPHIES OF MOUNTAIN HUNT.

guished Americans, who visited the camp. But at our separation for home, they were tenderly borne by their individual owners to the Sucker state as trophies of the days of army occupancy of the island. While here we also had the picture of poverty brought before us in its reality, when companies of old men, women and children of that class visited our camp to receive even the refuse of our mess kettles and tables, when we chanced to have any of that kind of articles on hand. These poorly clad, half clad, and scarcely clad at all, are not the saddest specimens of the ravages of poverty, and its attendant disease, which often reaches the point that prevents their leaving home, hovel, or whatever may be their place of tarrying, to go forth as foragers about the camps. One of our camera fiends got a snapshot of one of these bands, his comrades having succeeded

HUNGRY CUBANS AT MOUNTAIN PASS.

in lining them up for the occasion, while at the mountain pass camp. Still it should not be inferred that the habit of going so scantily dressed is a sure sign of abject poverty, for absolute nudity of children up to six years old is a common sight in this island. Even among those in the strata above what we would designate poverty, it is a stroke of economy and of common practice.

The conditions at this camp, above any other on this outing, seemed to be more conducive to an easy, "as you please" attitude in the soldier, from the highest rank to the humblest in the line. The day's march, the balmy restfulness of the quiet breeze, and all the environments, seemed to lend their aid in its production, as some of the

A HUNGRY TRIO WATCHING BILL GET SUPPER.

snap-shots of the occasion clearly evidenced. About 9:30 P. M., of the day on which we entered this delightful place, and after all at headquarters were snugly tucked away on their folding cots, or peacefully resting upon the bosom of mother earth, a voice was heard making inquiry for that particular point in camp, and soon an orderly from General Douglas' headquarters, which was located some distance in our advance, had scaled the wall and stood at the open front of headquarters tent with an order in hand, directing the colonel to remain in camp during the next day. After his departure a few brief comments followed, and all sank again into that peaceful quiet so characteristic of this end of the camp.

Accordingly the trumpet call on the following morning, Saturday, created no unusual activity in the camp, but the inquiry upon many lips was "do we have to break camp this morning?" or "I wonder if we will get a chance to go on the mountain today?" and many similar ones.

But knowledge of the order that reached the camp the night before having been spread, all uneasiness on this line was dismissed from the mind, and the boys began their hasty preparations for a real day's outing in the timber clad mountain. It was generally understood that camp would be broken Sunday morning and the homeward march continued, with the hope in many minds of reaching camp Columbia the same evening, thus ending the march and an eight days' outing. But as was common, at least in this army, we were doomed to disappointment, for by some hook-crook or carelessness, quite likely the latter, on the part of some one, the order to move did not reach our headquarters until 4 o'clock in the afternoon of Sunday. This was the signal for hasty work in camp, as supper had to be prepared and eaten, cooking utensils and other paraphernalia packed and loaded on the wagons before a start could be made. But all hands were joined together in their respective spheres, and as usual proved that we were equal to the emergency, for by 5:15 we were on the move to where, few, if any, clearly realized. A tramp of four

GIVING AN ORDER—COL. SWIFT AND CAPT. PARKER.

kilometers brought us to a little thatched village, at which point we started south at right angles to the road we had been traveling, and on which we were now to continue our march, notwithstanding it seemed to be almost the opposite direction from that of our destination. All went well except, that darkness was shutting out the scenes through which we were passing. Yet this did not seriously inconvenience us, as we had smooth footing for a distance of three and one-half kilometers, when, as if by a kind of magic, the macadamized road closed, and we entered a narrow way hedged on either side up to the cart track with a heavy growth of tropical vegetation, the kind, we could not determine, only as we felt the keen sting of a thorn when we pressed too far out in our narrow confines. But this was pleasant in comparison to what awaited us but a few hundred yards beyond, where we entered a deep cut which did not add anything to the comfort of our travel over a strange road in the dark. These cuts occurred at many points on the route, it being what is called, I believe, a sunken military road, and these cuts were designed to protect men from the enemy at exposed points by lowering the road so as to bring their heads below the level of the land. But to add to our discomfort, much of this dismal route was very stony, with deep ruts, while at other places it was overgrown with rank vegetation, except the pack mule track: besides its winding about as if designed to get the traveler "rattled" as to whether he was still going forward or had taken the backward trail. About five miles of this dreary, dismal tramp brought us to another village, Manangua, where we struck the terminus of another military pike of eighteen and one-half kilometers in length, leading to Havana, and on which we continued about four kilometers, when we found a suitable camping ground, and very soon occupied it, for we were a weary set of men; having marched about eighteen or twenty kilometers, and part of that over the roughest road we have met with in all our army experience, and that in the short space of five hours: going into camp about ten that night. Nothing daunted by this Sunday's march, Monday at 8 o'clock in the morning found us with camp broke and all packed ready when the command to march was given, and we started out on another fine road, with strange scenery on every hand, relieving somewhat the monotony, at least the weariness of mind, as we marked the usual one hundred and twenty pace per minute toward the city of Havana, to which, in this part of the island, like Rome, "all roads lead."

At high noon the band again struck up one of its familiar airs, and we marched into camp Columbia, saturated with perspiration, covered with dust and weary in body, having made about twenty kilometers, mostly under what seemed a summer heat in this tropical relgion.

Among the funny things that happened during this outing was the following, which occurred at General Douglass' Brigade Headquarters. Sometime earlier in the history of the brigade, some of the boys had smuggled a billy goat kid into the camp, not knowing just how Gen. Douglass might take to his goatship. But he very soon became the pet of all connected with the General's staff, the General included, and under such circumstances his goatship's propensities developed quite rapidly, especially his butting qualities. On the occasion referred to Capt. Snyder's (Brig. Q. M.) cot had by some means been pushed against the wall of the tent, forcing it out so that the tent wall rested on the pillow end, and which "billy" during the day had discovered in making his rounds of the camp; and as it suited his fancy for a day snooze, he appropriated it for a bed: quitting it later in the day doubtless for his evening meal and a stroll. But bed time came, and the Captain entering the tent found his cot in order and accordingly pushed the tent wall out and laid himself quietly down among his companions and soon was sweetly resting in the arms of Morpheus.

Meantime "billy" came back, and finding changes had been made, proceeded to prepare for his night's rest by removing the unseen intruder, for the captain was inside and he outside the tent. Accordingly he applied the battering-ram of his artillery, and the captain was startled by the weight of his butting capacity as their heads met, while "billy" stepped back to determine results before deciding on an increase of force. The captain, thinking his next cot neighbor, Captain Hale, had been getting off one of his tricks, soon came to a sitting posture and armed himself with one of his shoes, and then quietly "laid for his man" to make the next move, which he felt sure would come when he was thought to have again found grace with Morpheus. Just then "billy," having concluded that his first attack had driven the intruder from his appropriated quarters, placed his front feet on the head of the cot to investigate more closely before proceeding farther. Just then the captain, by the light of the moon, discovered his goatship's head as it pressed gently against the canvass, giving a clear outline of his graceful horns, and instantly he planted the heel of his No. — shoe square in "billy's" face just above his eyes, which so insulted his goatship's dignity—having never been treated other than with the ut-

ON GUARD--EARLY MORNING.

most kindness and indulgence—that he quietly sauntered off to seek a more congenial quarter, while the captain rubbed his head and tried to conciliate the insulted dream-god, Morpheus.

This trip certainly fitted us for what followed during the succeeding days, a cessation of drills and dress parades: a rest than which we never enjoyed more. But this happy state of things was not to continue long, for ere the week had run its course, lest our joints become stiffened and our muscles relaxed from excessive idleness, the Colonel ordered the resumption of our old trade, and the drill ground was again subjected to a good tramping every morning, and its smoothness tested by a regimental parade in the evening, while a renewal of the police work was not forgotten, but if anything, more systematically and vigorously pushed forward, looking to the thorough sanitation of our camp. But all our duties were not confined to our part of the camp. It remained for March 27, 1899, to reveal the time when the final review of the Seventh Army Corps was to take place. For some time the presence of General Alger, the secretary of war, had been expected in Cuba. That time had arrived, and so also had orders at our headquarters to take part in a grand review in his presence on the afternoon of the above date. Accordingly everything was put in readiness, even to a clean shave, and at 2:30 the lines were being formed for the march to the review ground fully a mile to our southwest, when our regiment was assigned first place in the order of review, the place which she was so eminently competent to fill. The conduct of the regiments on this occasion, including the cavalry and artillery, which brought up the rear, was not inferior to the excellent work done by the corps on former occasions, and when it is remembered that the corps was already disintegrating, some of the regiments having been sent to the states for muster out, there is great reason for pleasurable recollections of the excellent display made on this occasion. Especially had this regiment reason to be thankful for its painstaking, earnest efforts during its whole history, when we heard the

FOURTH ILLINOIS CORRAL, CUBA.

CAMP BARBER SHOP.

words of praise uttered in its favor by the highest authorities in our army, as the following, clipped from the Paris Beacon, reported by Ralph Wooley, clearly shows:

"A big review was held in honor of Secretary Alger Monday afternoon. Of course there are not many soldiers here now, but when they are all massed a good showing was made nevertheless.

"After the Fourth had returned from the review, officers' call was immediately blown. This caused the soldiers to think that orders to go home had been received and 'Illinois! Illinois!' was shouted in stentorian tones. 'There were no orders, but news almost as pleasing awaited the officers who were assembling. When all had gathered around him the Colonel said in part: 'Today, was held probably the last review of the seventh army corps, and I want to say that I am prouder than ever of my excellent regiment, which made its usual fine appearance in to-day's show. As the regiment passed the reviewing stand I overheard General Keifer as he leaned foward in his saddle and said to Secretary Alger: "Mr. Secretary, this, in my opinion, is the best regiment in the seventh army corps and always has been." The secretary readily agreed with the General, adding that he had been apprised of this fact before.'"

At this late day lumber for our flooring was being shipped in and from time to time a few loads were secured and the long desired and much needed improvement went forward, not reaching completion until the corps was breaking up for return to the United States. The few last weeks of our sojourn in camp developed nothing new or startling, the life of the regiment moving on in a kind of routine line, under which the men became restless, even impatient, over the long delayed order for their departure to the land of their birth and the home of their love. But like all things human this strain had its end, being broken by the following orders: the first of which was slow in getting to the rank and file in a definite, reliable way, perhaps because of its indefiniteness as to date of leaving, as its perusal will reveal.

HAVANA, April 1, 1899.
To Commanding General, Beuna Vista:

The division commander directs that the Third Nebraska, Ninth Illinois, Forty-ninth Iowa, Sixth Missouri and Fourth Illinois be prepared to go to the states as soon as transports arrive, of which you will be duly notified. These regiments should have their records prepared at once so there will be no delay in mustering them out. They will go in the orders named. The question of taking or leaving tentage will be decided hereafter. Their spare ordnance and ammunition should be turned in at once, and property responsibility settled so that there may be no confusion when it is decided they should start.

[Signed,]

. RICHARDS,
Adjutant-General.

O. C. 196.

By this it will be seen the date of departure is not given, and the order of removal put the Fourth Illinois at the last in the list of these regiments, to lift its gentle feet from the soil of Cuba. But later developments show that this privilege, for some reason, was at last denied us, as Colonel Swift predicted it would be soon after the order came to hand; since he knew, as no other man in the regiment, the wires that were being pulled to give that distinction to another regiment, and it is certain Egypt got the glory. But the mental tension left by the former order, was not to continue many days, as is seen in the following order which reached our camp about 1 o'clock in the afternoon of its date, and was soon the public property of the regiment.

HEADQUARTERS DIVISION OF CUBA,
HAVANA, CUBA, April 3, 1899.

Major-General Lee, Commanding Department Province of Havana:

GENERAL—The major-general commanding directs me to send, for your information and guidance, the following extract of telegram received last night:

"The first eight regiments (meaning the Third Kentucky, Department Matanzas; the Third Nebraska, Ninth Illinois, Forty-ninth Iowa, Sixth Missouri, Fourth Illinois, your department; and the Thirty-first Michigan and Sixth Ohio, department Santa Clara) named in your cablegram of April 1st, to come out of Cuba, have been assigned to ships as indicated in cablegram to you of April 1st. The assignments are as follows:

"Third Nebraska, Thomas; Ninth Illinois, Dixie; Forty-ninth Iowa, San Antonio and Vigilancia; Sixth Missouri, Seneca; Fourth Illinois, Plant System, Yarmouth, Olivette and Whitney.

"But it may not be possible to have these vessels to arrive in the order in which you have designated regiments to return to the United States. For instance, two ships to carry the Fourth Illinois will be in Havana April 3rd. It is desired that vessels which have been assigned to particular regiments shall bring those regiments out as indicated, and to such points as they will be directed before vessels leave Cuban ports. It will be necessary that adjutant-general be notified well in advance of date vessel will be ready to sail, so that you can receive instructions to what quarantine stations ship is to go, after conference here with the marine hospital service.

"These regiments will bring with them necessary tentage, cots, cooking utensils and ten days' rations, so that they can go into camp at quarantine station where ordered. If necessary, tentage brought with them can be left standing at quarantine, and, after baggage is disinfected, vessel may proceed with regiment to final point of debarkation.

"The surgeon-general marine hospital service insists that there shall be no mattresses for officers or men brought along, and it is so ordered. Records should not be packed with clothing, but should be available for work during quarantine detention.

"Colonel Ballinger is arranging for these camps, and desires that no troops start before April 5th. It is important that you report what parts of regiments are on different ships, so that they will be ordered to go to the same quarantine station.

"By order Assistant Secretary of War,
"CORBIN."
Very respectfully, your obedient servant,
[Signed]   W. V. RICHARDS,
                        Adjutant-General.

This, coupled with the fact that the paymaster was hurried into our camp late that afternoon to gladden our hearts by replenishing our depleted spelters and purses with the "root of all evil," that we might be able to secure something for the satisfying of the inner man while on the journey, in case we did not fall on some "lone isle" where these things could not be purchased for love or money; all tended to confirm the convictions in every heart that our days in Cuba were assuredly numbered, and would be speedily realized. Accordingly, every man in camp began the task of putting their souvenirs and relics (the larger part of their baggage) in shape for transportation, while the men that had been waiting for an opportune time to make his purchases in this line, hastened to the city under the protection of a pass, or otherwise, if too timid to attempt the procuring of one. Still night settled down upon us with no further omen as to the hour or date of departure; and at the usual hour, at least for pay day, which was always a little later than on ordinary days, the camp took on its usual quiet, when slumber closes the eyes and stills the mouth (except when he snores) of the otherwise persistent grumbler and kicker. But scarce had the wee hours of the morning of the 4th of April begun their stealthy approach, when an orderly from corps headquarters, treading rapidly on the threshhold of the exit door at 1 o'clock A. M., halted in front of the colonel's tent and gave the usual signal of the caller at a tent door; that is, a few vigorous applications of the finger-nails on the front of your canvas home, similar to those so commonly applied to the parts of the body in easy reach, when a big Cuban hopper, called a flea, makes application for a sample of your precious life fluid. The signal being answered by the colonel, a paper was placed in his hand, which was at once passed to Captain Parker, the adjutant occupying the next tent, who was soon on the headquarters street visiting the officers concerned and the leader of the band, to whom the following was communicated:

HEADQUARTERS DIVISION OF CUBA,
HAVANA, April 4, 1899.

Commanding General, Buena Vista:

Send in at once headquarters and three companies Fourth Illinois to go on Whitney, and five companies to go on Yarmouth, the remaining four companies will go on Yarmouth Friday next. Telegraph when troops may be expected at wharf.

By Command of Major-General Brooke.

[Signed.] RICHARDS,
Adjutant General.

O. C. 204.

HEADQUARTERS SEVENTH ARMY CORPS,
CAMP COLUMBIA.
HAVANA, CUBA, April 4, 1899.

Official copy respectfully furnished the commanding officer of the Fourth Illinois Volunteer Infantry for compliance and immediate report.

By Command of Major-General Lee.

———————,

Assistant Adjutant General.

This called out a genuine camp shout from the quarters of the band and certain other tents in this part of camp, while active operations began, looking to compliance with the order. At 6 in the morning the long wagon train began to centralize about headquarters, awaiting orders as to their disposition, for which they did not have to wait long, and by 9 o'clock Companies L, F, D and C, forming the first battalion, under Maj. L. E. Bennet, had tents down and rolled, all stores packed, and the same loaded on the wagons assigned to them. While all the improvised tables, benches and discarded articles were piled in heaps and committed to the flames, which did their work thorougly, this being the last act of our sanitation, leaving only the floors and a clean camp for the next regiment, if any should be so fortunate as to locate here. And soon the regiment was broken by this detachment moving out from them, leaving the beautiful camp with all its histories, to be seen again perhaps, only in the archives and picture galleries of our memories.

While it was not a sad parting as when we bid the last good bye to loved ones and friends, turning our backs upon the homes of our childhood near one year previous, when we started out with bouyant hopes that it would be ours to strike a blow in the liberating of the people of this island, in which we have been merely sojourners for three months: spending the most delightfully pleasant winter we ever experienced, thus escaping the severest of weather in our native state. To the music of our excellent band the agile feet of some three hundred men were keeping time, measuring off the regulation pace; as they passed out the north entrance of our camp into the road leading to Havana, retracing the steps that brought them from thence through the then strange scenery of a land whose customs and habits bore so distinctly the marks of antiquity. By eleven in the morning we had entered the San Jose wharf shed, when we rested, lunched and waited while the Cuban warehouse force were busily unloading our goods and transferring them to the Plant System steamer Whitney, which lay at anchor in the bay near the wreck of the Maine. About 4 o'clock in the afternoon the members of the staff present, the band and companies L, F and D boarded a United States tug and were steamed out to the Whitney and went aboard to await her readiness for the start on her voyage. Here for the first time the full import or rather the full text of the early morning orders began to dawn upon the minds of most of us in this battalion, when Company C was "turned down" at this point or detached from the battalion to make a period of its history in connection with the second battalion, which was just marching into the dock sheds as we were vacating them.

The Whitney is of medium size, a sidewheeler, with lower and upper decks, on the latter of which, amidship is located the state rooms, saloon or dining room, kitchen, offices and store rooms with pilot house still above.

The laws of our ports require all vessels landing at other ports to leave the harbor before sunset, which time was rapidly creeping upon up, as the rich tints of gold, crimson and blue began to blend in the western sky, while they deepened and changed behind the fleecy clouds that skimmed along the horizon, seemingly bathing their wings in the gentle rolling waves of the ocean, where like a timid child, it would hide itself from the searching gaze of the onlooker. Still while the time for our departure had drawn near an important part of our cargo, that is our commissary stores, were not yet loaded and the vessel bringing it from the dock was not in sight. But our ship's captain evidently had been there before, hence ready for the emergency that was upon us. Presently a peculiar quivering of the ship

was felt, while a screaking, cracking noise came from the hull of the vessel, which informed those familiar with it, that the anchor was being raised. Immediately following, the great paddles on the wheels at her sides began to move gently, as if fearful of disturbing the quiet of the murky filthy water of this bay; while the old ship stood still as if defying the action of her machinery and power of steam. But while these seeming pretenses to a movement from the harbor were being enacted, a large tug came around the vessels along the west shore with a speed that sent the waves rolling to port and starboard as her prow divided the waters before her, she rounded aft our ship and made herself fast to our bow. At once strong hands began the work of transferring her cargo, which proved to be the rations for our trip, into the hold of the Whitney.

By this time the objects on shore clearly revealed that we were on the move, for the great engines on our boat were breathing more heavily and the wheels were churning the waters of the narrow doorway of this almost rock bound harbor, while the sun still hung a little distance above the ocean horizon.

We had been on the dreary waste of ocean, which stretched far out before us, but a short time, when from old Moro's tower flashed out her brilliant light, while for miles along the shore west of the bay the electric lights of Havana city flashed and sparkled like a long row of diamonds set at irregular intervals. The sight was one not to be produced in pen picture or easily erased from the sensitive plates of memory. Thus while our approach to this quaint old city, about which clusters so much history, was so impressive, not less was that of our departure.

The evening shades had scarcely deepened into night, before we began to have that peculiar funny feeling that comes to one when the car of an elevator starts down with a rush, and there seems to be something just back of and below the sternum, that had not weight enough about it to keep pace with the heavier portions of the body, and you find yourself making involuntary efforts to swallow something that persists in seeking the light. But this one great difference is noticeable, that in the one case you succeed and in the other you don't, as was evidenced on this occasion, and especially while crossing the gulf stream; for some of the boys declare, they "threw up everything but their job in the army." This condition of things continued through the greater part of Wednesday, the sea calming somewhat as the day wore wearily toward its close, and we entered upon a more peaceful night to enjoy the sweets with which the dream god regales his votaries. Wednesday morning early, found some of us astir, anxiously looking like Noah's dove, for a place, even some lonely island, whereupon to set our feet. And as the light brushed back the gray dawn toward the west, the low sand beach of the keys about the bay of Tampa became visible and after an hour's easy sailing, we could see quite clearly the buildings and docks of the state quarantine station on Mullet Key in front, while to our left, was the light house and government quarantine station on Egmont Key. Between us and Egmont was a large vessel with her hull dressed in black, and her decks crowded with what seemed to be human beings, which as we drew nearer proved to be the Second Battalion of our regiment, whom we left on the docks at Havana. Through the fleetness of their ship, as we learned later, they were brought into the placid waters of Tampa bay twelve hours ahead of us, having gained sixteen hours on the Whitney, which, had it not been for the chagrin we felt at creeping in, as if we had been belated, as the boys sometimes were after visiting the city, we certainly would have cheered the gallant Yarmouth more enthusiastically.

For certainly we were ready to vote that the most unpleasant feature about our boat as a transport for soldiers, or even perhaps for cattle, was her lack of speed. Besides the rougher the sea, the slower she goes, since her wheels lost most of their utility by being partly or wholly out of the water.

After reporting at the state quarantine office we drifted about aimlessly in the bay for some time, until a health officer from the government station came out to learn our condition and arranged for us to disembark. Accordingly about 9:30 a lighter was pushed along side of us and the work of unloading began, and continued throughout the day and into the night, having removed the men from the Whitney about sundown and the last from the Yarmouth after dark. Once on Egmont Key and we began to get some idea of what the term "disinfect" means when applied to soldiers and their belongings in a quarantine station. As the soldiers passed one of the buildings they were required to surrender their entire pack, except guns, the whole of which was placed in an immense cast-iron boiler shaped vessel, and sealed up steam tight, while the boiling steam was forced through them for two or three hours. You can imagine what the straps on their haversacks, leather grips, gloves etc., were like, passing through this ordeal, while our trunks, boxes and hand baggage were all opened by us or by the fumigating force in such a way as came most easily to their hand, the contents partly removed or raised up and a decoction that smelled like, well, after the first whiff you quit smelling it if you could, for it would take your breath, or make you think you were getting sea sick. Nor would you be at all surprised that such a compound would destroy the life of any germ, having as it had in such great degree the "get there" penetrating qualities that would search them out

QUARANTINE CAMP, EGMONT KEY, FLA.

in the very fibre of the wood, and the power that would take the life it had thus sought out. With this fluid, harmless to anything but yellow silk and germs, they sprinkled pretty freely, as some of us discovered to our regret, four or five days later, then closed our trunks or boxes and with strips of paper sealed up the opening and around the lids, placing them by the hundred in a tight room and leaving them to their fate, that is, the germs. This latter process being harmless in itself to any fabric, the long delay before we could open and dry our garments, etc., caused mildew, but the steam process got away with things generally, so far as future utility or beauty was concerned. While all this was going on the boys were roaving, but not to their hearts' content, over the white sand, of which this island seems principally to be composed, in a corral of some ten acres, surrounded by a high wire fence that reminded one of Weyler's trochas in Cuba; beyond which, if one did, soldier like, make his escape, he was likely to get a dose of fine shot from the muzzle of a gun made to shoot that kind of missiles, in the hands of a civilian guard, or have the exquisite pleasure of remaining in quarantine for another ten days, and perhaps cause all the rest of us to experience the same undesirable pleasure. To say these restraints were chafing to men who had anticipated the glorious privilege of roaving this farm of Uncle Sam's of one-half by one mile in size and gathering the shells of the briny deep, is to state it very tamely indeed.

But the three days and four nights over, joyfully the entire lot of us, baggage and all, crowded upon the little Margaret, where we found little more than standing room. A three and a-half hours ride up the bay brought us to Port Tampa, where we again became detached bodies, forming three sections of a train which supposedly pulled out for Savannah, Georgia. But to our surprise we found ourselves

TRANSPORT MARGARET.

brought together again the following day about 3:00 in the afternoon on a siding four miles west of Augusta, Georgia, from whence we marched into camp MacKenzie, one mile distant, to find tents, mess shacks, and all other camp conveniences, even to electric lights on our streets. Hereafter eight days of camp life with morning drills cut off, but added vigorously to the evening dress parade, we were again joined by our companions of the third battalion who had passed over the same line but with added unpleasantness. Thus camp life was again upon us in all its features

CAMP MCKENZIE.

of routine, pleasant and otherwise, but with a fixed time for its culmination, that is, May second. As a preparatory to this, all books and accounts must be balanced and closed up, in order to the accomplishment of which a large increase in the clerical force was made in every company, and other offices; while the boards of survey must account for the shortage in expendible and non-expendible property of the Government, for the very exigencies in the movement of the army put it beyond the hope of any other fair or honorable solution. Besides this physical examination must be passed through again, to determine the possibility of pension claims from physical disabilities incurred in the line of military duty. While muster out rolls and discharges, all found their places in the short allotted time.

A week previous to mustering out the boys were ordered to turn in to the captains of their respective companies their knapsacks, haversacks, canteens and eating utensils, which looked as though they might get to eat at a table otherwise spread. But instead they only had them reissued at each meal and then returned again.

On April 27th they began turning in their weapons of warfare at the Augusta arsenal. Immediately after guard-mount, at 8:30 in the morning on the following date, our band was ordered to turn in its instruments also, a matter of regret to most of the command, since it so greatly changed the conditions in camp, cutting off, the enlivening and cheery music to which we had become so familiar and had learned to appreciate so highly. Thus every phase of camp life took on a changed appearance, which continued with but slight variation until we lined up, company after company, and passed through the very delightful part of our army program, the muster out. It was during our stay at Camp MacKenzie the very important and responsible duties of provost marshal were laid upon the sturdy shoulder of our worthy colonel, Swift, by whom, it can easily be guessed, the work was well and faithfully done; for a detail of the choicest men of his own regiment were placed in the city to execute his orders. Thus the time wore wearily on to the 2nd day of May, 1899, when the joy that had been warming in the hearts of the boys for several days, seemed to reach the boiling point, and they fairly boiled over at times, as one by one the companies were mustered out, and once more citizens, or milder, civilians of the United States. With all the disadvantages through which this regiment was called to pass, from its call to arms as state militia on the 26th day of April, 1898, it has nevertheless made for itself a record of high order, both as to its discipline, ability in tactics on all lines of duty, as well as on the march. It is therefore with pleasure and gratitude we remind the reader that the Fourth regiment has in no way lowered the good name of our state, whose sons have proven by the numbers that have rushed to arms in defense of the honor of the stars and stripes in two wars in less than half a century, with a loyalty and patriotism that has not been excelled by any state in the Union. In both these wars she has cheerfully aided sister states in the making up of their quota of men. And while it was not their privilege to enter the field of actual conflict and face a defiant enemy, the fact that they chafed under the circumstances and restraints that held them back from it, is full proof of their willingness and earnest desire to demonstrate to the enemy that were a "foe equal to his steel." Nor would the opportunity have revealed in them anything less than a courage commensurate with their desire. Neither has this regiment on any occasion had to take the back seat in the corps, when battle tactics were to be exhibited, dress parades and reviews participated in, or a heavy march executed.

The success that has attended it in all its varied duties and relations, calling out, as it has, the highest approval of those well fitted to judge of merit as well as effort, is not due to the diligence and efficiency of a few in its composite, but rests on the fact, that from the private in the ranks to the colonel at its head, there were, in no small numbers, men who were ready to, and did perform their duty promptly, energetically and faithfully. These are the facts that have led up to so many commendable statements like the following from President McKinley, who was moved to say as it passed in review before him: "It is the best volunteer regiment I ever saw."

In saying what we have, it was not to imply that there were no other regiments of true merit in this army corps, nor would we attempt to dim their just glory. But as they have made their own history, we leave it to them to publish it. For we believe it was an army of picked men, chosen for the most arduous task that confronted the nation in its conflict with Spain in Cuba, as the following clipping will reveal:

"HAVANA, April 17.—The last general order issued by Fitzhugh Lee to his command, the Seventh Army Corps, is in part as follows:

"An order has been received which moves the last regiment of the Seventh Army Corps across the sea to be mustered out, and the ranks of the organization will be forever broken. The record made by the officers and the men will forever be preserved on the pages of military history. No troops won greater reputation for discipline, drill, manly discharge of duty, soldierly conduct, and cheerful obedience to orders.

"The president's assurance that had the war with

Spain continued the Seventh Army Corps would have been selected to lead the assault on the Havana lines, proves that the corps possessed the confidence of the commander-in-chief of the army and navy, a confidence shared by his fellow countrymen.

"It is gratifying, in reviewing the career of the corps, to remember the harmony which existed among the 40,000 soldiers who answered the roll call at Tampa, Jacksonville, Savannah and Cuba. Whether volunteer soldiers of the North or South, they took the sunshine and the storm of camp together, and marched side by side under one flag, one cause, one country."

It was certainly an army of men, at the mention of whose names its honored and worthy commander would have no reason to blush or offer an apology.

NON-COMMISSIONED OFFICERS OF COMPANY G.

FOURTH ILLINOIS. 377

By unforseen causes, some cuts were not inserted at their proper places in the body of the book, hence they are placed elsewhere in the work.

NON-COMMISSIONED OFFICERS OF COMPANY F.

We here give a few poems referring to our worthy regiment.

WARNING TO ILLINOIS GIRLS.

[BY A SAVANNAH, GEORGIA, GIRL.]

Listen young ladies of Illinois
To a story I'll tell of your charming boys
Who came to our city in '98
To guard its citizens early and late.

They guarded our town, and captured the hearts
Of Maids and matrons down in these parts,
By their pluck and zeal, and manly ways,
And well the Fourth deserves the praise.

How well they marched on the grand review,
So well, indeed, that the president, too,
Said to their colonel, standing near,
'Tis the best drilled regiment passed by here.

And oh, how we cheered our boys that day;
And oh, how we wept, when they sailed away,
While since they are gone our girls are blue,
And talk of going to Cuba, too.

And indeed we'll go, if we hear again
That girls up north are threatening them
With dangers worse than Spanish foes.
We'll go to Cuba to sooth their woes.

We'll bring them back to our city fair,
Then every day'll be "Thanksgiving" here;
And we'll be so kind, and good, and true
They'll never go back again to you.

Now think of the boys you'd make exiles,
Delightedly basking in southern smiles.
First Willie McKnight, a charming lad,
Next in the procession then comes Dad.

And after him comes trooping others,—
Rolla and Babe, and Kincade brothers;
And right in line is our bonnie son Beam,
And all the men on the foot ball team.

There's many more I might mention yet,
Of the gallant Fourth, whom our girls have met;
Whom the girls all love, esteem and admire,
To sing their praises we never tire.

But suffice it now, and listen well,
For this is a secret I'm going tell,
The boys to their girls up north are true;
So don't get huffy, cross nor blue.

Don't threaten the lads with ire and wrath,
Lest Savannah girls may stand in your path,
To protect the Fourth with their lives they would,
The Fourth, so brave, so true and good.

L.

The above was written by a lady of Savannah, Georgia, about the date of the departure of the regiment for Cuba.

Having failed to secure the first poem written in reply to the foregoing, we give the second, and the final reply from the South.

OUR DEFENSE.

(A northern girl's reply to a southern girl's poem.)

The girls of the north-land,
The "Illinois Fourth land,"
    Beg favor to rise and remark
That the girl of the south-land,
The cotton and drouth land,
    Seems floundering 'round in the dark.
With thanks for her questions,
Advice and suggestions,
    We feel it our duty, you know,
To inform her politely,
Though plainly and tritely,
    We can manage to "hoe our own row."

We've short girls and tall girls,
And big girls and small girls,
    And girls of all sizes between;
We've maidens contrary-like,
Girls literary-like,
    Witching girls, girls like a queen.
We have fickle girls, faithful girls,
Awkward girls, graceful girls,
    Girls who old stockings will mend;
We have homely and pretty girls,
Dull girls and witty girls,
    Girls who a fortune would spend.

We've girls with true eyes,
Sweet, innocent, blue eyes—
    With eyes that are earnest and brown—
With eyes, softly yellow,
That vanquish a fellow,

      Glancing upward, then witchingly down.
Our sweet, gracious actions,
Our countless attractions
      Make us fair in our brave soldiers' eyes,
And few girls of Savannah,
In way, shape or "manneh"
      Can rival the beauty they prize.

We need not to worry,
To fret or to flurry,
      Or cause ourselves useless alarms.
All gossip we hear not,
All rivals we fear not,
      For we are secure in our charms.
In this we're confiding,
With faith strong, abiding,
      That no matter where they may roam,
Our boys will not tarry
Away when they marry,
      But will find their ideals at home.

We would not be selfish,
Or impish, or elfish,
      We're willing, in justice, to share
The girl of the south land,
The cotton and drouth land,
      May have those for whom we don't care;
But the girl of the north-land,
The Illinois Fourth land,
      Is queen of her own special throne,
And she'll keep not a part of,
But just the whole heart of
      Her hero in "Illinois' Own."
                Mattoon, Ill., May 13, 1899.

Some time, just before the Fourth Illinois left Savannah for Cuba, one of the literary young ladies of that city wrote and forwarded to *The Gazette* a poem with our young soldiers as the subject. The above is an answer, by a Mattoon lady, to the verse which said:

> Don't threaten the lads with ire and wrath
> Lest Savannah girls may stand in your path.
> We'll bring them back to our city, fair,
> Then every day'll be Thanksgiving, here.
> *Mattoon Gazette*, May 26, 1899.

SAVANNAH GIRL.

Again I bob up with a few modest rhyms,
In answer to Mattoon's most elegant lines,
To say that our girls refuse to be crushed,
Nor yet to the wall will they ever be pushed.

We too have our girls, so bonnie and sweet,
Whom the Fourth Illinois were delighted to meet;
Who can make up the beds, or sweep off the hearth,
Who lighten their labors with singing and mirth.

Who can cook a square meal, that your boys often shared,
When out at Camp Onward so badly they fared.
Good wives they'll make in the years as the come—
Fond, loving mothers and heaven of home.

I've no doubt you're all your fancy doth paint,
With eyes of the doe and face like a saint.
But our girls have beauty of lily and rose,
Are dainty and modest, have gracious repose.

They have hearts like yourselves, but scorn to malign
A lot of fair maids who to their friends have been kind;
But I'm sure in the hearts of the Fourth now at home
Sweet thoughts of our girls fill memory's throne.

We had no desire to win them from you,
But alas! many found our girls winsome and true,
And now at the north, in anger and strife,
You berate the poor man who came back for a wife.

And let me here add, for I know it is true,
(And this is no secret I'm confiding to you)
That many who left dear sweethearts up there,
Found out their mistake when our girls they met here.

How could they resist our sweet southern smiles
Or the coy charming graces of fair maidens' wiles?
We mostly gave friendship; 'twas all that we had,
For our love we held sacred for southern born lads.

You girls are, at least, not generous and kind,
For in "spite" you have answered, I beg to remind,
A girl who had written with kindest intent
Of the boys, for whom only warm praises were meant.

You all seem to think that our kindness was meant
For something of which, our girls never dreamt.
We lack not for lovers. If we won a few hearts
'Twas only because we acted kind sisters' parts.

And now as I come to the end of my lay
There's one other thing I really must say,
That sweethearts and lovers we have by the score
And don't have to travel to find a few more.

Tho' we frankly acknowledge your boys to be brave,
Our hearts to our own boys, we long ago gave,
Who are loyal and loving, brave, honest and true
As the Fourth or any who wore Uncle Sam's blue.

Savannah, June 6, 1899.   LOULIX.

The two following poems have been furnished us by friends of the regiment, and are inserted because of their relation and reference to it.

CHEER UP, CUBANS.

By Lucy T. Sumerlin.

Tune: " Tramp, Tramp, Tramp the Boys are Marching.

Come, ye grey coats and the blue,
Buckle on your armor new,
March in solid phalanx on to southern strands;
As Yankees, we are one
And as Yankees, we are done
Waiting for the Spaniards to withdraw their clans.

CHORUS:

Tramp, tramp, tramp, the boys are marching;
Cheer up, Cubans, they will come,
With our ships upon the sea
And our men to march with thee
We'll secure to you your freedom and your home.

Twenty million men or more
Can be drawn from shore to shore;
All the Yankees full of spirit, brave and true
Would then join the mighty host
For which Yankees well may boast
'Neath the stars and striper, our own red, white and blue.

CHORUS.

All the brave boys on the Maine
Who by treachery were slain,
And the battleship we prided much is gone;
Mothers, wives and babies too,
Cry for help to Yankees true,
From a land where cruel Spain has reinged so long.

CHORUS.

Shall the voice from the grave
And the men beneath the wave
Call for vengeance from this nation all in vain?
We will prove our claim to worth
When we bring down to the earth
All the tyrants and the cruel sons of Spain.

CHORUS.

The writer of the above, a resident of Mattoon, Illinois, is entirely blind.

CUBAN ISLE.

By Arthur T. French, a member of Company F, Fourth Infantry

(FROM ILLINOIS.)

I.

By the gulf stream gently flowing, Cuban Isle, Cuban Isle,
O'er the water wave-like growing, Cuban Isle, Cuban Isle,
Comes an echo on the breeze,
Reaching all the lands and seas,
And its mellow tones are these, Cuban Isle, Cuban Isle,
And its mellow tones are these, Cuban Isle.

II.

In your struggle now with Spain, Cuban Isle, Cuban Isle,
May your work not be in vain, Cuban Isle, Cuban Isle,
    'Till upon the map of time
    Trace your record out sublime
Blotting out the Spaniard's crime, Cuban Isle, Cuban Isle,
Blotting out the Spaniard's crime, Cuban Isle.

III.

When the tyrant smote your land, Cuban Isle, Cuban Isle,
Spreading death on every hand, Cuban Isle, Cuban Isle,
    Freedom from your land withdrew,
    Putting False against the True,
There were none more brave than you, Cuban Isle, Cuban Isle,
There were none more brave than you, Cuban Isle.

IV.

Not without thy wondrous story, Cuban Isle, Cuban Isle,
Can be writ the New World's glory, Cuban Isle, Cuban Isle,
    On the record of the years
    General Maceo's name appears
Gomez, Garcia and our tears, Cuban Isle, Cuban Isle,
Gomez, Garcia and our tears, Cuban Isle.

While we have confined ourselves principally to that period of our regiments history, which began when the last company, having passed the ordeal of a physical examination, took its place in the ranks and was duly mustered into the services of the United States, still, in passing the childhood and youth of this military organization with but a bare mention, as we have deemed it proper, yet its latter history should not be read in the same light in which other organizations are read, that went out from this and other states of the Union.

We must ever look at it in the clear light of the relation its individual members and companies sustained to each other and the government, during these years of its youth and childhood. For while in this and other states, men promptly answered the call to arms from every walk of life, joining companies in different localities, each holding no organic relation to the others as a regiment; this body was already an organized regiment which had made for itself a history of no secondary character, during a series of years while enrolled as the Fourth Illinois National Guard. Thus it possessed advantages over other regiments just formed, in that it was already to a great extent acquainted with and able to execute the tactics as laid down for the use of our army. Hence, barring the fact of its newly added material, by which the companies were recruited up to the maximum, it was prepared to enter at once the arena of conflict with no small prospect of achieving honor in the face of the enemy on a foreign soil.

It was this fact that tended greatly to chafe and iritate the regiment, when others, whose organization was much more recent and whose fitness, from a military point of view, was far inferior, were ordered to the front to participate in the short yet decisive conflict for the liberating of a struggling and oppressed people, who had prostrated themselves at the feet of our nation, pleading for deliverance with piteous tones and outstretched hands; hands lean and bony from want of food ruthlessly snatched therefrom, blood stained from their long and next to fruitless effort to gather from the fast wasting resources the merest subsistence. But instead of marching to this open door of active service, it was our lot to enter and fit up camp after camp, wearing away the days, weeks and months, in the most monotonus routine way conceivable, with no other incentive before us than the honor of attaining to a degree of skill in drill and camp duties, that were not to be excelled by any with whom we were associated in our brief tedious, and in a measure galling, army life and experience.

MORRO CASTLE.

U. S. MILITARY CEMETERY.

As many of our readers have visited what to every soldier in the Seventh Army Corps, is the sacred spot on Cuban soil, we give here a cut of the U. S. Military Burying Ground, near Playa, where we left the bodies of forty who were connected with the corps.

U. S. MILITARY CEMETERY.

The trenches in which these graves were formed were blasted out of the solid lime stone rock, after which they were partitioned off into places about thirty inches wide, with lumber, forming a box for each seperate coffin.

The Fourth was one of the few regiments in the Seventh Army Corps which did not leave any of its men in this sacred spot.

CAPT. AL. SNYDER, Q. M.   S. B. BLACKWELL, Q. M. SERGT.

AL. SNYDER.

Capt. Al. Snyder, whose portrait we have the privilege to present herewith, is a native of Edgar county, Illinois—was born on a farm near Paris on the 17th of February, 1853. His schooling, prior to his fourteenth year, was secured in the country district school near his father's home, except two years which were spent in the graded schools of Paris. From his fourteenth to the eighteenth year of his age he attended school in Paris, completing during this time the course of a private normal school of that city.

Having moved to Arcola, Douglas county, he in 1881 entered the state militia, becoming a charter member of Company A, was mustered in as second lieutenant, and later was promoted to the rank of first lieutenant; still bearing this rank, at a later date he was raised to the rank of captain and made quartermaster and commissary of the Fourth Regiment, Illinois National Guard, of which Company A formed a part. In consequence of his relations to this regiment, he was called upon to take a very important and responsible part in the strike of 1886 at East St. Louis, and at Centralia, Cartersville and Mounds, and at Chicago in the great strikes of 1894. At the call of the government for our state troops to take part in the war with Spain, he unhesitatingly answered the call, and was mustered into the United States service on the 20th of May, 1898, as regimental quartermaster, which position he filled until August 8th of the same year, when, by order of Brig.-Gen. J. H. Barclay, he was made acting brigade quartermaster of the Second Brigade, Third Division, Seventh Army Corps. On the 19th of October, 1898, he was made acting brigade quartermaster of the Second Brigade, First Division, Seventh Army Corps, by order of Brig.-Gen. Henry T. Douglas. Following hard on this, on the 20th day of the same month, by command of Major-General Green, he was promoted to acting assistant chief quartermaster of the Seventh Army Corps, while February 15th, 1899, brought another order from Brig.-Gen. Henry T. Douglas, placing him in the position of acting brigade quartermaster, Second Brigade, First Division, Seventh Army Corps.

Prior to muster out he returned to his former position

of regimental quartermaster, which he held when mustered out of the United States service.

While the quartermaster's position is one involving much and constant work, it also entails a very heavy responsibility. It need scarcely be said that Captain Snyder did his work well and met every responsibility with fidelity.

In civil life he is one of the recognized broom corn merchants of Arcola, as well as also being engaged in the insurance, real estate and loan business.

SAMUEL B. BLACKWELL, Jr.

Among Illinois' young National Guardsmen who were glad and proud to respond to the call of duty in the months which issued in the stirring year of 1898 was Samuel B. Blackwell, Jr., of Arcola, Douglas county, Illinois.

This young man was born in Arcola, Douglas county, Illinois, June 8, 1872, received his education in the public and high schools of that place, and embarked in the grocery business as a member of the firm of Blackwell & McCaine in 1893. At the age of eighteen years he enlisted in Company A, Fourth Illinois National Guard, served as a private one year, as a corporal two years and was then advanced to the office of quartermaster-sergeant of the Fourth Illinois National Guard, which position he has held five years. During the strike of 1894, in Chicago, he took his stand against riot, with other brave sons in the Fourth Illinois.

Duty and love for his country's beautiful Stars and Stripes showed this young American and soldier his duty, and he did it when President McKinley called for volunteers for our late war with Spain. On the morning of April 26, 1898, he left his home and friends to take his chances of life or death with his regiment to free Cuba. After a stay of one month in Springfield, Illinois, he left for Jacksonville, Florida, where he remained four months; from there the Fourth Illinois Infantry went to Savannah, Georgia, where it remained until its departure for Cuba, January 3, 1899, on the transport Mobile. As a part of the "Army of Occupation" in Cuba, the Fourth Illinois took its share of duties, and with his regiment Samuel B. Blackwell, Jr., arrived in his native state in May, 1899. The pleasure of credit for duties well performed, from proper authorities, was his reward. Cuba is free and glad to owe its freedom to such spirits of loyalty as the subject of this sketch.

REGIMENTAL BAND.

The Fourth Illinois Volunteer Infantry Band was organized at Camp Tanner, Springfield, Ill., under the leadership of W. L. Faris, of Jacksonville, Ill., April 29, 1898, consisting of members' names as follows:

W. L. Faris, Chief Musician, cornet, Jacksonville, Ill.
Como Trogdon, Principal Musician, baritone, Paris, Ill.
W. T. Stewart, Principal Musician, solo alto, Paris, Ill.
Charles Nall, tuba, Donnellson, Ill.
A. C. Owings, tuba, Litchfield, Ill.
Leo J. Frey, first trombone, Springfield, Ill.
John Twitchel, first alto, Virden, Ill.
Fred R. McKnight, second alto, Ramsey, Ill.; detailed from Co. I.
Albert Bassett, first cornet, Neoga, Ill.
Joy Woodman, solo cornet, Virden, Ill.
John McKnight, E cornet, Ramsey, Ill.
Carl Kirkpatrick, E clarionet, Virden, Ill.

FOURTH ILLINOIS BAND.

Edward Dewey, saxophone, Mt. Vernon, Ill.
William Patterson, snare drum, Paris, Ill.
Jess Gossett, bass drum, Casey, Ill.
Edward Howard, cymbals, Paris, Ill.

Left Camp Tanner, Springfield, Ill., with the regiment for Jacksonville, Fla., May 26, 1898; arrived at our destination May 29, 1898. William Santer, of Greencave Springs, Fla., enlisted as a private in Company K, Fourth Illinois Regiment, and detailed to the band to play baritone. He remained with the band until October 15, when he went home on a sick furlough, and October 21 he died. The Fourth Illinois Band played for his funeral at his home.

October 26 we received orders to go to Savannah, Ga., and arrived there October 27, took up quarters in Irish park with Colonel Andel. Here John McKnight, who, being detailed from Company B, Fourth Illinois Volunteers, was honorably discharged on account of physical disability October 30, 1898. We remained at Irish park until December 1, 1898, when the regiment was called off provost guard and took up quarters at Camp Onward. Here our chief musician, W. L. Faris, was honorably discharged December 10, 1898. Here the band was reorganized and detached from all companies, under the leadership of W. E. Daggy, with the following members:

W. E. Daggy, chief musician, cornet, Mattoon, Ill.
Camo Trogdon, principal musician, baritone, Paris, Ill.
W. T. Stewart, principal musician, solo alto, Paris, Ill.
Geo. Gibler, solo cornet, Mattoon, Ill.
Howard Style, solo cornet, Mattoon, Ill.
Albert Bassett, first cornet, Neoga, Ill.
Louis Higgins, first cornet, Neoga, Ill.
Frank Romizer, solo B-flat clarionet, Winchester, Ind.

Wm. Plen, first B-flat clarionet, Hutsonville, Ill.
Edward Dewey, first B-flat clarionet, Mt. Vernon, Ill.
Wm. Combs, second B-flat clarionet, Arcola, Ill.
Joy Woodman, E-flat clarionet, Virden, Ill.
Perl C. Newlin, piccalo, Casey, Ill.
John Twitchel, first alto, Virden, Ill.
Fred McKnight, second alto, Ramsey, Ill.; detailed from Company I.
Leo. J. Fry, slide trombone, Springfield, Ill.
Don Carlos Merritt, slide trombone, Charleston, Ill.
Mark Carruthers, tennor, Hazel Del, Ill.
A. C. Owings, tennor, Litchfield, Ill.
Harry Bassett, baritone, Neoga, Ill.
Raymond Coon, tuba, Mattoon, Ill.
Chas. Wall, tuba, Donnellson, Ill.
Richard Byers, snare drum, Charleston, Ill.
Edward Howard, bass drum, Paris, Ill.
Serg. Ben Walker, drum major, Carbondale, Ill.; detailed from Company C Dec. 15, 1898; returned to his respective company Feb. 10, 1899, at Camp Columbia, Havana, Cuba.
Serg. Harry C. Faulke, of Company K; detailed to the band as drum major Feb. 10, 1899.
Albert C. Owings; honorably discharged Feb. 16, 1899, at Camp Columbia, Havana, Cuba.
Bart Kelley; detailed from Company H to play tennor in the absence of A. C. Owings, who was formerly honorably dischared.
Wm. Patterson; detailed from Company H to play snare drum in the absence of Richard E. Byers, who is physically disabled.

Major J. C. McCord M.D.
Surgeon.

1st Lieut. A. E. Hill
Assistant Surgeon

1st Lieut. C. M. Co
Assist. Sur

st. Doon

DR. I. C. McCORD.

Dr. I. C. McCord, major and surgeon of the Fourth Illinois National Guard, was born at York, Clark county, Illinois, December 19, 1856. He is a son of Major D. O. McCord, surgeon in the Civil war, and was with his father during that little family unpleasantness from 1863 to 1865, and has vivid remembrances of Vicksburg, Island No. 10, (Jeff) Davis Bend, Memphis, Hellena and other historic points in connection with those stirring days. Having been raised on a farm, he devoted the summer to the occupation of a farmer, and applied himself to his books in the village school during the winter; having fully replenished the wood pile with long poles, which was to be transformed into fire and stove wood for the winter use, by the application of brawn and ax on the Saturday rest days, when a boy enjoys the rabit hunt. He also sought a broader education at the Wabash Academy and Edgar Academy, and later graduated from the Medical College of Ohio, Medical Department of the University of Cincinnati, in 1883.

His connection with the Illinois National Guard began some eighteen years ago, and during all this stretch of time he has missed attending but one of the state encampments, —in the summer of 1892, being on leave in Europe.

In these years he has run the gauntlet of military experience from private to that of regimental surgeon. He was ranking assistant surgeon of the state when appointed major and surgeon of the Fourth Illinois National Guard.

During the railroad strikes in the spring of 1893, he served as surgeon of the Fourth Illinois, and also during the Spanish-American war, except about four months during the existence of the Third Division of the Seventh Army Corps, when he acted as surgeon of the Second Brigade, Third Division of the Seventh Army Corps. And when the Fourth regiment, Illinois Volunteer Infantry, was mustered out, May 2, 1899, he was filling his place as major and surgeon therein.

LIEUT. GEORGE E. HILGARD.

Lieut. George E. Hilgard, M. D., assistant surgeon of the Fourth Illinois Volunteer Infantry, is a resident of Belleville, Illinois. With the class of 1893 he graduated from the high school of that city and the following fall he entered the St. Louis Medical College, continuing his studies for three years more, graduating from that institution in the year 1896. During the following two years he assisted the county physician, thus gaining much practical experience, the better fitting him for his chosen profession. During his school years, in 1895, he enlisted as a member of Company D, Fourth Illinois National Guards, and with it attended three annual encampments. During the third encampment he was placed on the regimental medical staff as assistant surgeon to Surgeon-Major T. C. McCord.

The only real duty encountered while in the Illinois National Guard, was during the famous cyclone period of May, 1896, which swept over the city of St. Louis. At this time the company was ordered to East St. Louis, where it was held as a guard for eleven days.

In February, 1898, he was commissioned as assistant surgeon of the Fourth Illinois National Guard. After the outbreak of the Spanish hostilities toward this country, the medical department was ordered to make certain changes—looking to its greater efficiency,—there being one major-surgeon and five assistant surgeons to the regiment. In order to determine those who were best fitted for such a position, a rigid examination was resorted to, and Lieutenant Hilgard was one of the three successful competitors. Major T. C. McCord and Charles M. Galbraith, being the other two.

As he was a centennial gift to his country, the Lieutenant was doubtless the youngest doctor in the division, if not in the entire corps,—he having had to wait one year for his diploma after graduating, owing to his being too young to practice under our state laws. His work in the regiment during its career in the Spanish-American quarrel, was of a most commendable character, and his efforts untiring. After the muster out of the regiment, Dr. Hilgard returned to Belleville, the place of his nativity, to continue in the practice of medicine.

HOSPITAL.

In the state militia service the fourth regiment's hospital corps consisted of Major and Surgeon T. C. McCord, of Paris; Captain and assistant surgeon B. F. Cook, Greenville; Lieutenant and assistant surgeon Charles M. Gailbraith, Carbondale; Lieutenant and assistant surgeon, George E. Hilgard, Bellville; Steward, Walter S. Lamon, Paris; Steward, Harlow W. Long, Newton; Steward, Charles B. Mallonee, Paris; Privates, Willis O. Augustus, Ed W. Dickenson, Will Blackman, Willard Matthias, George Boyd, Raleigh M. Woolley, Ira Huffman, Warren Wiley, of Paris; Percy Link, of Robinson; Andy C. Musgrave, of Hutsonville; Allen P. Dibble, of Mattoon.

The Fourth's hospital corps at this time was an entirely seperate organization from the regiment. In other Illinois regiments the corps were chosen from the ranks of the command; but that of the Fourth was recruited directly from civil life.

When war with Spain was declared the corps was sworn into the United States service with the regiment, and proceeded to Jacksonville, Florida. Upon arrival at this camp it was learned that Congress, in calling for forces had neglected to make provision for volunteer hospital corps, consequently those men belonging to these organizations were compelled to be sworn into the regular army for a period of three years, or until the war was over. At about this time an order was issued announcing that these corps should be enlarged in point of numbers, each regiment to furnish from twenty-five to thirty men all told. Accord-

FOURTH ILLINOIS HOSPITAL.

ingly fresh men, to complete the organization, were detailed by the twelve companies, and these, inclusive of the original corps, were then sworn into the regular army.

The new men to enter this branch of the service were as follows: Privates Elza M. Ragan, Harry L. Cullom, Leonard A. Osborne, Company E; Sergeant John P. Wilkins, Private Hans Gassman, Company A; Fred Huffman, Ed Lowe, Homer Putnam, James Logan, Charles Bagley, Company H; David Black, Company L; Hugo Goelitz, Company D; Carl Baker, Harry Stites, Company C; John Hoffman, Harry S. Huffman, Bert W. Caldwell, Company G; Edward Hill, Malcolm Hutchison, Company I; James Burge, Company K; Charles E. Little, Charles O. Burton, Jefferson Portlock, Company B; George Perry, Claude McCool, James Oglesby, Company M.

After being fully equipped with hospital accoutrements the majority of the men were permanently detailed to the division hospitals of the army corps, Steward Long and Privates Augustus and Boyd remaining at the regimental hospital for duty. Lieut. George E. Hilgard, Steward Charles B. Mallonee, and Privates Blackman, Dyas, Ewing, Woolley, Huffman (Ira), Hutchison, and Ragan, were sent to the Second Division Ambulance Company, while the remainder of the organization were ordered to report to the Second Division Hospital. In September the ambulance company was disbanded and the men sent to the division hospital. Steward Walter S. Lamon and Private Ed W. Dickenson were then detailed for duty at the medical supply depot in the city of Jacksonville, the former to assume charge of the establishment under Maj. James E. Pilcher, and the latter to act as clerk. Private Dickenson was honorably discharged in August. Subsequently Private Walter L. Ewing, of the ambulance company, was sent here also for duty.

Owing to the efficiency and general worth of the men sent from the Fourth into the medical department, more promotions fell to these men than all other regimental hospital corps in the Seventh Army Corps combined. This evidently was not a matter of chance or accident, but shows the care with which the selections had been made in the organization and recruiting of the corps.

Those of the privates to be made acting stewards after entrance into the regular service were: Acting Stewards A. C. Musgrave, Hans Gassman, Charles O. Burton, Raleigh M. Woolley, Charles E. Little, Allen P. Dibble and David Black. Promoted to lance acting stewards, a rank immediately below acting steward, were Harry Stites ank Hugo Goelitz. In other regiments the commanders of companies took advantage of the opportunities afforded in the call for men to recruit the medical department by unloading their objectionable soldiers into this branch of the service. This was not practiced among the Fourth's officers. In fact, the best men of each company were chosen for the work, and consequently reward in promotion was given them for the valuable and meritorious service rendered.

While in Jacksonville, Maj. T. C. McCord was detailed as brigade surgeon, and won for himself no small amount of distinction, so well did he conduct the affairs pertaining to this responsible position.

In November, 1898, after the regiment had moved to Savannah, Lieut. Charles M. Galbraith was ordered to report to the First Division hospital for duty, where he was placed in command of one of the companies. Upon several occasions, during the absence of Maj. John R. McDill, commander of the entire hospital, Lieutenant Galbraith acted in this capacity, always proving himself worthy of the trust bestowed upon him.

Before departure for Cuba it was decided by the chief surgeon of the army corps that each regiment should again have a small regimental hospital. They were to be a sort of a detention affair to retain men until their ailments could be thoroughly diagnosed. By this time Major McCord, Lieutenant Hilgard and Stewart Mallonee had been returned to the regiment from the posts to which they had been detailed for special duty.

To complete the regimental hospital company for service in Cuba, the following men were returned to the regiment from the first division hospital: Acting Steward Raleigh, M. Woolley, Privates Burge, Baker, Ira and Fred Huffman, Osborne, Ewing and Lowe. On departure for Cuba Steward Lamon was returned to the regiment.

One month later Ewing and Lowe were discharged while in Cuba; but the others remained with the regiment until mustered out. The men who were left on duty at the division hospital were individually discharged soon after the regiment was let out of the United States service.

MISS J. ENGELMANN.

[A sacrifice to the scourge at Jacksonville, Florida.]

Josephine Engelmann was born on her father's farm near Shiloh, Illinois, on the 16th of September, 1867.

She received only the education which that district afforded. She lost her mother when she was only twelve years old, and being the oldest of three children that were left, and being of a serious turn of mind, she made the best of the opportunities afforded, and under the guidance of her excellent father, Col. Adolph Engelmann, and her genial and highly gifted aunt, Miss Josephine Engelmann, developed into a noble womanhood. Having grown up in a family who had cut loose from all dogmatic beliefs, Josephine's intense desire for the spiritual and high, the craving of her nature for reverence and devotion, induced her to join the Methodist church, of which she was a true and faithful adherent up to her death.

MISS J. ENGELMANN.

When Colonel Engelmann was called to Belleville as postmaster, she became the mother of the little household, and the faithful helpmate of her father. After some years death claimed her aunt and soon after her father as his own. With the increase of her duties and responsibilities grew also Josephine's ardent wish and resolute determination to be the advisor and provider of her family, to be the means of developing her brother Otto, many years her junior, into that noble manhood of which the boy gave promise. Together they took care of a little farm, while Josephine added to their income by teaching school, first in the country and then at Belleville. Teaching was to her a religious act. She deeply felt the great responsibility resting with a teacher, of guiding the souls of her charges to find and love the beautiful and good, and great was her joy in being rewarded by the appreciative interest of the children. She also, for many years, with great interest and devotion, taught Sunday school at Belleville and at Shiloh. Thus years had flown, in which, amid all the arduous duties devolving upon this young woman, she persistently and eagerly made use of every opportunity of improving her mind and broadening her sympathies and sought to provide ways and means for her sister and brother to do the same.

When the war for the assistance of Cuban insurgents called our volunteers to arms, Josephine was thankful that duty prompted her young brother to stay with his orphaned sisters, although she was much in sympathy with this cause, thirsting ever to help the oppressed. But, when at the second call, Otto B. Engelmann felt it his duty to offer his services to the need of his country, she unflinchingly gave her approval. Her trembling heart had learned to place duty above its own desires. Otto Engelmann joined Company D Fourth Regular Illinois Volunteers on the 16th of June, fitted out with all that the love and devotion of his sisters could do for their young hero-brother.

With the eyes of love and solicitude every move of the regiment was watched, every line he wrote was weighed. When sickness began to strike down friends on all sides of the object of their solicitude, these girls lived between hope and despair, and when the news came that Otto was seriously sick, Josephine hastened to his bedside, to tear him from the claws of death, as she thought. Her mission was successful; not only did Otto recover, but she was also the means of bringing solace to many a sad heart by her sympathetic words and deeds.

But, alas, the dread disease had taken hold of her! Perhaps the anxiety and suffering had weakened her too much, or she had not paid sufficient attention to the approach of the disease. She went to the hospital on the 14th of October, and died on the 20th. Her body was sent home to be laid to rest in the family burial ground near Shiloh. The funeral was a touching tribute, paid by several hundred relatives and friends to this heroic girl, the true Christian, the noble woman. Could she have lived, the world would have been the better and happier for it; Josephine Engelmann's life would have been consecrated to the solacing and uplifting of humanity. Her noble example undoubtedly has inspired many a soul. Her influence and her memory live with us.

REV. H. W. TODD.

Rev. H. W. Todd, of Vandalia, Illinois, was, upon the recommendation of the regimental commander, duly appointed Chaplain of the Fourth Regiment Illinois Volunteer Infantry April 15, 1898. Reverend Todd served the regiment for six months, and owing to failing health resigned his position as Chaplain. Said resignation was accepted and he was honorably discharged November 1, 1898.

We regret that a more extended sketch could not be secured for this work.—J. R. S.

CAPT. H. W. TODD.   CAPT. J. R. SKINNER.

REV. J. R. SKINNER.

Born in Perry county, Ohio, December 25, 1846, his father dying before he reached the age of five years and the family breaking up two years later, he was thrown among strangers to struggle for himself. His early years were devoted to farming, blacksmithing and day labor while his education was practically neglected. But desiring the gospel ministry, he was encouraged by a friend, Rev. S. B. Leiter, D.D., to enter school and begin his literary preparations therefor. The counsel was accepted and Heidelburg University, Tiffin, Ohio, was the institution chosen for that purpose, and after years and parts of years of hard study and economy, that at times amounted to sacrifice, in June, 1873, he entered upon his chosen profession at Winimac, Indiana, near where, in 1876, he was united in marriage to Mary A. Good, who with their elder son entered the service of the United States, some months prior to his chaplaincy. He has served fields in Ohio, Michigan, Iowa, Kansas, Texas and Illinois, which latter state he has had the honor of representing in the chaplaincy of the Fourth Illinois Volunteers in their campaign as a part of the army of occupation in Cuba. As to efficiency and faithfulness in this capacity it is left for those intimate with his work to testify.

J. UPTON EVERS.

J. Uptan Evers, of New York City, now a representative of the Army and Navy International Christian Commission, was born in Reading City, Pennsylvania. Owing to his father's ministerial profession he resided in various eastern cities during childhood.

After graduating at the Academy and High school,

J. U. EVERS.

Mr. Evers studied law two years at Martinsburg, West Virginia, where he subsequently practiced in the magistrate courts. At the conclusion of his legal studies he entered Dickinson College at Carlisle, Pensylvania. Subsequent to his collegiate course he accepted a position in a prominent law firm of Baltimore, Maryland, where he assumed charge of a legal department.

Being strongly convinced that he ought to prepare for the ministry, he entered Drew Theological Seminary. While pursuing his theological studies, he received license to preach and assisted the pastor of Cornell Memorial church in New York City, doing considerable missionary work in the densely populated districts of the city.

When war was declared Mr. Evers' services were secured to represent Young Men's Christian Association work in various military camps. He labored at Camp Alger, Virginia, Camp Meade, Pensylvania, and Camp Wetherell, South Carolina, after which he went to Camp Columbia, Cuba.

Prior to camp work in the south, Mr. Evers was called to a pastorate in Hoboken, New Jersey, but upon realizing the urgent need of Christian work among the soldiers, resigned his charge, notwithstanding his congregation would not willingly consent to his resignation.

On the 6th of February, 1899, Mr. Evers arrived in Cuba, and began Y. M. C. A. work in the Fourth Illinois Volunteer Regiment, and the First Division Hospital at Buena Vista. About one hundred men of the Fourth Illinois Regiment were converted through the efforts of the Y. M. C. A. and the able co-operation of the chaplain, J. R. Skinner.

When the volunteer regiments were ordered home, Mr. Evers remained in Cuba to assist in permanently organizing Y. M. C. A. work throughout the island.

CHAPLAINCY.

The chaplaincy of this regiment dates back to a period much earlier than its call to the service of the United States. Reverend McNutt, of Effingham, Ill., having resigned shortly before the call of our country, Reverend H. W. Todd, of Vandalia, was chosen and commissioned as his successor, continuing in the position some six months, when he resigned to return home. To fill or occupy the vacancy thus occasioned, Col. Casimer Andel detailed Sergt. R. W. Ropiquet, a young attorney in Company D, who held the position until he received his discharge later in the fall. The position continued vacant until December 8, when Reverend John R. Skinner, of Arcola, Ill., was commissioned, reporting for duty the 22d of the same month.

On taking up the work that devolved upon us in the regiment, we found a large field for usefulness, but limited facilities as helps in the accomplishment of the work that needed so much to be done. But as the regiment was expected to take its departure for Cuba in a few days, it was not thought wise to attempt any preparations at Camp Onward for holding religious meetings. Neither was it thought prudent to hold service on the one Sabbath which we were permitted to spend with them in this camp, as we could scarcely keep warm around our little stoves in the tents. Yet the work to be done in Cuba must be prepared for, and accordingly Mr. A. E. Moody, of the Army and Navy Department of the Young Men's Christian Association, who has charge of their work in the Seventh Army Corps, was sought out at his headquarters in the city, and negotiations for one of their tents was entered into with him at once. And while nothing definite could be reached, yet there were sufficient gleams of success to encourage us to the pressing of our request after reaching Cuba. Accordingly, after about two weeks of hard work in getting his business and materials out of the almost limitless tangle into which the transportation with regimental goods had brought them, Mr. Moody informed us that the way seemed clear to furnish us a tent, secretary, and all necessary equipments for the use of our regiment. Every effort was made to hasten this bright outlook into a pleasant reality, but to our disappointment it was one of those conditions of things that move slowly and cannot be crowded. But during this time our first Sabbath on the island had dawned upon us after a night of almost incessant rain and windstorm, which demoralized many of the tents that were up, producing a very unpleasant condition under foot, besides the work of moving goods from the city to camp and the pitching of tents made it wholly impracticable to call the men together at the hour for service. The Sabbath following dawned upon us brightly, and at service call, 9 in the morning, the band with a couple of pieces of well-chosen music, called a goodly number of the boys about us in front of the guard tent, where it was our first privilege to address an army of men on the great question of their duties and responsibilities in reference to their relation to God and their fellowmen, a privilege we certainly enjoyed.

But the day that bade so well in its beginning, was made sad to us 'ere the noontide was reached by the drowning of one of Company K's men while bathing in the beautiful clear stream a short distance from camp. On the following Sabbath, the hour for service was so fully occupied by the departure of the Third Battalion on a seven days' outing and march, as to prevent our holding any service, and the next Sabbath we were doomed to a similar experience by the return of this battalion at the hour of church. But, being hindered at home, we assisted Chaplain Given, of the Sixth Missouri, one of God's noble, devoted men, while on the evening of this Sabbath we preached to the nurses of the Second Division hospital in their mess tent. During the last week in January we succeeded in securing from the Young Men's Christian Association mana-

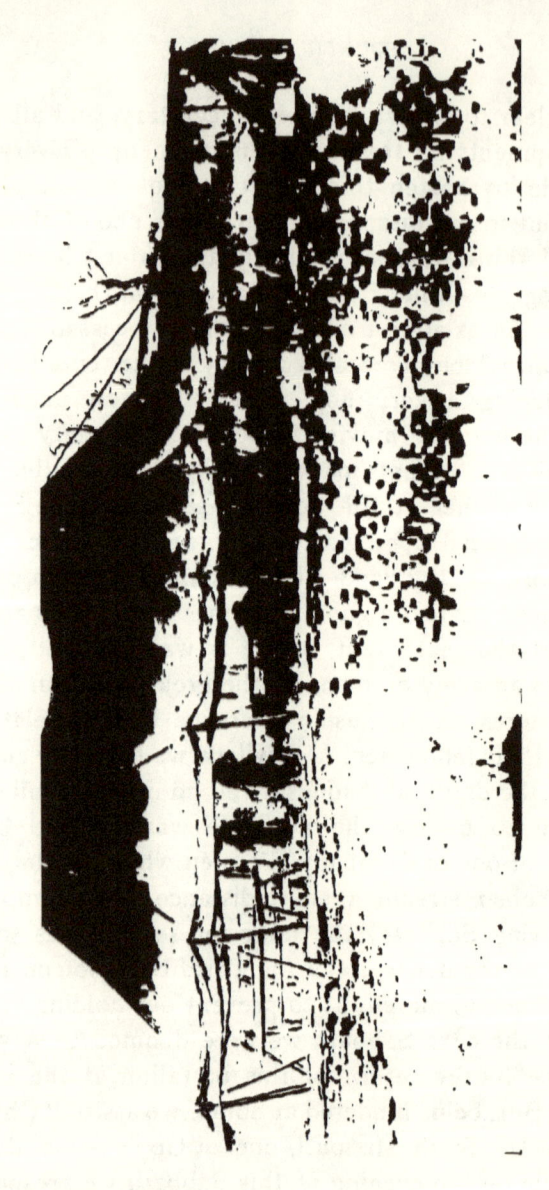

ger in the corps, a good tent forty by sixty feet, and brought it on the ground, but we were still doomed to disappointment, for at every move we found a shortage, in rops, poles, pegs, tackles and lumber, while the rains that intervened delayed the setting up of our tabernacle until the second week in January, when a band of volunteers from the regiment cheerfully gave us their assistance, and for the first time in its history, the canvas of a gospel tent was spread to the breeze, in the camp of the Fourth Illinois Volunteers.

Through the efforts of Mr. Mitchell, an efficient secretary of the Army Young Men's Christian Association, and the aid of several of the boys from the regiment, we succeeded in getting it seated and some conveniences for writing in place. And on Sabbath, February 12th, at 9 o'clock in the morning, we had our first service in the tent, followed by another at 7 in the evening, both of which were largely attended, encouraging our hearts for the future. But scarcely had we reached our humble tent homes when a strong wind from the sea began to rush in upon us, attended by a heavy downpour of rain that betokened disaster to our frail abodes. For early in the evening nature had begun to muster her cloud host, and continued it until the last star which had thrown its flickering rays out through the broken ranks, was hid back of its threatening panoply, while the bright sheen of the distant heavens seemed to be crouching away into hiding, before the threatening array. Along with this marshaling of the dark cloud host came the low but ever increasing murmur of the waves as they moved out farther and farther on the rock-clad beach, until what had been to us a murmur reached a crash and roar of contending armies as the wind whipped the gently rolling waves into maddened billows that rolled far out and broke upon the shore, scattering into mist and foam, to be carried by the furious storm and dropped like rain on the brush covered flats that border the ocean at this point.

The storm continued to increase and in a short time the moistened earth enabled the gale to draw the guy pegs, and our gospel tent was hurled, to the ground, demolishing lamps and seriously damaging the organ, while at the same time it gave the secretary a kindly warning by landing one of the center poles within a few inches of his tent, in which he was seeking rest.

But soldiers learn to make the best of conditions and therefore nothing daunted, preparations were begun to set it up again as soon as the gale, which continued through Monday and Tuesday, had subsided, and by Friday all was put in condition for use again, and on that evening another service was held, conducted by Secretary Mitchell, who was preparing to turn his work over to J. Upton Evers, prior to taking leave for his home in the States. In Brother Evers we found a true Christian young man who earnestly devoted himself not only to the work directly connected with the gospel tent, but also in visiting the hospital, carrying to the sick stationary, books, periodicals and good cheer, as well also in his private earnest appeals to the boys. At the tent and elsewhere he impressed upon them the importance of leading a godly life.

And it is but just we should mention that after considerable effort and delay, William Newton, of company H, was detailed as assistent secretary, who with Brother Evers, rendered efficient and faithful service during our stay at Camp Columbia. Contrary to our earnest expectations no services could be held on the 19th of February, on account of an order having been issued, ordering the regiment to start on a ten days march and outing on that date. Accordingly everything was astir Sunday morning and about 9:00 o'clock the regiment marched out of camp led by the band, followed by the Ninth Illinois and Second South Carolinia, the other two regiments of the brigade, started on their march to the city of Guines, which is located forty-nine kilometers south-east of Havana, and distant from our camp about thirty-five miles. Not desiring to attend the regiment on Sabbath morning, we secured permission to follow later. Accordingly we started in pursuit on Tuesday at 5:00 in the morning, having spent Monday hunting their trail, coming up to them at 4:00 in the evening, just as they were going into camp, which we will call Camp Swift, about one mile beyond Guines. We remained with the regiment until Saturday at 9:00 in the morning when we left them in camp at the mountain pass twenty-five kilometers from Havana, and came back to our own sunburned, storm-stained canvas house in the midst of an almost deserted quiet camp. The regiment not returning until Monday our gospel tent stood idle two Sabbaths. But on the 1st of March we had our first mid-week meeting with good attendance, and on the following Sabbath, we began a series of meetings, having the help of Chaplain Stringfellow of the Fourth Virginia, Chaplain Biederwolf of the One Hundred Sixty-first Indiana, and Chaplain Given of the Sixth Missouri during the week. Pay day coming unexpectedly on Saturday, so broke in upon the conditions in camp as to make it unadvisable to hold service on that evening. But on the day following at 9:00 in the morning we organized our bible class and had preaching service immediately afterwards, while in the evening Mr. Evens gave us a good practical talk. Up to this time, twenty-five soldiers had signed the following declaration and handed them to the secretary. "I hereby declare my acceptance of the Lord Jesus Christ as my personal Savior and my purpose by God's help to live a Christian life."

Name—— ——

Company and Regiment—— ——

Home address—— ——

Our band gave a concert in the tent one evening each week, besides we had a most thrilling lecture by Chaplain. Stringfellow on his experience as captain or chief of scouts in the confederate army, also one by Chaplain Bolton, of the Second Illinois, on "Something to shoot and how to shoot it;" which was a fine illustration of the scholarly ability and oratorical power of one of Wisconsin's ablest M. E. preachers.

Through the influence of General Secretary A. E. Moody, of the island Y. M. C. A. work, it was our exceptional good fortune to have with us one evening the gifted and eloquent Rev. Sam Small, who gave us one of his thrilling characteristic lectures, touching upon many phases of life as seen not only in the army, but as well in the civil, political and social relations of America. Y. M. C. A. Evanglist Smith, of Chicago, was with us several nights during our last week in Cuba, and gave us on each occasion a sermon full of gospel meat, and rich in counsel and advice to men. It was his privilege to hold the closing service on the night before our departure. Nor would we neglect to refer, and that with pleasure, to the efficient and effective aid rendered in our behalf by Sec. A. E. Moody, through whom we were enabled to have our gospel tent and its valuble supplies, as well also his talks on themes fitting so well the needs of our regiment. While it may seem improper to refer to our disappointments, yet the fact of our hasty breaking of camp deprived us of the anticipated pleasure of listening to Reverend Clark, Father of the Christian Endeavor movement, who was booked to address us in the gospel tent on the evening of the day we began our march toward the home land. We feel called upon to give it at least a passing mention. What the result of these efforts will be, as weighed and measured for eternity, cannot be estimated by finite minds, yet it is the hope and earnest prayer of those who have wrought therein, that many of the men who enjoyed these rich privileges in the closing days of their army life, will so profit by them in the moulding of their lives as civilians, and the consecrating of their hearts to God in Christ, as to realize the wonderful cleansing of his precious blood, and a title to the kingdom of heaven. Our regiment having been made up from so large a portion of our state and even beyond its borders, necessarily gathered in from the "good, bad and indifferent," morally; yet not more striking in this respect than those with which it was thrown, in the corps organization. Yet judging from the facts apparent on the surface, the family having the largest representation in our organization, being found in every company, was the popular "crap" family. Nor were they enlisted men only, but even in the corral and cook shack, and some of very sombre hue, this family can claim as its membership. Besides not a few have gotten well up the line under shoulder straps. But in the main they can be said to be a pretty fair sort of people, measuring up to the highest average of social life in that section of the state from which they came, and to the strata of society to which the various grades and hues of color belong. Still it is with pain of heart we feel called upon as a chronicler of the truth to refer to the fact of the demoralizing prevalence of profanity and other forms of sin that became notorious; and often under the erroneous idea that almost any sin was condonned by being a soldier. Still there were grand and noble exceptions in all these gradations, of true men, who like the sturdy oak or enduring granite withstood this storm and rushing torrent of sin and degredation, maintaining an equilibrium of manly character worthy of record.

With song service and expository talks on portions of scripture, we endeavored to give the boys of the Fourth and the First Division Hospital Corp during our stay in Cuba that which we trust will prove a blessing as well as a pleasure to them, and be looked back upon by them as a bright oasis in their army experiences. That the boys appreciated the gospel tent with its supply of books, tracts, papers, writing material and innocent games, was proven by the large crowds that commonly filled all the large tables during the hours of the day when not on duty in the camp or on the drill ground, and as an evidence of the amount of writing done there, ten thousand sheets of paper and a corresponding number of envelopes would supply the demand only about two or three weeks, showing also the expense connected with this excellent branch of Christian work.

ADENDA.

In presenting a few miscellaneous illustrations, indirectly connected with the history of this regiment, it may be well also to give a brief description of them and their surroundings, that the reader may get a clearer idea concerning their beauty and utility, or their opposite.

We will first ask the reader to go with us into the land so recently brought under the control of the United States as the scenes of this strange land will doubtless be of much interest.

Much that we have heard about the great Cuban army dims into a shadow when we confront the real, as we meet it in its own land and measure it by what we see. We present herewith a picture of a few of these brave warriors

SPECIMENS OF THE CUBAN ARMY.

in one of their "posts," viz.: the porch of a wayside residence and grocery. The general appearance and equipment is not such as to strike terror home to the heart of an American soldier. They ordinarly lack that manly bearing on duty, so characteristic of the more highly enlightened races.

In connection with this we insert a cut representing one and a portion of two others of a row of seventeen tents occupied by the warriors of the isle. Rude and simple in their construction, being built with a few posts set in the ground and ridge or roof poles placed thereon, and over these the long fern like leaves of the royal palm are placed, with points to the eves, sufficiently thick to turn the rains.

CUBAN SOLDIERS AND CAMP.

In connection with these the sheath of these same leaves, that surround the body of the tree, are spread out, making a large surface, often from eight to twelve feet. These, like the leaves, are used both for roofing and weather-boarding. The simplicity of this construction does away with the expense of nails, as thongs made from the inner bark of these sheathes are used to tie them in their places. The Cuban soldier in one sense is quite an inexpensive luxury.

In contrast with these one meets on almost every hill top in proximity with Havana, the famous barbed wire

BARB WIRE DEFENSE.

barricade, used by our Spanish neighbors as an outer defense of their fort, against this formidable Cuban army. While our illustration is a good one it cannot reveal the real strength of these barricades. They are often ten to twenty feet wide and so thickly woven and interwoven as to make an American soldier prefer a stone wall or earth works, if he is to do the storming of the enemy that lurks behind.

The posts to which these wires are fastened are so arranged that but few of the many wires, have a run of more than two or three feet, while to go through, one would have to cut from 150 to 200 of these twisted barbed strands in two places, which would be more than a few minutes job, and while he was working away, deliberately or otherwise, the fellow inside would have a fine mark on which to train his trusty rifle. If he were asleep or whiling away the time at a game of cards, and the click of wire cutters did not attract his attention, the strong hold might be taken with only the loss of blood that flowed from scratched hands. But that was not Uncle Sam's way of doing things.

He kept at a respectable distance and dropped a few shells just beyond the wire fence, until the other fellow evacuated and then went in through the gate, and saved the barbed wire for the free Cuban to fence his farm.

All through the interior of the island at every turn in the road, and if these were too far apart, built in the road and on commanding hills, the eye catches the familiar block-house, another of the time-worn Spanish defenses.

We here show a very good cut of one of these. In their day good protectors against rifle bullets, but in this day of improved guns our bullets would only get well heated in passing through one of these, for searing the hole it would make through the body of its victim, lying concealed behind these walls of brick. Sometimes they are constructed of stone, and we have seen them in the interior, of

BLOCK HOUSE.

frame weatherboarded with the shell or outer surface of the royal palm, sheathed with the same on the inside, and filled between the studings with dirt and small stones. These were built in various shapes, yet easily distinguished from other buildings by the port holes so in evidence.

Along with these properly come the people of this, to us, strange country, with some of their time-honored customs. It is truly a mixed race, with perhaps the race line distinction a little less sharply drawn than in our own land, yet a people, who, under ordinary circumstances, are contented and happy, with no little degree of the climatic desire for rest, ever nagging at them. Many of their customs and ideas are of an antiquated type, or rather they still live in the centuries of the past. Hence, with one of the most

A MIXED RACE.

A CUBAN PLOWING.

beautiful lands, and on which nature has bestowed with a lavish hand, we meet with the old wooden plow of the type used in the age of Moses, with a few slight improvements, while the faithful ox, who has caught the rest fever also, is persuaded on in his task with the goad as of yore. Still in spite of these antiquated tools and methods, nature produces in rich abundance.

The tandem teams are at first a strange sight to the American, but, like all the odities in this land, one with which he soon becomes familiar. From two to eight mules or ponies, weighing from five to eight hundred pounds, are one of the common sights on the fine military roads; while the immense carts, weighing often much more than our

428 HISTORY OF THE

TANDEM TEAM ON MILITARY ROAD.

GEORGIA OX CART.

common wagons, and the correspondingly large loads, are in great contrast with the teams.

One chief reason for the two wheeled vehicles being so commonly used here is, the system of taxing vehicles per wheel, and another is the greater ease with which the team can draw the same amount of weight than when on a four wheeled vehicle. But we need not go beyond the borders of our own fair land to see conditions and things of the antiquated type as our picture of an ox cart reveals, and which is not an uncommon sight in that section of Georgia where our camps were located.

In striking contrast with the fine mansions with their open courts and gardens, filled with nature's richest bloom and tinted foliage, is that of the residences of the lower

THATCHED HUT.

class in the country and oft in the suburbs of the cities, which is only a thatched hut. The one here pictured to the reader is a good specimen, and stood on the border of Camp Columbia. Over the common pole frame, made by tying one pole to another, the long palm leaves are tied to constitute a roof, while the leaf sheath is spread out and tied to the wall frame perpendicularly for siding.

These abodes form the homes, very often, for more than the family, for dogs, pigs, fowls, fleas and, well, the *so forth*, all abide under the same roof.

Just across the road from this hut, and hard by one of the Spanish fortifications, seen in the background, stood

HANGMAN'S TREE.

one of the peculiar trees of this island, and which had acquired the title of hangman's tree, from the fact, as we were told, that on its projecting limb some seventy-five or eighty persons had been hung during the wars of Spain and Cuba.

As to the truth or falsity of the statement we do not vouch, but it gave to this tree a notoriety that cost it its life, and removal from its long occupied place. Little by little had the soldier's knife, saw, hatchet and other tools cut away small pieces, until it was near the point of falling, when one evening about 10 o'clock, just before the Seventh Army Corps broke camp for the home trip, the moon not failing nature in her brightest robes, a lieutenant and the writer returning from a ride up the beach, came by just as a little group of bluecoats assembled to look very closely at the deep scar in its trunk,—that is all they were doing as we passed, and not a tool for cutting was in sight, but lo the next morning saw only the haggled top of a stump to perpetuate the shame of that spot.

But more and larger souvenirs of the hangman's tree were on exhibition in certain parts of the corps in a day or two, than ever before.

Something of the governmental preparation to meet all the necessary demands that fall upon it in supplying the Army of Occupation in Cuba, may be gathered from a miniature view of her immense quartermasters store house, located at Quemados, within the bounds of Camp Columbia.

While the waiting wagon train indicates something of the demands that were made upon this, one of the most important, laborious and difficult branches of work connected with the army.

QUARTERMASTER'S STORE HOUSE, QUEMADOS.

Among the revered landmarks of the city of Havana is that of "The Cathedral," a view of the interior of which is here given, and which needs but little description. At the bottom left hand corner a portion of "the tomb of Columbus," the corner from which the marble slabs that form the slanting wall, were removed to gain access to the remains of the once dishonored discoverer, and from which it is generally believed his dust was taken lest it be dishonored by the "uncultured Americans."

We never saw anyone but monks or priests at worship in this sacred place, which was open every afternoon.

Passing just beyond the northwest limit of the city we came to the Cristobol Colon cemetery, one of the most

INTERIOR OF THE CATHEDRAL.

beautiful and at the same time loathsome burial places of the world. Its gateway, monuments, tombs, catacombs, and public buildings, are certainly not often excelled. The monument erected to the memory of the firemen who lost their lives in a heroic struggle against the flames that threatened the city some years since, is said to be one of three that stand as competitors for rank as the grandest in the world.

But while one-half of this large enclosure charms you with its beauty and richness, the other half is equally loathsome.

In the northwest corner of the main ground, which is enclosed by a high, strong stone wall, is found another wall, less defiant, yet some 8 feet high, and 100 by 130 feet square, with its enclosure excavated in the limestone rock 35 feet deep, and which is filled to a little above the level of the surface with the bleached bones of human beings. This is the "human boneyard" of an inhuman people. We here give a cut of it—one of the most shocking scenes in this lovely land.

The dimensions of this awful tomb we cannot vouch for, but received them from one who claimed to have gotten the facts. But as to the millions of skeletons said to rest (i. e., until bluecoats began to seek for skulls, cross bones, teeth, etc., to carry home as mementos) in this vast grave are so great that we do not venture to repeat it as a fact.

But hard to believe as this is to some, still more shocking is what leads to the filling of this pit with human bones, viz.: That of the burial tax which the ruling church power of that island has been collecting for years. The sum exacted is so great that only a portion of the poor can meet it, and that only for a few, perhaps five years, the shortest period, we are told, for which it is collected.

HUMAN BONE YARD.

Such are ordinarily placed in the grave in an almost nude state and lime thrown on the body and covered a few inches deep with dirt, and at the expiration of the tax period the bleached bones are exhumed and borne in baskets to the "bone-yard." Sometimes it happens that these large, double-decked, poor man's hearses, containing two trays to the deck, come in with four occupants, and the trays are taken out one at a time, laid at the edge of the grave, and then turned over, dumping its contents into the grave; the liming is attended to and another treated in the same way, until, as we have been told by eye witnesses, ten bodies had been thus roughly dumped into one grave, when a thin covering of dirt was thrown upon them.

But another, we suppose poorer class, are hauled directly to a kind of morgue at the center of the south wall of the cemetery, where the bodies are placed on tables and subjected to a process of liming which soon prepares the bones for bleaching in the common grave of the poor. In the less pretentious burial grounds of this land, all of which are strongly walled, the bones are usually thrown in a pile in one corner, and the writer has seen various bones of the human body that the dogs or buzzards had carried into the road beyond the rocked enclosure. But the time of this uncivilized, unchristian practice we believe is past.

Before our departure from this lovely land, the United States authorities had required the covering of the "bone yard" with earth, as a sanitary measure.

Thus, while the rich man's body is borne away in all the splendor of liveried coachmen, with their gorgeously decked "four-in-hand," and costly gilded hearse, to his last resting place on which a perpetual tax is arranged for, his neighbor is treated little if any better than the domestic animals of our country.

It was in the better part of this noted cemetery that, on

the 17th day of February, 1898, nineteen bodies of the brave men who died in their quarters in the ill-fated Maine, were interred; and later others were laid by their side until more than fifty bodies of those noble seamen had found their last resting place in the soil of this sacred enclosure, where only a simple cross bearing these words, "Victims of the Maine," mark their last resting place.

As this is in so great contrast with the gorgeous surroundings, already a movement is on foot to erect a suitable monument in place of the wooden one that now points the American to the spot, most dear to him of all he here looks upon.

In passing from these scenes of this newly conquered Spanish province, we wish to call attention to an aged burying place of our own land, and one indirectly connected with the history of this as well as other regiments of the Seventh Army Corps.

It is "Bonaventure," which is located a short distance from the city limits of Savannah, Ga. This is one of the oldest and most noted burial places in the United States, and at the same time one connected by very important links with the early history of the "Sunny South."

We perhaps cannot do better in describing this beautiful and historic place than to insert, by permission, a short extract from the "History of the 161st Indiana Volunteer Infantry," in which Chaplain Biederwolf says: "Bonaventure is said to be one of the most beautiful cemeteries in America, and the history and romance connected with it makes it doubly interesting; the estate, first owned in colonial times by an English nobleman, was sold to John Mulryn, whose only daughter was given in marriage to Josiah Tatnall and the union was typified by planting those now aged and hoary live oaks in a mono-

MAINE GRAVES.

BONAVENTURE CEMETERY.

gram, comprising the letters 'M' and 'T' still traceable in the shape of the sylvan aisles between the stately trees. Josiah Tatnell was a great soldier, serving in the wars of 1812 and of 1846, and was commander of the Merrimac in its battle with the Monitor.

"He became governor of Georgia, and lies buried today in Bonaventure, near the spot of his birth. The place is full of sacred associations and its gigantic trees, hung with their long heavy moss tresses, seem to speak of mourning and weeping."

The cut we give but tamely represents the scene as viewed in its real beauty. The long bunches of gray moss that hang from almost every bough, like the tresses of some fair lady gracefully floating under the sway of the gentle evening zephyr, must be seen to be appreciated.

Passing from these scenes in the home of the dead it will be a relief to look upon and contemplate something closely identified with life and its sweetest pleasures. The city of Havana, though beautifully situated, and charming in its surroundings, yet was seriously marred as a place to live on account of the scant supply of pure water. And while Cuba has an abundance of this article, and of the finest quality, its unequal distribution leaves many charming localities destitute, save the streams that flow through the crevices of the rock far below the surface.

To meet the needs of Havana city, the idea was conceived of conveying water into it through aqueducts from the limpid streams in the country. After several partially successful attempts, the present system, or aqueducts of the Vento, was begun as recent as 1859, with a view of securing an ample supply from the inexhaustible Vento spring, one of the many fountains of this country that sends out a small river from its mouth. Vento spring is some eight miles south of the city, near the hills, and on the very margin of the clear, rapid flowing Almandares river, and yet sufficiently elevated above the sea to need only the force of gravitation to carry it through the immense artificial channel that ascends the little hills and descends into the plains, always just below the surface of the long stretch of country, that lies between the fountain and the city.

Though the present appliance has cost the magnificent sum of over three millions of dollars, it is far from being completed according to original plans, but has been connected with the aqueduct of Ferdinand II, proving itself adequate to the demands of the city, and even more. For the United States government tapped this stream at the

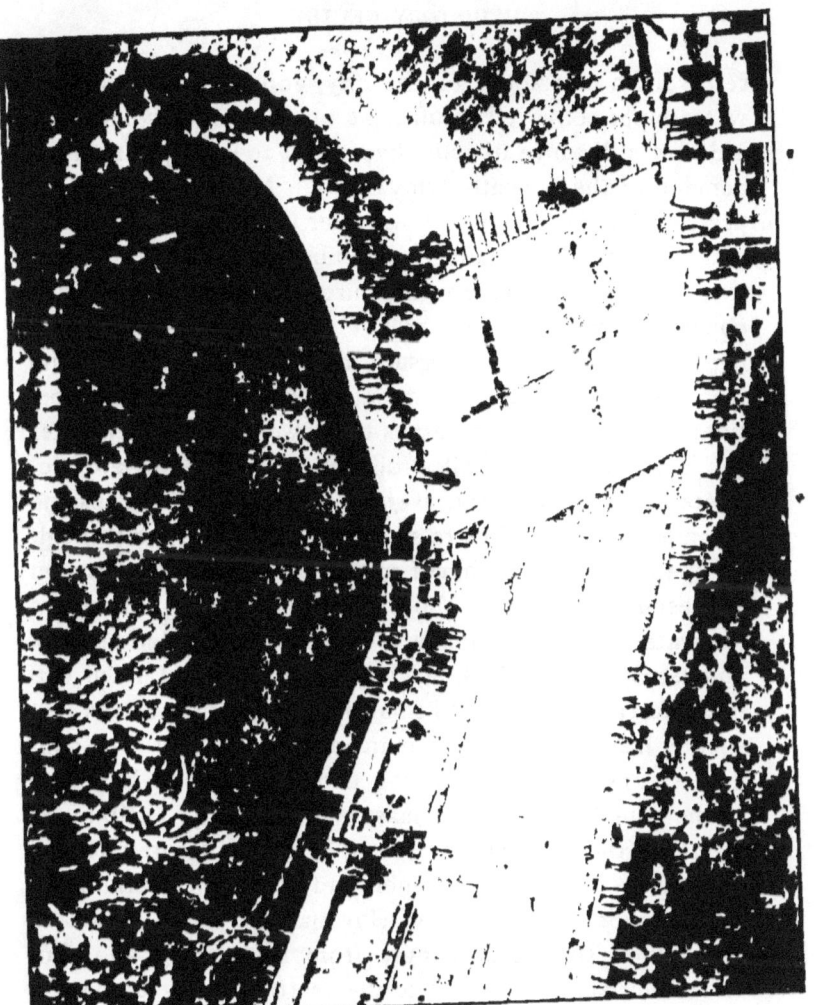

VENTO SPRINGS.

reservoir, a mile south of the city, and by means of large water pipes conveyed a sufficient quantity of this pure limpid flow a distance of some five miles, to supply the entire demand of the Seventh Army Corps. Not having sufficient pressure for flushing purposes, after its long run through a cramped artificial channel, an immense tank 22 x 24 feet was erected on a frame work, thirty feet high, at the headquarters of our regiment, the fate of which is referred to on page 329. The added pressure from the tank erected in its place sends the water with great force to the remotest portions of the camp, and flushes the sewer pipes, which enter the sea some four miles distant. To attempt an adequate description of this wonderful spring would consume too much space; suffice to say that the spring rises through an opening in the bottom of a large deep basin, constructed of masonry, as seen in the accompanying cut. From this the water enters the aqueduct, which is constructed of brick and cement, over which at regular intervals of about two hundred yards are erected small houses from six to ten feet square, inside of which are man holes opening into the aquduct for purposes of repairing damages that might accrue to the aqueduct, with the least possible delay. It may be said that these houses or towers are kept securely locked and often inspected. Rumor had it that General Lee's plan of capturing the city of Havana was, to get back of it and cut off the water supply from this spring, and thus force their surrender. As to the truth of this plan we are not prepared to say, not having consulted the General about it, as we suppose the originators of the rumor did not either. But don't think for a moment the forces of Spain were asleep to the importance of this point.

Our foot ball team needs no introduction or elaborate "write up," as the manly appearance of its men tell of its

FOOTBALL TEAM.

fitness to achieve honor in its line. We number and name them for easy recognition by their friends. 1 Sergt. R. H. Barton, Company C; 2 Corp. O. P. Louden, Company C; 3 Corp. Fred H. Hays, Company M; 4 Bert Railsback, Company M; 5 Musician W. T. Mather, Company L; 6 W. O. Wallace, Company D; 7 C. L. Golden, Company M; 8 Corp. W. McKnight; 9 Roy Harris, Company M; 10 L. C. Baker, Company M; 11 Corp. O. Kaufman, Company L; 12 F. Cady, Company M; 13 J. Eckenrode, Company L; 14 J. Kaser, Company L; 15 H. Balding, Company L; 16 Lieut T. F. Louden, Company C; 17 C. Harmon, Company L; 18 H. Bundy, Company M.

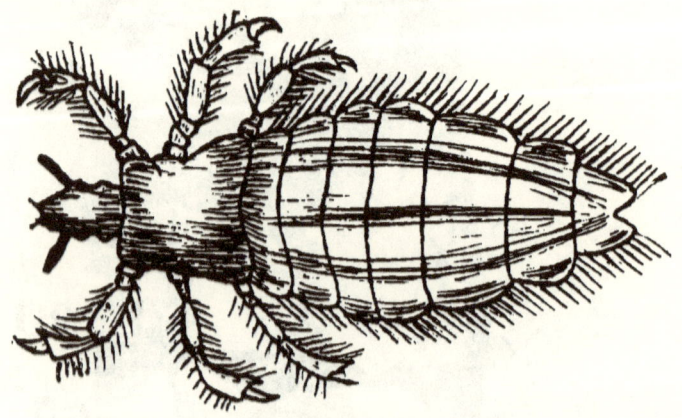

A GRAYBACK.

While perhaps there are but few who have not heard of that pestiferous little tickler, the "grayback," yet doubtless the multitude have never seen him. Therefore, we have thought it proper, since we cannot introduce him in person to the reader, never having had the pleasure of looking upon him ourselves, to do the next best thing to it, viz: to present to you a picture of his grayback-ship. And if you are blest with a strong imaginative faculty, you will be able to discern the familliar letters U. S. that you have so often heard spoken of, clearly outlined on his back, even though he may be of the Cuban species.

While this cut is very much enlarged, yet doubtless it does not present him any larger than you would suppose him to be, if he were engaged in a flank movement, or making some strategtic turn in order to appropriate a portion of the vital fluids of your system, or perhaps on a double time movement seeking out a safe retreat from a pursuing finger, in some near by seam of your trousers.

We are indebted to private Hallie Brown, of Montcello, Indiana, an ex-member of Company I, One Hundred Sixty-first Indiana Volunteers, who made the pen drawing, from a photograph of his verminship, from which this etching was produced; also to his father, E. R. Brown, for the privilege to use it in this volume. If any soldier fails to recognize this his camp friend, it certainly will be because he is a "tender foot" or novice in army camp life, or because the enlarged condition of his "bugship" brings out strongly so many of his commonly unseen delicate features, as to conceal his identity. "But it's his bugship just the same."

As "variety is the spice of life," we deem it prudent to add a little to this volume by sandwiching an address delivered at Vandalia on the occasion of the reception of Company I, on its return from Cuba, by comrade George Cheney, a private in that company.

ADDRESS.

Mr. Chairman, Ladies, Gentlemen and Friends:

A darkey preacher once visited a conference of his Methodist white brethren. As the sole representative of his race present, he was called upon for an address. He arose and said: "My dear brethren, I feel very much like a huckleberry in a bowl of milk." I opine that my present feelings are very similar to those of the colored orator.

Nevertheless, it gives me great pleasure to express to you the sincere appreciation and deep gratitude which we feel for this sumptuous banquet and hospitable reception which you have accorded us. But mere words cannot express the depth and intensity of the emotions which agitate our hearts on this occasion of our reunion with families, friends and neighbors. Far more eloquent and expressive than mere words is the joy that beams from the eye, and the gratitude that trembles in the voice.

Yet the feelings of joy and happiness are not unmingled with those of sadness and sorrow, for we are not all here. Hall, Ryan, Smith, McLaren,—our eyes seek for them in vain. They have crossed the stream of silvery sheen, and pitched their tents on the further bank of the River of Life. They have joined the band of immortal patriots on the other shore and wait and beckon for those who survive.

Citizens of Vandalia, one year has flown to the dim regions of eternity since our nation stood on the verge of a great international struggle. The ominous mutterings of an approaching storm were heard and the dark waters and thick clouds of war had obscured the heavenly light of peace. The angry lightning of public indignation painted the war cloud a lurid hue and the angry voice of public protest rolled along the national horizon in thunder peals. All felt that a struggle was inevitable. The spirit voices calling from the dark waters of Havana harbor, the prayers of the widows, and the cries of the orphans had ascended to the judgment seat of a long suffering God, who ordained that a nation whose beacon light was liberty, fraternity, equality, whose might was equal to its will, whose mercy was equal to its wrath, whose judgment was sure and whose vengence was swift, should deliver the beautiful captive from the cruel hand of the tyrant robber and assassin.

A short but terrible struggle was anticipated. Many prophesied that our peerless navy would be swept from the sea; that our inexperienced regulars and untrained volunteers would meet swift defeat. We deceived ourselves miserably. But with these forebodings in their mind, the sons of freedom, true to their teachings and inheritance, rallied to the battle cry of freedom, offering their lives on the altar of patriotism, a cheerful sacrifice for the defense of an oppressed and struggling people and of the honor of their country.

Obedient to the summons of the alarm bells of war, the boys of Company I, with rifles glinting in the sunlight, marched proudly away to the noise of drum and cymbal, fife and trumpet, with visions of the awful grandeur of war floating before their excited imagination, and now having done all that opportunity permitted, they have returned with the blossoms of spring—a badly disappointed, a sadder and a wiser set—the "bottle" scarred veterans and heroes of two hundred and fifty dress parades and twenty-five reviews.

Not long had we been from home before we learned the truth of Sherman's aphorism. It wasn't all music and hallelujah, hip and hurrah boys, well wishes and God speed you's, chicken sandwiches, pies and cakes from home, dress parade, reviews and marches before cheering thousands and pretty girls with tears in their eyes.

It was a deal of mud and dirt, weary hips, monotonous drills, rice that rattled as it went down, beef that looked as though it wanted to hook into the gravy in which you couldn't stick a fork, and to which the boys used to say:

Oh, steer! oh, steer! why are you here?
You've served long years of toil and abuse,
And now you're here for the poor soldiers' use.

Hard skirmishes with live hardtack 'til Tom Curry, much averse to anything like labor, told us to break the tack in two, find which way they were going, then put their heads together and let 'em push. Painful meetings with old friends in the form of canned beef, so-called, of Alger fame. We wept as we paused irresolute and contemplated the tragic trick of old Mike or Tom. Uncle Sam: We'll never forgive thee, giving us our old family "hoss" to eat.

We also learned what it meant to be the first man with two in a bed and three in the middle.

Despite the hardships of the first days in a military camp we were devoted to our duties and tried hard to become strictly military. Some mighty queer tactics were executed in the verdant days of our apprenticeship. Most of them were put into execution along the guard lines. Guard mount was in the evening and the sentinels were instructed to challenge all persons seen on or near their posts at night. When day arrived and the sun began his journey across the heavens, the faithful sentinels, still obedient to their instructions, halted everything in sight. When the relief came around the sentinel calmly pacing his post, became suddenly startled, (he'd only seen them a quarter of a mile away) and challenged. Halt! Who's there? Corporal with the relief. Advance corporal with the relief and be recognized.

Nevertheless one had to strictly understand his business in order to get across those lines. One night Governor Tanner attempted to cross the lines but was promptly halted. Said he "It's all right, I'm Governor." "I don't give a cuss," said Cy, "if you're the shade of Julius Cæsar, you can't get across this post." But there was a way to get across. The way to a soldier's heart is through his stomach, and it is a mighty short road between, too. A vigilant officer might sometimes in the dead of night have heard the challenge, Halt! who's there? Friend with a bottle. Advance friend with the bottle and pull the cork. If a man knew that countersign he could generally get across.

But the guard line of the Irish Seventh was proof against the Springfield colored gentry. One night a "coon" had tried repeatedly to get through, but was finally arrested by an Irish recruit, who called, "Corporal of the guard, number siven, I've got a damn nager." Just then the darkey hit him on the noddle with a brick and took French leave. Upon recovery, Mike looked around for his missing game, and halloed, "Corporal of the guard, niver mind, the damn nager's gone."

But all was not pleasure or fun. Galling trials were to be undergone, for a young American who breathes the spirit of liberty and independence with the every breath of life, is not the most amenable to discipline. The continual salaaming to officers, turning out of the guard to do the honors to supercilious, arbitrary, bumptious fellows, who regarded us as untrained animals and themselves as little gods, was exasperating to the untrained soldier. Company I is to be congratulated on its wise selection of officers. They are men and treated us as men. They did not forget that the enlisted man did not sink his manhood when he joined the army; that he volunteered and was enlisted by the government to fight for his country and not for the convenience or accommodation of a set of officers. That's the reason they have come home with their men, while the others didn't dare to.

Our feelings toward the other class were well expressed by a little red headed Irishman at Springfield during a bantering argument with Lieutenant Mullins, of the Fifth. Mullins was a Martinet, who insisted on the honors being properly done. We had been up all night on guard and did not feel in the humor to turn out at the every appearance of His Highness. After about a dozen rounds, with severe lecturings thrown in, we came to the boiling temperature. Red acted as the nozzle of the kettle and sang out, "I told the boys when I came here that I wanted a job that I could hold, and I've got it. This is the first job I ever got that I couldn't quit." "Why don't you go home, then?" said Mullins. "Didn't I try to go home the other night and the guard wouldn't let me? From what I've seen around here, if these struttin' officers would tell a feller to butt stumps I guess he'd have to butt." The volunteer soldier loves a leader, and will follow him "into the jaws of death, into the mouth of hell," but a driver he hates.

We had but one opportunity of getting even with the officers, and that was on one rainy day in Springfield, when the boys, in fun, put four lieutenants, six captains and one major through a paddling machine, just as their mothers used to do. We found, after we got into the service, that it wouldn't do to monkey with the buzz saw any more. It would have been about as wise as to fool with the business end of an army mule, and that, as old vets know, isn't Solomon like.

After the mud, rain and cold in Springfield, sober satisfaction prevailed when we were ordered to proceed to Tampa. We thought we would join Shafter, and soon be in the thick of battle. But here, as at numerous other times, we were disappointed. It seemed an old game, in which the Fourth continually got the wrong end of the stick. Instead, we were ordered to reinforce the other regiments conducting the ever-memorable siege of Jacksonville. We had expected glorious battle. We got into a scrimmage with stumps, cactus, weeds and briars. With spade, axe and pick, we finally conquered, but we couldn't see anything heroic in cutting poles, grubbing stumps, digging ditches and other things. We sweat and smelled just like we would at home in a potato patch. We did get to make some bayonet charges on an old picket fence. You could see that fence quiver for a quarter of a mile when the boys gave their battle yell. But we became popularly known as the "Florida Land and Improvement Company."

In addition to our other trials we had another in the person of a chap named Bancroft—officially, General Bancroft. He was, as the boys said, "a warm member." We stood more in awe of him than did ever any small boy of his paternal razor-strop. This fellow used to get up before breakfast and scare the whole guard detail into a fit of the jim-jams. He was a strict disciplinarian, and many a fellow suffered for being a minute late. Once the tables were turned on him. It was announced to the guard one evening that the General would inspect the lines that night. The guards, carefully cocked and primed, were warned just how to shoot off, and told the hour he would arrive. For some reason he delayed. When he did arrive, he stumbled onto a "rookey." In answer to the challenge he said, "General Bancroft." "Well," said the "rookey," "you'll catch thunder; you're two hours late." Another time he put a fellow through a severe catechism. "How do you salute?" "I don't know." "What would you do if I should come across your post?" "I don't know." "What would you do if a fight should start or a fire break out?" "I don't know." "Well, you are an ignorant fellow. What would you do if you were at home?" "I don't know." But that fellow was rattled. There are just three things a soldier will do first when he gets home: First, get a square meal; second, have his picture taken; and third, kiss his best girl if he has one, and if he hasn't, he ought to have.

For a time we felt life under General Bancroft to be more durable. The boys used to threaten to transfer or resign. Moffett said the next time he would join the Salvation Army so as not be so close to headquarters. About this time a long, lean, attenuated individual known to the boys as Jersey, went to Major Elliott with a fine half morocco bible under his arm, a present from his sweetheart, who adjured him to study it faithfully, and startled the Major by asking him for a transfer. "Why Jersey what do you want to transfer to?" "To the Salvation Army." "What do you want to transfer to that for?" "My girl sent me a bible and I don't know what to do with it. The boys say it's a dandy, that she must have given $3.50 for it, but there is a crap game going on down here and if some feller'l give me two dollars fur it I think I'll let her go."

While General Bancroft was severe he was a man and a gentleman. Be it said to our credit that we learned to appreciate and respect him.

Last winter an old veteran told me that if a soldier had not had one hundred graybacks on him at one time, moving off with both feet simultaneously at once, as Colonel Andel said, he had never seen service. That was a little extravagant, but I'll tell you a little secret if you'll promise not to tease us about it. Agreed? Well we've all seen service. Great was the consternation when the seam squirrel struck camp. The old Confederate gray back seemed to be still true to the Lost Cause, though all else had forsaken it, for he industriously pestered the boys in blue just as he did in the sixties. Or mayhap I do him an injustice. He might have been doing his best to enlist in the blue in order to get at the Spanish Don. Some of us held a meeting,—adopted a set of resolutions denouncing the louse tribe in general, the graybacks in particular, and declared that not a seam squirrel should set foot on our soil.

One day Tom Adams hailed me with, " Geo. you got any graybacks?" "No sir," said I, "I don't keep such things." "Well they're in your squad." "The dickens they are, whose got 'em?" "Wib and Roy and Frank." "Well by jimminy we'll quarantine 'em." As I went to my tent I mused. If they've got 'em its barely possible I have. They're pretty decent fellows and I've been sleeping right next 'em. So after some inquiry as to the habits and habitat of the animals, I removed my habiliment and commenced a search, feeling that it was entirely useless. Well, I doubled and counted back time and again, omitted all mention of the nits, and still I was ahead. I couldn't dodge or deny it, I was the lousiest man in the squad.

The boys set huge caldrons of water on the fire and put in kerosene, salt, vinegar and anything else that they had ever heard would kill a louse. I thought, now that I'm disgraced, milder and less laborious methods would suit me better, and so I got a specific exterminator.

Jacksonville witnessed the hardest, most trying period of our service. Never will we forget the terrible months of July, August and September under the blazing sun and in the blistering sands of Florida. Every day strong men fell from the ranks before the onslaughts of a mysterious, unseen, but terrible foe, and were borne away by the ambulance on its ceaseless rounds by day and night to the tented hospital on the hillside. Every day, as the soldiers visited their suffering comrades, they saw the light of life flutter, grow dim, and at last go out. Every day the somber hearse, bearing its sad burden, followed by a group of the mourning comrades of the dead, told of another patriot gone to his last reward. Every day the station resounded to the echoes of the salute, the muffled drum's sad notes, and the sweet and solemn melody of the bugle, as the last sad rites were paid to the soldier dead.

Amidst these sad scenes we witnessed sublime heroism in the acts of those noble women, the trained nurses, who so unselfishly sacrificed large salaries, comparative ease and comfort, and some their lives, for the onerous and dangerous duties and hard conditions of a military hospital to save the lives of our dying boys. Said Satan: "Yea, all that a man hath will he give for his life." And many a boy today owes all that he has to those patriotic women.

Before these angels of life and mercy came into our lives, the sick soldier boy lay on his poncho or blanket in the sand and died in the clothes in which he had gone to the hospital. Delicacies sent to the soldiers never reached them. Stimulants and food for their benefit were misappropriated. They received scant care and unskillful nursing.

But after the arrival of these women, oh, what a change. Tents were floored. Iron bedsteads, with mattresses and plenty of sheets and night clothing, made their appearance. Medicines and delicacies found their way to the boys. They received care as tender and thoughtful, and more skillful, than a mother or sister could have given. Day and night these sweet-faced, tender-hearted and iron-nerved women moved from sufferer to sufferer, softly, sweetly speaking words of cheer and comfort, smoothing the pillow, raising the cooling cup to the fevered lips, fanning the burning brow, administering the health giving draught, and checking the flow of the crimson tide of life; or sat by the side of the dying, catching the last message of love to the folks at home, wiping the death damp from the brow, and speaking words of faith and hope to steady the nerves when the awful moment arrived and the dying one stood face to face with the great unknown. For their noble work in the Civil War, Abraham Lincoln said: "God bless the women of America," and from my humble corner I echo a fervent Amen.

And, Oh! how hungry the sick boys used to get. They used to lie and talk of the good things they would get when they got well 'til some fellow unable to stand it longer would hollow, " shut up, I'm hungry enough without that." One evening the physician raised their diet list. They lay awake half the night thinking of the morning meal. But the arbitrary attendant cut the ration in two. The patients did much grumbling and made many sarcastic remarks, 'til the nurse who was not a good representative of the profession, in great wrath exclaimed: "Well, if you want to kill yourself, you can eat a cow for all I care." "Bring on the cow and the calf too."

For the doctors the boys had little use and much contempt. They used to say the doctors would give a fellow a pill for a sore toe. Peter Akeman had an ailment of some kind and called on the doctor for relief. Sawbones gave him some pills. A few days later he had an entirely different complaint and got more pills, Pete declared out of the same bottle. Said he, "Say, doctor, how do these b-b-blame things know where to go to?"

Right glad were the boys to leave Jacksonville for Savannah. At Savannah the boys first saw a genuine manifestation of the noted Southern hospitality. Their generous treatment by the citizens won the boys' hearts completely, while the efficient service, manly conduct and gallantry of the boys won the esteem of all the Savannah citizens, both white and black. Not too much can be said for the loyalty and patriotism of the southern people. The state of Illinois owes a vote of thanks to the people of Savannah for their generous and friendly treatment of the boys of Illinois.

Here they won laurels in eliciting the highest meed of praise from our President that could be given a volunteer regiment. Said he: "It is the best volunteer regiment that I have ever seen. The correct distances, perfect lines, military bearing and easy swinging step mark them a splendid organization of men." Illinois got her reputation up down there, for it takes good daddies and good mothers to raise such fellows.

It was with deep regret on the part of both citizens and soldiers that the Fourth took its leave for Cuba. Our voyage was another trying experience. During our journey by rail much trouble had been experienced in keeping the boys on the cars. We were always warned not to get off. So a certain Captain, true to habit, drew his men up in line shortly after we had weighed anchor and said very earnestly: "Now men, we'er off for Cuba and I don't want a damned one of you to get off the boat."

As the ship began to roll and toss and heave, we also began to roll and toss and heave, and soon we cast our bread upon the waters. As "Runty" said we threw up everything but our reputations. We might have felt relieved could we have gotten rid of those also. One fellow was doing especially well by the fish, when a sympathetic comrade inquired: "Why, Joe, are you sick?" "Sick! The Devil! Do you 'spose I'm pukin' for fun?" When we got off we were a hopeless, helpless looking set. Even our shadows looked bilious. We had been touched for all we had.

Cuba we found to be a beautiful land of fertile fields, gorgeous flowers, waving palms, crystal streams, days of golden sunshine, glorious starlit nights and beautiful women.

The American soldier has a keen eye for beauty, especially in the fair sex. To him it is no trifling thing. He sympathizes with Hyatt of a certain story. Hyatt and Wyatt were close college chums. Coming down the staircase one day Hyatt said to Wyatt, "Who is that plain, homely creature there in front?" Said Wyatt, "That's my wife." "Wyatt, how did it happen that a man of your ability, education, experience and prospects, married such a looker as that?" "Well, now, Hyatt, don't be too hard. Beauty is only skin deep, you know." "Well for heaven's sake, skin her then."

But notwithstanding the beauty and agreeableness of our surroundings, the hearts of the boys yearned for Illinois. Anything pleasing happened, the shout was Illinois. Anything displeasing or disappointing occurred, the wail was for Illinois. In their waking moments they talked of Illinois, and locked in the soft but strong embrace of slumber they murmured Illinois, Illinois. If the transport had gone down amidst the tossing billows, the last head that bobbed above water would have shrieked Illinois or something else.

Every night borne on the rushing pinions of the imagination they went back to the old home and saw father and mother, brother, sister or some one else. When day dispelled the illusion they'd laughingly say, Well I's up home last night and saw Bud. Had the biggest chicken in the barnyard. God bless thee Illinois. Thou hast the best cattle, the finest horses, the fairest fields, the greenest meadows, the noblest streams, the shadiest forests, the prettiest girls, the sweetest homes and the best, the fondest, the kindliest old folks of any spot on God's green earth. When we leave thee again Oh! Illinois, Uncle Sam will be in dire straits. We are glad to be with you again. We have not had a hard time; a pretty good time for soldiers we guess; but soldiering is no fun at best. We realize that our sacrifices were pale in comparison with those of the heroes of the Revolution, who marched and fought, shoeless, hatless and ragged, leaving their foot prints in blood on the frozen ground; or with those of the boys of '61, who battled on the red field at Shiloh, charged through the clouds at Missionary Ridge and stormed the heights of bloody Kenesaw. We know we cannot go down in history with the veterans who withstood the storm of shot and shell at Gettysburg, or perished in the Wilderness of death, or at Spottsylvania, Cold Harbor or Appomatox.

But let no man point the finger of scorn at any boy who wore the blue in '98 and '99. Let no sneer pass the lips of the frivolous. Let not the arrows of cruel satire and ridicule be leveled at him who considers it unfortunate that he did not participate in battle. He has performed the fullest measure of duty that the God of battles, the fortunes of war and the destinies of nations permitted. He has performed his duties in a manner that won him the admiration and praise of not only our chief magistrate, but of foreign soldiers and statesmen as well. He enlisted to fight, and confidently expected and ardently wished to see action. True, he might not have been so brave on the firing line. He might have had sudden chills or St. Vitus dance; his trousers might have needed little Grovers on their rear; but even those feelings are not alien to tried veterans.

During a certain battle of the civil war a heavy musketry fire was in progress. Men were falling fast. It was a time when the oldest and bravest would have gladly been in their tents. A rabbit, scared out of the brush by the terrific fire, went full tilt for the rear. As his little white tail bobbed up and down, hither and thither, in and out amongst the tall grass, General Vance, afterward governor of South Carolina, shouted after him: "Go'er, cottontail; if I hadn't a reputation I'd be with you."

As before said, they enlisted to fight, and its no fault of theirs, that they're not every one lying dead on the field of Santiago. And in a larger sense than first appears, the credit for our brilliant victory belongs in some measure to those who did not see action. It is reserve force that wins the victories of nations, as well as the triumphs of the orator, the success of the physician, the statesman or the business man. It is idle to believe that our victory could have been so soon and so easily won with an army composed of only those who fought at Santiago and Manilla. It was the knowledge that still two hundred thousand soldiers just as willing and capable as those who fought at Santiago, were ready to take the field, that caused Spain to see the hopelessness of her struggle. It is not flattering to American pride to believe that out of our army of two hundred and seventy-five thousand men only thirty-five or forty thousand were brave enough to fight.

These men sacrificed time, money and opportunity, home and friends and social position to do and die for their country. In this they were disappointed, but as they look abroad upon the brightened prospects of the world and of mankind, they feel that the sacrifice has not been in vain.

From their example our country has learned a new lesson of itself. It has learned that the sordid greed for wealth and material gain has not dulled the sense of honor nor quenched the fires of patriotism burning in the breasts of the common people. We have learned that no longer is there a North, a South, an East or a West, that the sentiment of our whole people in our country, our whole country and nothing but our conntry, one flag, one cause, one country, one heart. We know that no selfish consideration of material gain will ever cause our nation "to take its hand from the sword hilt to put a penny in its purse," when a duty toward humanity is to be performed.

While we know that every grand Empire and aspiring Republic that have passed from earth, have been slain with a dagger of fine gold; despite the selfish cant of Mammon's helots, we may be assured that the foundations of our national power are still strong. When a great nation champions the golden rule among nations, stays the hand of the assassinating robber. and oppressor, strikes the shackles from the limbs of the political slave, assists struggling manhood, avenges outraged womanhood, lights the torch of liberty amidst the darkness of tyranny, dries the eyes and lifts the fallen form of weeping, suffering humanity and puts bread in the mouth of starving childhood, we may be assured that Almighty God has a work for that nation to perform. But let us hope that the dawn of the twentieth century will usher in a newer and better era. Already we have heard the harbingers of the coming day, for out of the depths of Russia there has come a voice earnestly pleading for peace. Already the eastern sky is aglow and burnished arrows of light shot from the golden bow of morning dart to the zenith.

Let us hope that it may be the golden age of peace, of fraternity, of equality. When wars and struggles, national and international, shall be no more; when every son of God may peaceably eat his bread in the sweat of his own brow; when the sword shall be be beaten into the plough share, and the spear into the pruning hook; when the lamb shall lie down with the wolf; when a little child shall lead them; when joy, love and peace reigning supreme shall swell with emotion the human heart, issuing forth in one world-wide universal song. and ascend to the far off heavens all aglow with the dazzling radiance of the star of Bethlehem, shining o'er the glorified form of the Prince of Peace seated on his jewelled throne. Angel choirs with psalter harp and dulcimer will echo the glad refrain in psalm and hymn. The celestial harmony, rolling along the golden streets, through the pearly gates and o'er the jasper walls, on, on, on through the starry universe, will blend with the music of the spheres, carrying the glad song to faraway worlds to us unknown, while echoing and re-echoing on the boundless shores of the universe, where beat the waves of eternity's time, will be heard the soft, sweet murmur of the Angel hymn, "On Earth, Peace, Good Will to Men."

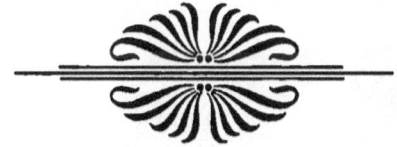

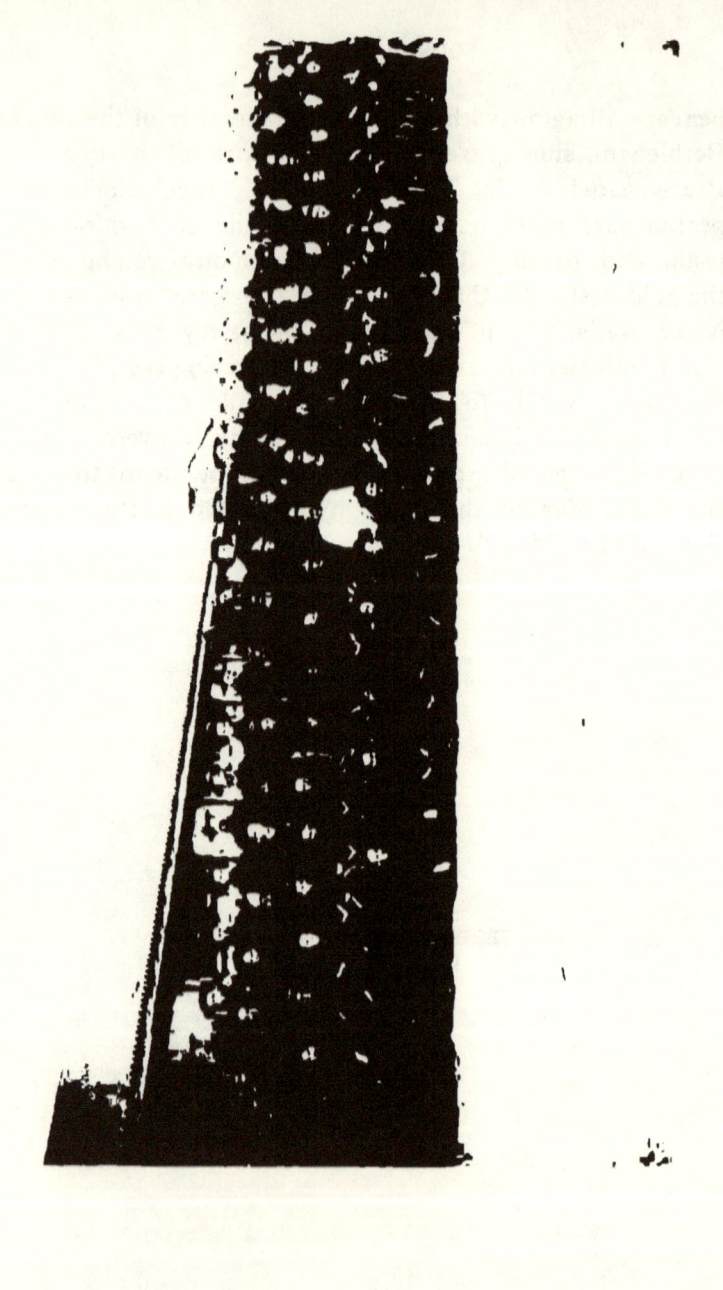

www.ingramcontent.com/pod-product-compliance
Lightning Source LLC
Chambersburg PA
CBHW022111300426
44117CB00007B/665